How the University Works

CULTURAL FRONT
General Editor: Michael Bérubé

Manifesto of a Tenured Radical
Cary Nelson

Bad Subjects: Political Education for Everyday Life
Edited by the Bad Subjects Production Team

Claiming Disability: Knowledge and Identity
Simi Linton

*The Employment of English: Theory, Jobs, and the
Future of Literary Studies*
Michael Bérubé

Feeling Global: Internationalism in Distress
Bruce Robbins

Doing Time: Feminist Theory and Postmodern Culture
Rita Felski

Modernism, Inc.: Body, Memory, Capital
Edited by Jani Scandura and Michael Thurston

*Bending Over Backwards: Disability, Dismodernism, and
Other Difficult Positions*
Lennard J. Davis

After Whiteness: Unmaking an American Majority
Mike Hill

Critics at Work: Interviews 1993–2003
Edited by Jeffrey J. Williams

Crip Theory: Cultural Signs of Queerness and Disability
Robert McRuer

*How the University Works: Higher Education and the
Low-Wage Nation*
Marc Bousquet; Foreword by Cary Nelson

How the University Works

Higher Education and the Low-Wage Nation

Marc Bousquet

Foreword by Cary Nelson

NEW YORK UNIVERSITY PRESS
New York and London

NEW YORK UNIVERSITY PRESS
New York and London
www.nyupress.org

Library of Congress Cataloging-in-Publication Data
Bousquet, Marc
How the university works : higher education and the low-wage
nation / Marc Bousquet ; foreword by Cary Nelson.
p. cm.
Includes bibliographical references and index.
ISBN-13: 978-0-8147-9974-1 (cloth : alk. paper)
ISBN-10: 0-8147-9974-4 (cloth : alk. paper)
ISBN-13: 978-0-8147-9975-8 (pbk. : alk. paper)
ISBN-10: 0-8147-9975-2 (pbk. : alk. paper)
  1. College teachers—Salaries, etc.—United States. 2. Universities
and colleges—Employees—Salaries, etc.—United States. I. Title.
LB2334.B58 2007
331.2'8137812—dc22   2007029790

New York University Press books are printed on acid-free paper,
and their binding materials are chosen for strength and durability.

Manufactured in the United States of America

c 10 9 8 7 6 5 4 3 2 1
p 10 9 8 7 6 5 4 3 2 1

To Heather

For an Organization of Intellectual Workers

I consider it important, indeed urgently necessary, for intellectual workers to get together, both to protect their own economic status and also, generally speaking, to secure their influence in the political field.

On the first-mentioned, the economic side, the working class may serve us as a model: they have succeeded, at least to some extent, in protecting their economic interests. We can learn from them too how this problem can be solved by the method of organization. And also, we can learn from them what is our gravest danger, which we ourselves must seek to avoid: the weakening through inner dissensions, which, when things reach that point, make cooperation difficult and result in quarrels between the constituent groups.

. . . The intellectual worker, due to his lack of organization, is less well protected against arbitrariness and exploitation than a member of any other calling.

An organization of intellectual workers can have the greatest significance for society as a whole by influencing public opinion through publicity and education. Indeed it is its proper task to defend academic freedom, without which a healthy development of democracy is impossible. An outstandingly important task for an organization of intellectual workers at the present moment is to fight for the establishment of a supranational political force as a protection against fresh wars of aggression.

—Albert Einstein, 1949

Contents

Acknowledgments

This book could not have appeared without the unflagging support and encouragement of a long list of activist intellectuals, especially those who comprise the editorial collective of *Workplace: A Journal for Academic Labor* (www.workplace-gsc.com). These include, among many others, Dick Ohmann, Paul Lauter, Gary Rhoades, Bill Vaughn, Katherine Wills, Eileen Schell, Bruce Simon, Christian Gregory, Steve Parks, Laura Sullivan, Karen Thompson, Cary Nelson, Michael Bérubé, Vicky Smallman, Randy Martin, Steve Watt, Matt Gold, Tony O'Brien, Gregory Bezkorovainy, Ali Zaidi, Susan O'Malley, Vinny Tirelli, Greg Meyerson, Julie Schmid, Kirsten Christensen, Felicia Carr, Ray Watkins, Noreen O'Connor, Barbara Foley, Jamie Owen Daniel, Rich Daniels, Bill Hendricks, Don Lazere, Joe Aimone, Mary Refling, and Kent Puckett. Some of the collective, like Aimone, are responsible for drafting me into the movement; others, like Refling, Daniel, and Smallman, for keeping the movement going; still others, like Nelson, Lauter, and Martin, for continuing to provide intellectual leadership and generous support at critical junctures in the journey. All of them have contributed in some very significant way to this project, in ways simply too various to catalog.

Of foundational importance was my experience at the City University of New York, where I first began to understand the prospects for greater equality and democracy represented by public higher education. Among my CUNY comrades I especially have to thank Eric Marshall of the Adjunct Project and Leo Parascondola, Barbara Bowen, Stanley Aronowitz, and George Otte, who first suggested I attend a union meeting. At CUNY and thereafter, my friend Granville Ganter's contributions to this project ran the gamut from critic and copyeditor to matchmaker and mixologist.

I doubt that I would have written this book without the years I spent as an assistant and then tenured associate professor at the University of

Louisville, in a right-to-work state with a powerless faculty, and where public university coaches and presidents cart their compensation home in wheelbarrows while spectacularly failing to serve student need. While in Louisville, I was especially grateful for the friendship of fellow transients Susan Erdmann, Stephen Dougherty, Wayne Ross, and Sandra Mathison and for the indispensable intellectual partnership of a courageous network of activist graduate students, especially Chris Carter (now at the University of Oklahoma), Tony Scott, (University of North Carolina–Charlotte), Laura Bartlett (University of Ohio–Marion), and Steve Wexler (California State–Northridge). Upon arriving at Santa Clara, I benefited from research support and a subvention in partial support of this book. Thanks to John Kloss for permission to reprint his academic labor cartoons. With respect to Thomas Nast's cartoon "The American Twins," I am very grateful for the gifts of time and knowledge donated by Delinda Buie, Mildred Franks, and Harry Rubenstein, curator for labor history at the Smithsonian Institution.

Portions of this project have appeared, sometimes in different form, in *Social Text, JAC (Journal of Advanced Composition), College English, Workplace, Works and Days, Cinema Journal,* and *minnesota review.* I'm grateful to the editors for permission to reprint, but also in many cases for meaningful intellectual contributions to this project, notably Lynn Worsham, Jeanne Gunner, and Randy Martin. Among the editorial supporters of this project, I have to emphatically thank Pittsburgh neighbors, rival editors, and friends David Downing and Jeffrey Williams. For over a decade, Williams has supported this project with a steady stream of queries, challenges, reading suggestions, offprints, invitations, complaints, and introductions. Under his leadership, *minnesota review* remains one of the few venues for thoughtful scholarship regarding academic labor. At the helm of the *Works and Days* collective, Downing has helped dozens of cultural-materialist scholars develop their work in thoughtful exchanges with invited senior critics. In devoting an issue of the journal to concerns raised by some of my earlier essays, he delayed the appearance of this book while improving it immeasurably. I owe similar thanks to my editor at New York University Press, Eric Zinner, for grasping the potential of the material on undergraduate labor (patiently waiting for me to deliver it) and, especially, for his courage in remaining with this project after the strike of graduate employees on the campus that is home to the press.

Every word of this book is indebted to my partner, Heather Julien.

Foreword

Resistance Is Not Futile

Cary Nelson

Marc Bousquet is the Virgil of postmodern academic labor, leading a professoriate in denial through the Dantesque wastes of a system whose sins daily grow more numerous. For this reader at least, chapter 4 was the nadir, the ninth circle of academic hell. There you will meet Susan Erdmann, a teacher who meets her college students at a UPS hub after midnight, struggling to speak to them above the din of machinery. And you will meet the students themselves, students routinely exploited as cheap labor by higher education and its cooperating industries. This is a "partnership" between UPS and the University of Louisville and other area schools, one of many across the country. The students slave five nights a week at minimum wage; if they last long enough, they earn tuition support. Few of them do. Fewer still ever graduate. Most instead accumulate workplace injuries. This is a world I certainly knew nothing about, I am ashamed to say, before reading this book.

Marc's work on the nature of the contemporary university is the single most important recent advance in our understanding of the structure of higher education. This series of interlocking essays gives us the first persuasive account of the university that emerged in the last quarter of the twentieth century. This powerful and defamiliarizing critique has the potential to lift the veil from our eyes and expose the nature of the economic system that now regulates the lives of students and faculty alike.

As Jeff Williams reminded us in a special issue of *Works and Days* devoted to Marc's work—and as cannot be overemphasized—this project grew out of theorized activism. Marc formulated the logic of the job system in the mid 1990s, in the heady days of the Graduate Student Caucus organizing for change in universities and in the Modern Language Association. Those were the days when the MLA president blared, "Graduate students will serve on the Executive Council over my dead body." But they were also the days when graduate students and their allies did indeed begin to serve and won many victories, despite the unstinting antagonism of most of the MLA's organizational leadership. Marc's theory of the job system developed as an analysis in response to the coopted blindness of faculty, the conservatism of disciplinary organizations, the failures of our own self-understandings, and the remorseless advance of reliance on contingent labor throughout the academy. His work builds on the systematic employment injustice that many of us have worked hard to expose, but it takes our understanding of this injustice to a new level of coherence and integration.

As a result of the multiple delusions that professional ideology has installed in us, some of us believe the academic job system needs but modest adjustments at the margins, while others are certain the system will in time repair itself, and still others of us believe it requires drastic reform. Part of what Bousquet is arguing throughout this book is that the job system is functioning exactly as it has evolved to function—delivering cheap instructional labor precisely when it is needed, disposing of experienced instructional labor when it becomes more expensive, breeding compliance in all its participants. The last year in which the notion of apprenticeship had any validity for the profession was 1970. Since then, the country has not had the will to produce the number of full-time faculty positions required to meet its instructional needs. In other words, there has consistently been a large number of undergraduates to be taught. In that sense, there never really has been an overproduction of Ph.D.s, although we *have* recklessly produced Ph.D.s without doing the work to guarantee them jobs.

As Marc analyzes it, the new Ph.D. is the predictable waste product of a system that is in no way dysfunctional. The system is immoral and degrading, but perfectly efficient. And, indeed, most of us do everything necessary to keep it working, including maintaining the fiction of a "job market" when, in fact, we all know that, for decades, most Ph.D.s have systematically been destined for radical proletarianization or the scrap heap. What's more, we keep bringing in new cheap graduate student labor so as to make hiring more expensive Ph.D.s unnecessary. As enrollment climbed, we invented a massive part-timer system to exploit Ph.D.s even more aggressively than graduate students. On campus after campus, faculty might just have said no, most usefully with collective bargaining agreements either mandating limits to the percentage of part-time employees or prohibiting them entirely. Every other tactic of mass action was available to halt the installation of the present job system as well, from work slowdowns to demonstrations to strikes. But very few faculties chose these options; instead, they chose to look away, while sustaining their own privileges.

A generation of senior faculty thoroughly interpellated into the job system's logic has come to the end of its usefulness. Not long ago, the organizing committee of Harvard's prestigious English Institute met to plan the following year's program. When they looked to salt the event with promising younger scholars, these luminaries came to the agreement that such people were nowhere to be found. No good work, they concluded, was being done by anyone under fifty. My own experience is that I do not have to look farther than my own department to find inspiring work by young scholars. But a certain species of academic superstar believes he or she *is* the profession. No wonder they are comfortable with their belief that nothing can be done to transform the job system. Exploitation, after all, doesn't matter, since there's no one beneath their level worthy of fair and decent treatment.

The betrayal of their younger colleagues by some of our most distinguished scholars is certainly one of the more depressing features of the current landscape, since it suggests that intellectual achievement itself can be bankrupted when its rewards are grounded in inequity and indifference. But, of course, such attitudes are not universal among senior faculty. And in a curious way, the callousness of prestige may provide some necessary instruction for those who need to be awakened from unwarranted idealization.

Certainly, every major economic and structural trend in higher education suggests that the future will include further declines in faculty compensation, independence, and intellectual freedom. A large number of undergraduates, as Marc reminds us, are themselves already just part-time students, deflected from their studies by jobs. And higher education as a whole continues to drift fitfully toward a narrow mission of job training and away from the more complex democratic mission of empowering critical citizenship. One of the more powerful features of Bousquet's work is his ability to integrate an analysis of higher education's evolving mission with its instructional and workplace practices.

The only solution, as Marc demonstrates, is a collective project of theory and action. The mutual project of theorizing our situation is essential if we are to free ourselves from the powerless subject positions that all the institutions of higher education have collaborated in articulating for us. Only a mixture of analysis and radicalizing experience can undermine the identities that now keep exploited academic labor in its place. Neither will suffice on its own. Marc's work exemplifies the critical, dynamic interaction between theoretical analysis and activism that is the academy's only hope.

Yet, what, we may ask, can we hope for: What models of higher education have a chance to survive the effects of commodification, quantification, and corporatization? Marc believes the university can recover its powers of critique, but only after we admit its thorough penetration by capital. Indeed, throughout its history, the university has never had complete autonomy. What it *has* had, to use the Althusserian term, is a set of continually renegotiated and variable forms of relative autonomy. Take a simple analogy: when you enter an enclosed courtyard in Oxford or New Haven, the noise of the street is only partially muffled, yet the effect is enough to provide a reflective space for focused critical reflection, for concentrated intellectual work. Contrary to what the late Edward Said argued, fearing that higher education would lose its independence if it were to be politicized, that space is already a product of political struggle. The struggle, however, is not to sustain an impenetrable ideal garden but, rather, a space intermittently less subject to transgression and distraction. The university is now being subjected to sustained political, cultural, and economic assault. To deny that is to cede the future to corporatization and a form of higher education with little purchase on cultural critique.

There is no escaping the great challenge, hurdle, impediment, and—indeed—fundamental ground of any thorough effort to bring theory to bear on the thirty-five-year employment crisis that has defined professional life for so many humanities graduate employees and Ph.D.s. Having devoted a century to analyzing literary objects of adulation and a few decades to interrogating less appealing regimes of power, the job system compels us to turn inward. It is ourselves we must scrutinize, however reluctant we are to do so. We are the people who staff and maintain the system that exists. It operates not merely with our consent but with our sustaining labor. The regret so many of us express amounts to little more than rationalizing consolation. Most of what we do every day perpetuates—indeed, normalizes—every inequity and every abuse presently structured into academic employment. We have met the enemy, but we will not admit that it is us. Marc Bousquet's groundbreaking book will help awaken us.

To bring theory to bear on ourselves, as he has done, is to reverse the elaborate mechanisms for displacement and denial that have been in place for all our lives. We have seen one body of theory after another encrypted, to apply Derridean usage, as a form of specialization. Every body of theory with broad implications for understanding our own practices has sold its potential for professional critique in exchange for institutionalization. Psychoanalytic criticism set the pattern, becoming a subfield and a matter of individual choice rather than a place that would require everyone to think about departmental life, professional identity, and institutional codes. Marxist theory, suspected of being unwilling to accept the benefits of capitalism uncritically, was for decades virtually banned in the American academy, but in the end, it gathered a band of acolytes who were willing to curtail political analysis of the academy in exchange for personal freedoms and rewards and an implicit agreement to locate politics elsewhere, both in the text and in the nation. For a time, feminist theory mounted powerful critiques of institutionalized sexism, but it, too, has in many places settled for the comforts and conflicts of departmentalization. *similr to Ohmann + campus politics*

The one institutional site where one might have hoped for a theorized account of the job system was the Modern Language Association. But that has not been how the association has defined its role. As Marc shows, for more than thirty years, the association has fought tooth and nail against every impulse toward frankness. For fifteen years, the MLA lied about the seriousness of the problem. Then it began a series of strategic retreats, admitting only so much of the truth as would not threaten the status quo, fighting every reform initiative and nominating as its officers people who would proceed to defend a system of heedless privilege, thereby sacrificing the theoretical precepts they used to read literature when it came to analyzing the profession. As Bousquet points out, the MLA in every initiative has at once asserted our powerlessness, its nobility, and the inevitability of all existing economic arrangements. It treats the fake job market, religiously tracking its every twist and turn, as an inevitable fact of nature rather than as a fundamentally exploitive matter of choice. It is clear that we need a properly theorized and honest account of how such professional societies function and how they might be induced to become agents of change. Marc has started that account here.

To theorize the contemporary university is to recognize that there was nothing inevitable about its formation. It did not have to be, and it can still be dismantled. Set a $200,000 limit to faculty salaries and a $300,000 limit to upper administrative salaries. Limit coaches to $300,000 as well. At my institution, even the president's assistants earn $300,000; I'd cut their salaries by 50 percent. Redirect the money saved to hiring assistant professors, raising part-timer salaries to parity and graduate student employee wages to the cost of living, and eliminating all tuition payments for poor and lower-middle-class students. Deny administrators the right to fund gratuitous pet projects at the expense of a principled campus salary schedule. If administrators refuse to comply, sit in their offices, sit in front of their cars, block campus streets, block access to buildings, picket their houses. Use nonviolent civil disobedience to force change. Or, if that seems too confrontational, form a union and negotiate these matters at the bargaining table. Increasingly, graduate employees and contingent faculty are doing just that. The key decisions about the job system are made on your own campus when budget priorities are set. Take the money in your own hands. You have nothing to lose but your colleagues' chains.

1

Introduction

Your Problem Is My Problem

> We have taken the great leap forward and said, "Let's pretend we're a corporation."
>
> —John Lombardi, president, University of Florida, 1997

Over the past forty years, the administration of higher education has changed considerably. Campus administrations have steadily diverged from the ideals of faculty governance, collegiality, and professional self-determination. Instead they have embraced the values and practices of corporate management. Consequently, the new realities of managed education strongly correspond to the better-understood realities of managed health care. For example, both education and health have been increasingly marketized—transformed into sites of unprecedented capital accumulation by way of the commodification of activities and relationships. Public assets and activities intended for the public good have been transferred into private hands. Workers in both health and education have seen the compulsory acceleration of market behaviors (such as competition for resources and profit-seeking) in their professional cultures. In both fields, the management of professional activities has resulted in the return of the sort of dizzying inequalities formerly associated with the Gilded Age. Under the principle of revenue maximization, managers direct professionals to provide ever more elaborate boutique services to the wealthy. At the same time, under the principle of cost containment, they constrain professionals to offer degraded service or even deny service to the vast majority of the working class.

Most people intuitively understand the consequences for health of managed care. Because the calculus of profit demands continuous reduction in the costs of care, especially the expensive labor time of highly trained professionals, the "management" of care implies the substitution of lesser-skilled and lesser-paid workers, such as nurse's aides, for highly skilled and higher-paid physicians. Fewer people get to see doctors. Doctors have fewer options for treatment and diagnosis. Many critical health care decisions are made by nonmedical management or by doctors with strong incentives to accommodate their managers. More of the expense and burden of care is shifted to patients and families. Under a profit regime, the standards of care are established not by the measure of lives saved but by the measure of financial risk: At what point do the fiscal liabilities for malpractice exceed the dollar savings of using fewer, cheaper, less experienced, and less elaborately trained personnel? Up to the limit of malpractice exposure, health-care providers have real incentives to use older equipment, take smaller precautions against infection and complication, shorten hospital stays, and deny access to the best procedures in favor of cheap procedures.

Less well understood is how the logic of the HMO increasingly rules higher education. For example, management closely rations professor time. Thirty-five years ago, nearly 75 percent of all college teachers were tenurable; only a quarter worked on an adjunct, part-time, or nontenurable basis. Today, those proportions are reversed. If you're enrolled in four college classes right now, you have a pretty good chance that one of the four will be taught by someone who has earned a doctorate and whose teaching, scholarship, and service to the profession has undergone the intensive peer scrutiny associated with the tenure system. In your other three classes, however, you are likely to be taught by someone who has started a degree but not finished it; was hired by a manager, not professional peers; may never publish in the field she is teaching; got into the pool of persons being considered for the job because she was willing to work for wages around the official poverty line (often under the delusion that she could "work her way into" a tenurable position); and does not plan to be working at your institution three years from now. In almost all courses in most disciplines using nontenurable or adjunct faculty, a person with a recently earned Ph.D. was available, and would gladly have taught your other three courses, but could not afford to pay their loans and house themselves on the wage being offered.

Most undergraduate education is conducted by a superexploited corps of disposable workers that Cary Nelson describes as a "lumpen professoriate" (Nelson and Watt, *Academic Keywords,* 208), often collecting wages and benefits inferior to those of fast-food clerks and bell-hops. According to the Coalition on the Academic Workforce survey of 2000, for instance, fewer than one-third of the responding programs paid first-year writing instructors more than $2,500 a class; nearly half (47.6 percent) paid these instructors less than $2,000 per class (American Historical Association). At that rate, teaching a full-time load of eight classes nets less than $16,000 annually and includes no benefits. By comparison, research faculty with half their workload in "publish or perish" activities usually teach four or fewer classes in a year. Persons who have acquired $30,000 to $100,000 in debt en route to a Ph.D. cannot afford to work for those wages. More often than not, working for those wages is the reason they acquired debt in the first place. In fact, without some kind of assistance, few can afford to work for two or three times that amount.

Higher education employers can only pay those wages in the knowledge that their employees are subsidized in a variety of ways. In the case of student employees, the massive debt load subsidizes the wage. For poorly paid adjunct, or contingent, faculty, who are women by a substantial majority, the strategies vary but include consumer debt and reliance on another job or the income from a domestic partner. Like Wal-Mart employees, the majority female contingent academic workforce relies on a patchwork of other sources of income, including such forms of public assistance as food stamps and unemployment compensation. It is perfectly common for contingent university faculty to work as grocery clerks and restaurant servers, earning higher salaries at those positions, or to have been retired from such former occupations as bus driving, steelwork, and auto assembly, enjoying from those better-compensated professions a sufficient pension to enable them to serve a second career as college faculty. The system of cheap teaching doesn't sort for the best teachers; it sorts for persons who are in a financial position to accept compensation below the living wage.

As a result of management's irresponsible staffing practices, more students drop out, take longer to graduate, and fail to acquire essential literacies, often spending tens of thousands of dollars on a credential that has little merit in the eyes of employers. The real "prof scam" isn't the imaginary one depicted in Charles Sykes's fanciful 1988 book by that title, which concocted the image of a lazy tenured faculty voluntarily absenting themselves from teaching. Instead, the prof scam turns out to be a shell game conducted by management, who keep a tenurable stratum around for marketing purposes and to generate funded research. The tenured are spread so thin with respect to undergraduate teaching, however, that even the most privileged undergraduates spend most of their education with parafaculty working in increasingly unprofessional circumstances. As the union activists of the nontenurable will tell you, the problem is not with the intellectual quality, talent, or commitment of the individual persons working on a nonprofessorial basis; it's the degraded circumstances in which higher education management compels them to work: teaching too many students in too many classes too quickly, without security, status, or an office; working from standardized syllabi; using outsourced tutorial, remedial, and even grading services; providing no time for research and professional development. Working in McDonald's "kitchen," even the talent of Wolfgang Puck is pressed into service of the Quarter Pounder.

Despite the tens of billions saved on faculty wages by substituting a throwaway workforce for professionals scrutinized by the tenure system, managed higher education grows ever more expensive. Tuition soared 38 percent between 2000 and 2005, outpacing nearly every other economic indicator. Where does the money from stratospheric tuition and slashed faculty salaries go?

At for-profit institutions, the answer is obvious: it goes into shareholder pockets. Currently enrolling about 8 percent of the 20 million students in financial-aid-eligible institutions, publicly traded education corporations have shown eye-popping return on investment. Between 2001 and 2003, for instance, the average annual return on publicly traded education corporations ranged from 63 to 75 percent (Cho). Since a sizable fraction of these large profits come from tax dollars in the form of financial aid, there has been growing scrutiny of nearly every major player in the for-profit sector. Recently, ITT, Corinthian, and Apollo have all endured substantial federal or state investigation; Career Education underwent investigation by both the Department of Justice and the Securities Exchange Commission, while simultaneously defending a rush of lawsuits from investors and employees (Morgenson; Blumenstyk, "For-Profit Colleges"). In early 2006, the New York State Board of Regents placed a moratorium on new programs by for-profit vendors, after "perceived abuses" at institutions enrolling 60,000 students and receiving more than $100 million in aid from the state (Lederman). I'm persuaded by Jeff Williams's elegant formulation describing the defunding, privatization, and commoditization of higher education as the creation of a "post welfare-state" university. But I wonder if we might not press even harder at the matter by describing this restructuring of higher education as the "corporate welfare" university?

The explosive growth in the profits of education corporations comes at a time of intensifying corporate profits globally. In the five years after 2001, the Standard and Poor's 500 showed a record-setting twelve straight quarters of profit gains averaging 10 percent or more. In 2005, the United States, United Kingdom, and Japan each showed all-time highs in profit share as a percentage of gross domestic product. This could mean that education corporations were lifted by a generally rising tide of profitability. Alternatively, insofar as education profits were well ahead of most other industries, there might be features unique to higher education, enabling it to take special advantage of the conditions particular to this historical profit opportunity. The latter seems more likely. Goldman Sachs, which reported most of these figures, attributes at least 40 percent of the record expansion of corporate profit margin directly to corresponding financial losses by workers, especially the erosion of wages and benefits due to casualization, outsourcing, deregulation, and globalization (Greenhouse and Leonhardt).

It seems probable that the larger-than-average success of education profiteers has quite a bit to do with a larger-than-average ability to extract concessions from its workforce. Lacking even the veneer of a tenurable stratum, the dollars squeezed from a 100 percent casual faculty joined tax money and tuition from the country's poorest families in enriching the shareholders of education vendors.

But in nonprofit education, which only "pretends" to "act like" a corporation, where have the billions gone? At first glance, there are no shareholders and no dividends. However, the uses to which the university has been put do benefit corporate shareholders. These include shouldering the cost of job training, generation of patentable intellectual property, provision of sports spectacle, vending goods and services to captive student markets, and conversion of student aid into a cheap or even free labor pool. So one sizable trail to follow is the relationship between the financial transactions of nonprofits and the ballooning dividends enjoyed by the shareholder class.

The shareholders of private corporations aren't the only beneficiaries of faculty proletarianization and the tuition gold rush. Because public nonprofits have been receiving steadily lower direct subsidies from federal and state sources, there has been a general belief that higher tuition and staff exploitation have somehow been accomplished by sharp-eyed, tight-fisted managers with at least one version of public well-being in mind, if only within the narrow framework of "reduced spending." But that belief is open to question, since managers have been spending fairly freely in a number of areas.

One area in which nonprofit education management has been freely spending is on themselves. Over three decades, the number of administrators has skyrocketed, in close correspondence to the ever-growing population of the undercompensated. Especially at the upper levels, administrative pay has soared as well, also in close relation to the shrinking compensation of other campus workers. In a couple of decades, administrative work has morphed from an occasional service component in a professorial life to a "desirable career path" in its own right (Lazerson et al.). Nonprofits support arts and sciences deans, chairs, associate deans, and program heads comfortably in six figures. Salaries rise into the mid six figures for many medical, engineering, business, and legal administrators. University presidents have begun to earn seven figures, close on the heels of their basketball coaches, who can earn $3 million annually and are often the highest-paid public employees in their states. There are also notably those who directly administer capital. In 2003, the administration of Harvard University compensated the individual who managed just *one sector* of their endowment to the tune of $17 million. This rate of pay was 1,000 times higher than the compensation doled out by that same administration to Harvard's lowest-paid workers. In thirty years of managed higher education, the typical faculty member has become a female nontenurable part-timer earning a few thousand dollars a year without health benefits. The typical administrator is male, enjoys tenure, a six-figure income, little or no teaching, generous vacations, and great health care. Nontenurable faculty are moderately more likely, and nonteaching staff substantially more likely, to identify themselves as belonging to an ethnic or racial minority than the tenure-stream faculty. Administrators are less likely to identify themselves with minority status the farther they are up the food chain.

There are lots of other areas in which nonprofit administrators have spent even more. With the support of activist legislatures, they've especially enjoyed playing venture capitalist with campus resources and tax dollars by engaging in "corporate partnerships" that generally yield financial benefit to the corporation involved but not the actual campus

(Washburn, *University, Inc.*). More prosaically, they've engaged in what most observers call an "arms race" of spending on the expansion of facilities. And as Murray Sperber and others have documented, they've spent recklessly on sports activities that—despite in some cases millions in broadcast revenue—generally lose huge sums of money. The commercialization of college sport has raised the bar for participation so high that students who'd like to play can't afford the time required for practice, and students who'd like to watch can't afford the ticket prices. Traditionally, the phenomenon known as "cross-subsidy," the support of one program by revenue generated by another program, primarily meant a modest surplus provided by the higher tuition and lower salaries associated with undergraduate education; this income was used to support research activity that was unlikely to find an outside funding agent. Under managed higher education, cross-subsidy has eroded undergraduate learning throughout the curriculum and become a gold mine supporting the entrepreneurial urges, vanity, and hobbyhorses of administrators: Digitize the curriculum! Build the best pool/golf course/ stadium in the state! Bring more souls to God! Win the all-conference championship!

Why have those who control nonprofit colleges and universities so readily fallen into the idea that the institution should act like a profit-seeking corporation? At least part of our answer must be that it offers individuals in that position some compelling gratifications, both material and emotional. This is an age of executive license. In addition to a decent salary and splendid benefits, George W. Bush enjoys the privilege of declaring war on Afghanistan and Iraq. College administrators commonly enjoy larger salaries and comparable benefits. They, too, have the privilege of declaring war—on their sports rivals or on illiteracy, teen pregnancy, and industrial pollution. It feels good to be president. As a "decision maker," one can often arrange to strike a blow on behalf of at least some of one's values. What must be swept under the rug is that the ability to do these things is founded on their willingness to continuously squeeze the compensation of nearly all other campus workers. The university under managerial domination is an accumulation machine. If in nonprofits it accumulates in some form other than dividends, there's all the more surplus for administrators, trustees, local politicians, and a handful of influential faculty to spend on a discretionary basis. It's often assumed that some vaguely defined yet all-powerful force called "economics" or "market pressure," perhaps from the above-mentioned for-profit education corporations, has made all of this pain, the degradation of teaching and learning, "necessary."

For instance, in what is otherwise one of the better essays on the rise of for-profit education, Ana Cox suggests that for-profit institutions have a profound influence on the management of nonprofit higher education. As she puts it, a "creeping for-profit ethos" has spread from the University of Phoenix outward, to the nonprofits.

This is a very commonsensical assumption, and it is correct in the general sense that nonprofits have adopted revenue-maximizing principles borrowed from the larger world of profit seeking. But it's wrong about the heart of the matter. Who is influencing whom? While for-profits enroll about 8 percent of students in institutions receiving financial aid, they capture only 2.4 percent of those enrolled in institutions granting degrees. For-profits collect just 5 percent of the $395 billion spent on higher education in the United States (Blumenstyk, "For-Profit Education"). They remain strongest in distance and nondegree education, in the tradition of correspondence schools such as Donald Trump's 10,000-student "Trump University" (Osterman). There are certainly some ways that the low, single-digit market share of degree-seeking students enjoyed by the for-profits places pressure on certain segments of nonprofit education, especially community colleges. But it is hardly the case that for-profit schools taught nonprofit higher education how to cheaply deliver a standardized, vocationally oriented curriculum designed by tenured administrators and implemented by a massively casual instructional force. That practice was perfected decades earlier by the nonprofits themselves, while billionaire University of Phoenix founder John Sperling was still a labor activist and president of a chapter of the American Federation of Teachers, struggling to better the situation of faculty exploited by his nonprofit higher education employer. The dishonest staffing of the nonprofits taught Sperling, a one-time idealist and faculty unionist, how to harvest surplus value more ruthlessly than Nike and DeBeers, not the other way around.

As a matter of policy, accreditation, and sometimes law, the nonprofit institutions themselves intentionally crafted the low standard of a majority nonprofessorial faculty between 1972 and the 1990s. It was this low standard, set by the nonprofits for themselves, that, in turn, permitted the explosive profits of commercial education providers circa 2000. As a result, the accreditation system, dominated and ultimately corrupted by the administrator class that had engineered these low standards in the first place, was fundamentally helpless to protest that the for-profits had too few highly qualified faculty members. While the Big Ten and the Ivy League were aggressively expanding the meaning of "faculty" to include untrained graduate students, retirees, moonlighters, and anyone else able to work for Wal-Mart wages, who could argue that the for-profit competitors to community colleges should be held to higher standards?

The Culture of the "Corporate University"

There are many ways of understanding what we mean when we speak of the "corporatization" of the university. One valuable approach focuses on the ways campuses actually relate to business and industry in quest of revenue enhancement and cost containment: apparel sales; sports marketing; corporate-financed research, curriculum, endowment, and building; job training; direct financial investment via portfolios, pensions, and cooperative venture; the production and enclosure of intellectual property; the selection of vendors for books, information technology, soda pop, and construction; the purchase and provision of nonstandard labor; and so forth (e.g., Barrow; Bok; Kirp; Newfield, *Ivy and Industry*; Noble, *Digital Diploma Mills*; Sperber; Washburn, *University Inc.*; White). Through these activities, most individual campuses and all of the various independent and self-governing institutions of the profession are commercialized: they are inextricably implicated in profoundly capitalist objectives, however "nonprofit" their missions.

Included in this line of analysis are diverse bedfellows. The unabashed right wing of this approach celebrates commercialization, especially the annual $17 billion for-profit education industry itself; such adherents include, in addition to Trump and Sperling, celebrity junk-bond felon Michael Milken. The left wing of this approach is led by such contributions as *Campus, Inc.* and *University, Inc.*, respectively, Geoffrey White's scathing collection of exposes of "corporate power in the ivory tower" and Jennifer Washburn's monograph on the "corporate corruption of higher education." There is also a "center" to this discourse. The center comprises widely read recent efforts by prominent university administrators such as Harvard president Derek Bok (*Universities and the Marketplace*) and the acting dean of Berkeley's Goldman School of

Public Policy, David Kirp (*Shakespeare, Einstein and the Bottom Line*). The common theme of centrist efforts is the claim that there is no alternative to "partnership" with business and "making peace with the marketplace." Distressingly, more than a few unions of the tenure-stream faculty have adopted a position similar to those of Bok and Kirp, accepting the partnership with corporate enterprise as a "necessity" and adopting the protection of tenure-stream faculty rights to intellectual property as a higher priority than, for instance, addressing casualization and the installation of a radically multi-tiered workforce.

An important alternative understanding of the transformation of the university focuses not on commercialization but on organizational culture. Among the best-known examples of this approach include Bill Readings's study of the ideology of excellence, in connection with the active effort by university administrations to transform institutional culture, and Sheila Slaughter and Larry Leslie's and Gary Rhoades and Sheila Slaughter's examinations of "academic capitalism," the phenomenon through which university management both encourage and command faculty to engage in market behaviors (competition, entrepreneurship, profit-motivated curiousity, etc.). In both cases, the particular merit of the projects is the sense of human agency. Changes in the academic workplace come about as a consequence of clearly understood and clearly intended managerial, corporate, and political initiatives with the explicit intention of inducing the faculty to relinquish certain values and practices. Individually and collectively, faculty members make choices when they adopt new organizational cultures.

The organizational culture approach avoids the "victim of history" narrative popularized by Bok and Kirp, in which there is no alternative to commercialization. It also sees the university as a complex and contradictory place, in contrast to the vestal-virgin or ivory-tower tropes dominating such accounts (Newfield, "Jurassic U."). At least since the early 1970s, when labor economist Clark Kerr theorized the "multiversity" and David Reisman chronicled the rise of "student power" over "faculty dominance," it has been extremely useful to view the academy as a complex organization hosting multiple, generally competing, institutional groups, each with its own evolving culture, and, further, to see cultural change as related to the struggle between the groups—to see the vigor of 1960s student culture, for instance, as closely connected to the rise of student power relative to the powers of administration. Most studies follow the lead of 1970s scholarship in considering the rise, through the 1960s, of at least three increasingly distinct cultures: faculty, student, and administration. During that period, the lion's share of the attention was on student and faculty cultures. However, the circumstances supporting the flourishing of those cultures have eroded. With the increasing economic segmentation of higher education, and the long period of political reaction beginning circa 1980, the sense of a vital "student culture" is generally absent from U.S. mass culture and scholarly literature alike (with the exception of the graduate-employee labor movement, of which more below). Because the traditional figure of the tenure-track professor is now a small minority of the instructional force in U.S. higher education, the sense of a "faculty culture" has also been undermined. As a result, investigating faculty culture means investigating the multiple subcultures of the persons doing the work formerly done by the tenurable faculty: part-time pieceworkers, graduate-student employees, undergraduate tutors, and full-time nontenurable instructors.

Even as the 1970s sense of strong faculty and student cultures has dissipated, management culture has moved in the other direction entirely—becoming ever more internally consistent and cohesive. The culture of university management has the power and, crucially, the intention to remake competing campus cultures in its own image. In fact, the extent to which we increasingly see campus administrations as dominant over other campus groups has much to do with what we see as the success of administrative culture: that is, its capacity to transmit its values and norms to other groups. As I relate in chapter 3, since the 1960s the faculty have certainly organized—with greater and lesser success, depending on immense variables—but, in the same period, campus administrations have enjoyed a massively increasing sense of solidarity. The managerial caste has grown by leaps and bounds and is tightly knit. Through a complex and vigorous culture of administrative solidarity, university management sees itself as a culture apart from faculty. More than just "apart," management is often aligned *against* the faculty (say, when the faculty seek to bargain collectively or to make "shared" governance meaningful). Even when it is not aimed at defeating a particular faculty initiative, management culture is pitched toward continuous struggle with faculty culture. Informed by the rhetoric of "change," an administrative solidarity continuously shores itself up in opposition to the attitudes, behaviors, and norms felt to describe traditional faculty culture. Faculty values and practices targeted for change generally include those associated with relative autonomy over the direction of research and conduct of teaching.

In large part, the self-recognition by management of an emerging culture of its own flowed from the extent to which university administration through the 1970s increasingly took traditional faculty beliefs and practices as an object of study. Informed by trends in corporate management, the "educational leadership" discourse increasingly zeroed in on what Ellen Chaffee and William Tierney dub "the cultural drama of organizational life" (1988). Management theory turned away from the human-resources model of developing individual potential. Turning to a more social-psychological frame, managerial discourse began to describe "the underlying cultural norms that frame daily life at the college" (37) as the root of most managerial problems (i.e., as an obstacle to organizational change). This phase of management theory—the leadership discourse—also saw organizational culture as the wellspring of all possibilities. As the new crop of "institutional leaders," "change agents," and "decision makers" saw it, transforming institutional culture could accelerate change, reduce opposition, and sweepingly create in individuals the desire to change themselves to greater conformity with the institutional mission.

If this sounds Orwellian, or a bit like Foucault goes to business school, it should. In adopting a management theory founded on the dissemination of a carefully designed organizational culture, campus administrations were like most U.S. corporate management in putting to practical use the lessons in cultural materialism they'd learned in humanities classes. It's no exaggeration to say that, through management theory, the ranks of corporate executives and campus upper administrators are wholeheartedly cultural materialists to a greater extent than the faculty of most humanities departments.

Rather than as dedicated cultivators of human resources, they now envision themselves as an intellectual vanguard—as the institution's meta-culture: change agents whose change agency is expressed through cultural invention, whose leadership strategies are aimed primarily at "the social construction of collegiate reality" (Neumann, 389). Plainly put, higher education administration pervasively and self-consciously seeks control of the institution by seeking to retool the values, practices, and sense of institutional reality that comprise faculty and student culture. And they have succeeded wildly. A significant fraction of tenure-stream faculty readily engage directly in the commercialization of research, the enclosure of intellectual property, market behavior such as competition for scraps of "merit pay" rather than a collective demand to keep up with the cost of living, an increasingly managerial role over other campus workers in connection with the continual downsizing and deskilling of traditional faculty work, and so forth. And as they do, we are seeing them embrace exactly the "culture of quality" and "pursuit of excellence" that the administration has intentionally designed for them.

One tantalizing question begged by management's wildly successful social engineering of faculty culture is this: Under current conditions, to what extent do the tenure-stream faculty represent the possibility of an opposition, a counterculture? With the spread of acceptance among the tenure-stream faculty of academic-capitalist values and behaviors, and acquiescence to an increasingly managerial role with respect to the contingent, there is little evidence of anything that resembles an oppositional culture. Indeed, it has become increasingly difficult to speak of anything resembling faculty culture apart from the competitive, market-based, high-performance habitus designed for them by management. One study of this question regarding community college faculties in the United States and Canada concluded that, despite evidence of antago- nism between the faculty and administrations on individual issues, and a degree of concrete opposition located in faculty unions, tenure-stream faculty were generally subject to a profound "corporatization of the self" that produced a pervasive "environment of employee compliance with institutional purposes" founded in management's success at foster- ing a primary identification with the employing institution "over and above" an alternative affiliation with, for instance, one's discipline, any sense of a separate faculty culture, or even the union (Levin, 80–81). Of course, there are exceptions, and self-consciously militant faculties have made their mark in California, New York, Vermont, and elsewhere, in- cluding the South. But even most collective-bargaining faculties have not fully addressed such core issues of administrative control of the workplace as the massive creation, over the past twenty years, of a ma- jority contingent workforce.

There is nonetheless an emergent and vigorous culture of faculty op- position—just not in the tenurable minority. Instead, the rising faculty culture belongs to the unionization movements of contingent faculty and graduate employees, who together comprise what the American As- sociation of University Professors accurately terms the "new majority faculty." On the face of it, it would seem even more difficult to speak of a "culture" of the contingent workforce. This is a group whose precarious position is overwhelmingly designed to disable solidarity, face-to-face encounters, and the emergence of a sense of common culture and communal interest. Moreover, graduate employees and adjunct faculty face not only the employer as a challenge when organizing but also other workers, including tenure-stream faculty and their unions who, Keith Hoeller points out, have in many cases bargained the multi-tier system of academic labor into existence (Hoeller, "Treat Fairly"). It is a group whose hold on the term "faculty" itself is precarious, as Joe Berry has underlined: "Every time a [tenure-track faculty member] or administrator uses the word 'faculty' to refer only to the full time tenure track faculty, one more piece of grit is ground into the eye of any contingent within earshot" (87). Still, they have succeeded in forging an emergent culture of opposition—a culture that sustains and promotes a movement to transform policy, standards, knowledge, appropriations, and the law itself.

This book is a product of that culture. As a graduate student employee and contingent faculty member on several New York campuses in the early and mid 1990s, I participated in campaigns for representation in my union and in my disciplinary association, founded a journal devoted to the struggle (*Workplace: A Journal for Academic Labor*), and circulated an analysis of the particular role that graduate education plays in academe's uniquely successful system of superexploitation (this eventually appeared as "The Waste Product of Graduate Education: Toward a Dictatorship of the Flexible," partly included below). That participation was itself a major part of my graduate education. In the process, I discovered that those of us in the movement understood the system of academic labor far better than the vast majority of senior scholars writing about it in a discourse that I came to label "job-market theory." This discourse was peculiarly detached from our working reality, yet many of us (and all of our faculty mentors) accepted it as a description of our lives and prospects. The leading text of "job-market theory" throughout this period was the contribution of labor economist and Princeton President William G. Bowen who, in a book coauthored with an undergraduate, erroneously projected a major increase in the "demand" for teachers with the Ph.D. (Bowen and Sosa).

As I relate below, the interesting question is not whether Bowen was wrong and the contingent workers were right in a particular instance. The better question is: Why were we right? None of us were economists, and no authorities disputed Bowen. (Other than, fascinatingly, novelist, then-director of the National Endowment for the Humanities, and English Ph.D. Lynne Cheney, who did so from her experience as a contingent worker, not from her pulpit in the administration.)

Ultimately, I came to believe that we were right because the academy's contingent workforce has a superior standpoint for understanding the system of our work. This isn't a theoretical claim. Over the past twenty years, the analysis of the academic labor system provided by contingent faculty and graduate employees—including those who have reported that oppositional knowledge and contributed to it, especially Cary Nelson, Gordon Lafer, Eileen Schell, Randy Martin, Joe Berry, Barbara Wolfe, and Michael Bérubé—consistently provides a superior description of academic workplace reality than such official sources of information as the disciplinary associations, the Council of Graduate Schools, and the managerial discourse.

In addition to more accurate description, I also believe the standpoint of the contingent faculty and graduate employee generates a more just claim on our attention and action than the standpoints occupied by administration or even the faculty in the tenure stream. The commitment of administration to continuously eject the graduate employees and contingent faculty from the system is one dimension of their overriding ambition: to render all employees other than themselves "permanently temporary."

Job-Market Theory

Like many scholars of my cohort, I entered graduate school in 1991 informed by a common sense about academic work that was significantly influenced by the 1989 Bowen report, which projected what it emphasized would be "a substantial excess demand for faculty in the arts and sciences" by the mid 1990s, with the consequence that early in the new millenium we could expect "roughly four candidates for every five positions." The department administrators who recruited me into the profession were of the thoughtful and concerned variety: they were up on the literature and very glad to inform me that something called the "job market" would radically improve just six years in the future. There had been a cycle of bad times for holders of the Ph.D., they admitted, but prosperity was just around the corner. During the early 1990s, buoyed in part by the election of a Democrat to the White House, liberal news-papers and major disciplinary associations recirculated the Bowen projections with a sense of relief and general optimism: With the certain onset of universal health coverage, could full employment for English faculty be far behind?

David Lawrence, MLA's staffer for its association of chairs of English departments (ADE) wrote with typical emotion when he enthused, "Friends, the future we've all been waiting for is about to arrive" (1). For a decade afterward, disciplinary associations and scholars on the state of the profession, such as David Damrosch, gave serious credence to the Bowen projections of "increased demand" for the academic employment of holders of the doctoral degree. As late as 2001, the report of the American Philosophical Association on employment issues, re-published on many department websites, continued to give credence to the Bowen projections, even though the first years of the projected boom had instead conclusively showed only a massively intensifying bust. It wasn't until five years after the report—shortly before it was quite clear that the projections would fail to materialize—that the *Chronicle of Higher Education* finally ran a short item questioning the validity of the report (Magner, "Job-Market Blues"). Slowly through the second half of the decade, most disciplinary associations somewhat reluctantly gave up favorably citing the Bowen projections of a rosy future.

As many readers will know, instead of a jobs bonanza, the 1990s and the first decade of the new millennium have seen an intensification of the pattern established in the 1970s and 1980s. In many academic fields, especially the humanities, as few as one in every three holders of the Ph.D. can expect to eventually find tenure-track employment. Those who do succeed will spend more time toward the degree (bulking the curriculum vita, teaching more, racking up debt), and more time in non-tenurable positions after receiving the doctorate. It is easy enough to measure the gulf between the 1.25 jobs per candidate projected by Bowen and the reality of 0.33 job per candidate. The reporters of the *Chronicle of Higher Education* and one or two angry reviewers of Bowen's subsequent work have made a point of revisiting the rather startling gap between projection and reality (Magner, "Job Market Blues," "Study Says"; Rice).

But the more important and interesting question is analytical: What was wrong with Bowen's assumptions that he strayed so outrageously into fantasy? And what was it about these projections that generated such a warm and uncritical welcome? In chapter 6 of this volume, I provide a detailed critique of Bowen's breathtakingly flawed methodology and examine the way his flawed results were taken up by the most visible disciplinary association in the arts and sciences, the Modern Language Association, from whose Manhattan digs, then in Astor Place, job-market theory was dispensed to the mainstream press.

In brief, Bowen's method was to impose neoliberal market ideology on data that, instead of demonstrating a stable "market" in tenure-track jobs, attests to the unfolding process of casualization. Most egregiously, for instance, when confronted with data that increasing numbers of doctoral degree holders had been accepting nonacademic work since the 1970s, Bowen ignores the abundant testimony by graduate students that this dislocation from the academy was involuntary. Instead, he imposes the ideology of "free choice" on the phenomenon, generating the fallacious claim that this ever-upward "trend" showed that even more people will "choose" similarly. The result of this tautology was that he projected a spiraling need to increase graduate school admissions—in order to compensate for the imaginary, ever-increasing cohort of people that he wrongly portrayed as choosing nonacademic work. Although all of the available testimony from graduate students themselves suggested an involuntary dislocation from their plans of tenure-stream employment, Bowen opted to present the traditional, deeply ideological figure so central to his disciplinary knowledge—the "freely choosing" figure of "homo economicus," which was widespread in neoclassical economic modeling and a mainstay of neoliberal policy thought after 1980.

This error was only one element in an overall set of ideological assumptions. In modeling the academic labor system as a market, Bowen introduced an unwarranted analogy to other markets in the business cycle and assumed a "natural" boom-bust pattern. He also excluded the majority of academic workers. In order to manufacture an empirically existing "job market" out of data that indicated a labor system running on the continuous substitution of student and casual labor for tenure-stream faculty, Bowen had to virtually exclude the labor of students, full-time lecturers, and part-time faculty from his model of the labor system. Somehow he manages to populate his "universe of faculty" with only 12,000 part-timers. By contrast, the 1993 National Study of Post-Secondary Faculty (NSOPF) saw more than 250,000 and felt this number was deeply undercounted (National Center for Education Statistics).

Furthermore, Bowen's projections rest on the counterfactual assumption that "institutions always *want* to have more faculty and will add faculty positions *when they can afford to do so*" (Bowen and Sosa, 153; emphasis theirs). In reality, every nook and cranny of the public discourse on the question held reams of evidence attesting that what institutions really wanted was to accumulate capital and conserve labor costs by casualizing faculty positions by any means available: early retirement, expanded graduate programs, outsourcing, distance education, deskilling, and the like. Bowen's response to the "bear market" in academic hiring during 1970–1989 was, in a sense, predetermined: he started out looking for the complementary swing of the pendulum, what he viewed as the inevitable bull market in academic hiring, and he found it. Sometime between 1994 and 2012, Bowen was sure, things would turn around. After all, "markets" always do.

Bowen is hardly alone in erroneously imposing market ideology on data about the structure and relations of academic labor. The interpretive engine driving Bowen's projections—the notion that there is a "job market" in academic labor (a notion which in its folk-academic usage has to be held distinct from the better applications of labor market analysis) remains nearly universal throughout the academy. Job-market theory is a significant vector through which managerial thought spread to faculty and graduate students as part of what I call a second wave of dominant thought about the situation of academic labor after 1945. (There is an earlier, prewar period of struggle over academic labor that was emblematized by John Dewey's cofounding of both the American Federation of Teachers and the American Association of University Professors. Surveyed by Clyde Barrow and Christopher Newfield, as well as by education historian John Thelin, this is the period of white-collar industrialization from which we derive such managerial innovations as the credit hour and such labor victories as "academic freedom.") Originating in the surging self-confidence of higher education management, managerial thought after 1970 became a "wave" insofar as it entered the culture, thought, and scholarship of other education constituencies. During the past quarter century, the worldview of faculty and students has repeatedly threatened to collapse entirely into the management viewpoint.

Nonetheless, there are many lines of alternative thought. Often, quite strong formations survive in connection with an earlier first wave of dominant thought about the situation of academic labor after 1945;

these include the analysis and commitments associated with the movement for unionization of the tenure-stream faculty in the 1960s and 1970s. The once-vigorous movement for unionization of the tenurable, now in a phase of "survivor institutions," was itself largely a component of a much larger surge of organizing activity that gathered momentum in the 1950s, the radicalization of and movement to unionize public employees, including schoolteachers. It cannot be said that the professoriate provided leadership to this movement. Rather clearly, schoolteachers, municipal clerks, firefighters, police officers, and their unions showed professors the way. During its heyday, however, the ideas of faculty unionists pervasively infiltrated the thinking of management, students, and the public. As I note in chapter 3, Clark Kerr and the Carnegie Foundation gazed at the movement for unionization of the tenurable faculty with intense trepidation, projecting that the decades of student power would be followed by decades of faculty power.

Originating as management's oppositional knowledge in response to the emergence of faculty and student power, second-wave knowledge about higher education working conditions gained currency steadily through the 1970s, achieved dominance through the 1980s, and remains dominant at this writing. The intellectual roots of the managerial second wave are in neoclassical economics, the neoliberal political regime, and the pervasive discourse of management theory. For the vast majority of working managers, as well as most nonmanagerial persons indoctrinated by management thought, this second-wave ideology is more of a "vulgar liberalism" than a committed neoliberalism—a kind of accidental neoliberalism produced by the wildly inaccurate application to higher education working conditions of dimly remembered chestnuts from Econ 101.

One of the earliest, most adopted, and least contested discourses of the managerial second wave, job-market theory captured the imagination of most faculty and many graduate employees with the clarity and elegance of its central tenet: tenure-track job advertisements can be considered the "demand," and recent degree holders the "supply," for an annual job "market," overseen by professional associations such as the MLA. While this language originally served as analogy, for most producers and consumers of job-market theory the terms hardened under neoliberalism into a positive heuristic, serving as a kind of half-baked approximation of labor-market analysis. (Responsible labor-market analysis, for starters, would have accounted for casualization.) This language appealed to the tenure-stream faculty, including the organized faculty. The notion of a "market in jobs" allowed tenure-stream faculty to approach the problems of graduate employment in ways entirely separate from the ways they approached their own workplace issues. Even faculty who saw the need to bargain collectively on their own behalf took up job-market theory with relief. Through it, the issues of graduate employment appeared susceptible to a simple solution—the balancing of supply and demand by concerned academic citizens (perhaps administrators or graduate faculty). As a result, it was possible to believe that these were not issues that had to be confronted by the unions themselves.

Job-market theory separates the workplace issues of the graduate employee from the workplace issues of the faculty and sweepingly defines the workplace relation of faculty to students in paternal, administrative, and managerial terms. Whatever actions faculty might take to secure their own working conditions, job-market theory defines their responsibility toward graduate students and former graduate students not as a relationship of solidarity with coworkers but, instead, as a managerial responsibility. In multiple roles—as graduate faculty, in professional associations, as management—the tenured saw their responsibility to graduate employees through the lens of participating in the administration of the "market."

From a labor perspective, job-market theory disables the practice of solidarity and helps to legitimate the tiering of the workforce. Even to the most idealistic and committed observer, the job-market model offered the seductions of a quick, technocratic fix. For more than three decades, the model has sustained the general conviction that the system of graduate education produces more degree holders than necessary, and that this "overproduction" can be controlled "from the demand side" by encouraging early retirements and "from the supply side" by shrinking graduate programs.

Reality is very different from the model. In the reality of structural casualization, the jobs of professors taking early retirement are often eliminated, not filled with new degree holders. Nor does reducing graduate school admissions magically create tenure-track jobs. Most graduate schools admit students to fill specific labor needs. One of the core functions of graduate programs is to enhance flexibility, always presenting just enough labor, just in time. As a result, management cannot reduce graduate-employee admissions without making other arrangements for the work that graduate employees would otherwise have performed. Universities that have cut their graduate employee rolls have consistently preferred to make other flexible arrangements, hiring part-timers or nontenurable lecturers and not new tenurable faculty. Insofar as these new flex workers are themselves inevitably former graduate employees, there can hardly be said to be any net improvement.

In this context, the idea of a job market operates rhetorically and not descriptively, serving largely to legitimate faculty passivity in the face of this wholesale restructuring of the academic workplace by activist legislatures and administrations. By offering faculty the fantasy of supply-side control from the desktop, the job-market fiction provides an imaginary solution—the invisible hand—to a real problem.

Under casualization, it makes very little sense to view the graduate student as potentially a "product" for a "market" in tenure-track jobs. For many graduate employees, the receipt of the Ph.D. signifies the end, and not the beginning, of a long teaching career. Most graduate students are already laboring at the only academic job they'll ever have—hence, the importance for organized graduate student labor of inscribing the designation "graduate employee" in law and discourse.

From the standpoint of the organized graduate employee, the situation is clear. Increasingly, the holders of the doctoral degree are not so much the *products* of the graduate-employee labor system as its *by-products,* insofar as that labor system exists primarily to recruit, train, supervise, and legitimate the employment of nondegreed students and contingent faculty.

This is not to say that the system doesn't produce and employ holders of the Ph.D. in tenurable positions, only that this operation has become secondary to its extraction of teaching labor from persons who are nondegreed or not yet degreed, or whose degrees are now represented as an "overqualification" for their contingent circumstances.

The Waste Product of Graduate Education

Grad students existed not to learn things but to relieve the tenured faculty members of tiresome burdens such as educating people and doing research. Within a month of his arrival, Randy solved some trivial computer problems for one of the other grad students. A week later, the chairman of the astronomy department called him over and said, "So, you're the UNIX guru." At the time, Randy was still stupid enough to be flattered by the attention, when he should have recognized them as bone-chilling words.

Three years later, he left the Astronomy Department without a degree, and with nothing to show for his labors except six hundred dollars in his bank account and a staggeringly comprehensive knowledge of UNIX. Later, he was to calculate that, at the going rates for programmers, the department had extracted about a quarter of a million dollars' worth of work from him, in return for an outlay of less than twenty thousand. (Stephenson, *Cryptonomicon*, 97)

Discussing the enthusiasm he and the Sloan Foundation had for funding William Massy's *Virtual U* management training game, Jesse Ausubel wrote that "everyone else" in the university has "a very partial view of a complex system," but one person—the president—"finally sees the institution synoptically [through] financial flows." Through the game, newly appointed presidents and upper administrators "can see totality in a few minutes or hours that in real life would take decades." The medium through which this synoptic view is possible, Ausubel confesses, "is basic: money." Every decision in the game "translates directly or indirectly into a revenue or expense." Under the general neoliberal onslaught, this managerial conversion of all values into financial flows and the corresponding understanding of all human systems via market logic serves as the only available heuristic for thinking at the level of totality.

In this airless environment, even the slightest displacement of management's logic yields insight into a very different underlying reality. For instance, it is perfectly common for scholars of professional work more generally to employ the heuristic of a labor monopoly rather than a labor market. (The best application of a labor-market mode of analysis to academic work might include the concept of segmentation—asking, for example, how is it that women comprise a vast majority in the casual sector and a distinct minority in the tenured sector?) Monopoly control of professional labor generally reflects a social bargain made by professional associations that exchange a service mission with the public for substantial control over the conditions of their work, generally including deciding who gets to practice. In a professional police culture, for instance, only the graduates of police academies may practice, and the police unions, like professional associations, supervise this instruction and apprenticeship, thereby safeguarding the employment conditions of these recruits against the depradations of would-be amateur and volunteer police practitioners (and the city managers who would employ them). From this perspective, the ideology of the job-market analogy may be seen as having obscured the very useful description of the academic labor system in perfectly scholarly and conventional terms as a failed monopoly of professional labor.

That is, postsecondary educators generally fulfill the service mission that constitutes their half of the bargain; in return, society continues to grant them monopoly control over degrees. But the labor monopoly fails because degree holding no longer represents control over who may practice.[1] Indeed, the inescapable observation must be this: under casualization, degree holding increasingly represents a *disqualification* from practice. The ultimate refutation to job-market theory is that, in observing that the holder of the doctoral degree is the "waste product of graduate education," we are only moving toward an acknowledgment of simple fact.

Degree holders frequently serve as university teachers for eight or ten years before earning their doctorate. In English departments, a degree holder will have taught many writing classes, perhaps also a literature survey or theme class, even an upper-division seminar related to her field of study. Many degree holders have served as adjunct lecturers at other campuses, sometimes teaching master's degree students and advising their theses en route to their own degrees. Some will have taught thirty to forty sections, or the equivalent of five to seven years' full-time teaching work. During this time, they received frequent mentoring and regular evaluation; most will have a large portfolio of enthusiastic observations and warm student commendations. A large fraction will have published essays and book reviews and authored their departmental web pages. Yet at precisely the juncture that this "preparation" should end and regular employment begin—the acquisition of the Ph.D.—the system embarrasses itself and discloses a systematic truth that every recent degree holder knows and few administrators wish to acknowledge: *in many disciplines, for the majority of graduates, the Ph.D. indicates the logical conclusion of an academic career.*

As presently constructed, the system of academic work requires instructors to have the terminal M.A. or M.Phil. or to have the doctorate "ABD" (all but the dissertation). Ideally, these teachers will have a well-paid partner or other means of support enabling them to teach for wages below the poverty line for an extended period of time without undue suffering.[2] Without a degree and presupposing another source of income, people of this description can and do teach virtually forever. The system cannot run without people who are doing or who have done graduate study, quite frequently persons who can be represented as on some long trajectory toward the terminal doctorate. As presently constructed, the academic labor system requires few if any new degree holders—but it gasps and sputters when there is a tiny interruption in the steady stream of new graduate students (hence, the appearance of employment contracts in admittance packets).[3] The system "really needs" a continuous flow of replaceable nondegreed labor. It can also use degreed labor willing and financially equipped to serve in the subprofessional conditions established for the nondegreed, but the majority of people with degrees cannot afford to do so.

What needs to be quite clear is that this is not a "system out of control," a machine with a thrown rod or a blown gasket. Quite the contrary: it's a smoothly functioning new system with its own easily apprehensible logic, premised entirely on the continuous replacement of degree holders with nondegreed labor (or persons with degrees willing to work on unfavorable terms). The plight of recent degree holders encapsulates this logic. Let us say that Jane Doe has taught sections English 101-97 and 101-98 for the past seven years and, for the past four, women's studies 205, a special topics course fulfilling a university-wide diversity requirement. Upon earning the degree (or in many circumstances much earlier), Doe becomes ineligible to teach those sections, unless given a special waiver or postdoctoral invitation. The reason most universities limit the number of years a graduate student is "eligible to teach" is to ensure that a smooth flow of new persons is brought into the system. The many "exceptions" to these eligibility rules are the expression of this labor pool's flexibility, enabling the administration to be confident that it can deliver low-cost teaching labor "just in time" to any point on the factory floor.

Because of the related erosion of secure employment opportunity for young workers throughout the global economy, this system has no trouble bringing in new persons. Applications to graduate programs primarily designed to prepare future faculty have steadily climbed, despite the poor chances of finding tenurable employment.

The system's only problem is disposing of these self-subsidizing student teachers after it has extracted six to ten years of their labor, to make room for a new crop of the same. This logic of replacement creates many local ironies. Because people who are declared "ineligible to teach" by a graduate program frequently serve as flexible labor at other campuses, it is often at the junior colleges and other less-prestigious locations where the most experienced and dedicated flexible faculty can be found. The flexible labor at research universities with graduate programs are primarily new graduate employees and therefore will generally have between zero and five years' part-time experience. By contrast, the flexible labor at most other campuses, including junior colleges, will often consist of persons who have exhausted their fellowship years (and may or may not have received a degree as a result). They will therefore commonly have between five and twenty years of experience. These local ironies are important because they make clear that the system's logic is not designed to provide better teaching even at the richest schools: it is designed to accommodate capital accumulation, which transpires with greater efficiency at the richest schools. At wealthier private research schools, where grad employees may teach one or two courses in only two or three years of their fellowship, parents, students, and scholarship donors will pay tuition and expenses that approach $50,000 a year in order to be taught by trainees, nearly all with less than the equivalent of one year's full-time pedagogical experience.

The academic labor system creates holders of the Ph.D., but it doesn't have much use for them. This buildup of degree holders in the system represents a potentially toxic blockage. The system produces degree holders largely in the sense that a car's engine produces heat—a tiny fraction of which is recycled into the car's interior by the cabin heater, but the vast majority of which figures as waste energy that the system urgently requires to be radiated away. The system of academic labor only creates degree holders out of a tiny fraction of the employees it takes in by way of graduate education. Leaving aside the use of M.A. students as instructional staff, doctoral programs in the humanities commonly award the Ph.D. to between 20 and 40 percent of their entrants. In many disciplines, the system only employs perhaps a third of the degree holders it makes. Like a car's engine idling in the takeout food line, the system's greatest urgency is to dispel most of the degree-holding waste product.

From the perspective of casualization, the possibility of a toxic buildup of degree holders is not, as commonly maintained by job-market theorists, the result of "too many" graduate students. On the contrary, it is precisely the nature of permatemping to arrange that there are always "just enough" graduate students and other nondegreed flex workers to be delivered "just in time" to serve the university's labor needs. It is in the interest and logic of the system to have as many graduate students as it can employ while producing the fewest number of degrees—or, better yet, to produce persons with degrees who don't make a claim for permanent academic employment. This is one reason that graduate-school administrations have recently promoted the Marie Antoinette or "let them eat cake" theory of graduate education: "Why, if they cannot find teaching work, let them be screenwriters!" This is a kind of excrement theory for managers, through which the degree holder figures as a horrible stain or blot, an embarrassment that the system is hysterically trying to scrape from its shoes. By institutionalizing the practice of preparing degree holders for "alternate careers," the system's managers are creating a radiator or waste pipe to flush away persons whose teaching services are no longer required precisely because they now hold the degree.

Persons who actually hold the terminal degree are the traumatic Real puncturing the collective fantasy that powers this system. Degree in hand, loans coming due, the working partner expecting a more fair financial contribution, perhaps the question of children growing relevant, the degree holder asks a question to which the system has no answer: If I have been a splendid teacher and scholar while nondegreed for the past ten years, why am I suddenly unsuitable?

Nearly all of the administrative responses to the degree holder can already be understood as responses to waste: flush it, ship it to the provinces, recycle it through another industry, keep it away from the fresh meat. Unorganized graduate employees and contingent faculty have a tendency to grasp their circumstance incompletely—that is, they feel "treated like shit"—without grasping the systemic reality that they *are* waste. Insofar as graduate employees feel treated like waste, they can maintain the fantasy that they really exist elsewhere, in some place other than the overwhelmingly excremental testimony of their experience. This fantasy becomes an alibi for inaction, because in this construction agency lies elsewhere, with the administrative touch on the flush-chain. The effect of people who feel treated like waste is an appeal to some other agent: please stop treating us this way—which is to say to that outside agent, "please recognize that we are not waste," even when that benevolent recognition is contrary to the testimony of our understanding. (And, of course, it is only good management to tell the exploited and superexploited, "Yes, I recognize your dignity. You are special.")

By contrast, the organized graduate employee and contingent faculty share the grasp of the totality of the system that proceeds from the understanding that they are indeed the waste of that system. They know they are not merely treated like waste but, in fact, are the actual shit of the system—being churned inexorably toward the outside: not merely "disposable" labor (Walzer) but labor that must be disposed of for the system to work. These are persons who can perform acts of blockage. Without expelling the degree holder, the system could not be what it is. Imagine what would happen to "graduate programs preparing future faculty"if they were held responsible for degree-granting by a requirement to continue the employment of every person to whom they granted a Ph.D. but who was unable to find academic employment elsewhere. In many locations, the pipeline would jam in the first year!

The difference in consciousness between feeling treated like waste and knowing one's excremental condition is the difference between experiencing casualization as "local disorder" (that authority will soon rectify) and having the grasp of one's potential for transforming the systemic realities of an actually existing new order. Where the degree-holding waste product understands its capacity for blockage and refuses to be expelled, the system organizing the inside must rapidly succumb.

Theorizing Blockage

There are many ways of writing about the casualization of academic work. As I elaborate in chapter 2, the most inclusive frame is one that addresses the malignant casualization of the work process globally. In this frame, the designation "student," including undergraduate and even child labor, emerges as a bonanza in global capital's voracious quest for low-cost, underregulated labor. In chapter 4, I explore how in the United States and globally the designation "student" has evolved into a legal fiction designating a form of "worker which is not one": someone who can be put to work but does not enjoy the rights of labor. Students are just one category of workers without rights—persons who work but who, in a growing web of law in service of exploitation, are construed as "not workers" for purposes of the statutes that provide worker protections, such as the National Labor Relations Act (NLRA).

This global "informalization" of the work process can only be met by the most inclusive forms of unionization. Mobilization of the academic community will inevitably require tearing down the barriers between academic work and other kinds of work. We will have to set aside the often-crippling exceptionalism associated with "mental" labor generally.[4] Ultimately, the most helpful standpoint from which to initiate action will be one that sees contingency as a global condition engineered by capital for labor, and which understands the university as a dynamic node of post-Fordist employment from the sweatshop to the classroom.

In this enlarged context, it is fair to ask, Why bother to talk about the doctoral degree holder at all, when the experience of contingency is general, or at least generational? Isn't it frivolous to speak of an "excrement theory" of graduate education when the democratic promise of higher education is eroding everywhere around us? Don't we just need more clear positive knowledge regarding flex work? In the big picture of global exploitation, just how important are the problems of underemployed holders of doctoral degrees anyway?

Alternatively, without a theory of the waste product—the system's constitutive exterior—we have so far utterly failed to see that the effects of academic casualization are immanent throughout the system (not merely "local" to the casualized). For thirty years, the bad knowledge of "markets" for degree holders has enabled faculty unions and disciplinary associations alike to accommodate the creation of a multi-tier labor system, the most dramatically tiered labor system in North America. Faculty bargaining agents have accepted the collective fantasy regarding the waste of the labor system: that graduate employees are being "trained" for future jobs, not toiling in the only academic job they will ever have. Subtract the largely imaginary relationship of most graduate-employee laborers to a future job, and the systemic effects of that labor are visible as the effects of casualized second-tier labor in any workplace: management domination of the work rules, speedup, moonlighting, and grossly depressed wages for everyone.

The system of disposable labor has been consistently mistaken as a problem only for the relatively small constituency of the graduate student and other contingent faculty.

For instance, the total compatibility of the cheap teaching system with capital accumulation has enabled most schools (or the public funding them) to either (a) pay off shareholders handsomely or (b) spend money on other things besides teaching labor—engage in vast building programs, create enormous endowments, launch new program: vices, and so on. From this perspective, one might sentimentally ᵈᵉₚ... the way that graduate students are exploited by being cycled out of the system after a period of service and debt accumulation, but then go on to feel that "other constituencies" are surely benefiting from new stadiums, business centers, and prisons. This view suggests that the money saved by cheap teaching surely benefits some people, and if the only people harmed are a few graduate students, or persons whose other sources of income allow them to teach as a kind of philanthropy, what's the big deal?

One of the most useful aspects of the knowledge of graduate-employee and contingent faculty unionists is the way it addresses the system as a totality, enabling us to see that few people situated in the education ecology really benefit from the system of cheap teaching.

From "I Feel Your Pain" to "Oh Shit! Your Problem Is My Problem!"

It is declared to be the policy of the United States to eliminate the causes of certain substantial obstructions to the free flow of commerce and to mitigate and eliminate those obstructions when they have occurred by *encouraging the practice and procedure of collective bargaining* and by protecting the exercise by workers of full freedom of association, self-organization, and designation of representatives of their own choosing, for the purpose of negotiating the terms and conditions of their employment. (Daniel Silverman, Director, NLRB Region 2, applying the language of the NLRA to the NYU case; emphasis in the original)

The "third wave" of knowledge regarding the academic labor system emerged in the early part of the 1990s. It is grounded in what has grown into a fifty-campus movement of graduate-employee unions (GEUs) and the flourishing campaign to organize contingent faculty, which has racked up a string of successful drives at both public and private campuses in the past several years. Many aspects of both movements have been documented in the legal literature surrounding the struggle for recognition, in an important series of films by Barbara Wolf and in well-known books since 1994 by Cary Nelson, Steve Watt, Michael Bérubé, David Downing, and Eileen Schell, together with two special issues of

Social Text edited by Randy Martin (one of which appeared, expanded and republished as *Chalk Lines: The Politics of Work in the Managed University*). The movement has given rise to collections of its own, notably Deborah Herman and Julie Schmid's *Cogs in the Classroom*, Michael Dubson's *Ghosts in the Classroom*, Eileen Schell and Patricia Lambert Stock's *Moving a Mountain*, and my own effort with Tony Scott and Leo Parascondola, *Tenured Bosses and Disposable Teachers*.

The medium most associated with the movement is the Internet, which hosts, in real time, the unfolding knowledge and burgeoning solidarity of the movement. Especially significant are the websites of various contingent faculty bargaining units and campaigns cooperating in the Coalition of Contingent Academic Labor (COCAL), and the graduate-employee websites indexed by Jon Curtiss's Coalition of Graduate Employee Unions (CGEU). The Internet also hosts noteworthy weblog commentary by the "Invisible Adjunct," among others, and *Workplace: A Journal for Academic Labor* (at www.workplace-gsc.com), at this writing entering its tenth year of continuous publication.

During union activity, such as organizing campaigns or the landmark strike of New York University graduate employees beginning in November 2005, Internet commentary effloresces. These typically involve independent, organizer, and institutional sites and weblogs. In the most visible events, debate will also spike in the weblog-powered "commentary" functions attached to reporting in online media, such as the institution's student newspaper, alumni publications, the web portals of local mainstream media, and the trade press. The onset of the NYU graduate employees' strike gave rise to a blizzard of online debate, largely mediated by the undergraduate newspaper and such venues as the discussion forums attached to *Inside Higher Education*. These debates involved undergraduates, tenured and contingent faculty, anti-union graduate employees, organizers, activists, New Yorkers living nearby, and alumnae from across the country.

Despite its vigor, third-wave academic labor knowledge is continuously under active erasure by the positive and commonsensical knowledge of the foundations, disciplines, institutes, and media. To some extent, this erasure takes the simple, ideological form of the power of second-wave market knowledge to interpellate concerned faculty, undergraduates, taxpayers, and public analysts, not to mention graduate employees themselves. As I try to make clear in chapter 5, the relationship of a discipline's intellectual content to its structural role in the labor system shapes even the most sympathetic adherents' sense of what can be said and thought, not just what can be done.

For graduate employees, the overwhelming consciousness of one's disposability all too frequently lends the aura of concreteness to the ideology of "market." But the erasure of graduate-employee labor knowledge also takes the more active forms of direct suppression. In organizing campaigns, the suppression of labor knowledge by administrations can take the form of nonrenewal of the fellowships and assistantships of organizers, as well as punitive recommendations by advisers—even, occasionally, expulsion. It can take the form of illegal harassment, as Joel Westheimer charged in the NLRB complaint he successfully settled with NYU after being denied tenure at NYU subsequent to testifying in support of graduate-employee unionists (Fogg). Most often, though, direct suppression of labor knowledge by administrations and disciplinary institutions takes the form of the kind of pervasive information warfare conducted, for example, by MLA's staff and executive council in response to resolutions by the organization's assembly in support of Yale University's GEU. In this instance, typical of the control that the staff and officers of MLA sought to impose on the organization's processes of self-governance throughout the 1990s, organization staffers mailed out a twelve-page propaganda leaflet attempting to shore up the administrative position on the labor dispute (hoping, unsuccessfully, that the membership would decline to ratify the measure). As Bérubé notes, this completely one-sided document was circulated, without any sense of irony, under the claim that it attempted to preserve "diversity of opinion" on the question, and it became part of a continuing pattern by MLA officers and staff of containing graduate-employee dissent (56–58).[5]

The fundamental unit of third-wave or graduate-employee consciousness regarding the structure of academic labor can be contained in two words: We Work. But coming to this fundamental consciousness is not only a question of overcoming the ideology of apprenticeship and the disciplinary powers of academic institutions, it is a question of struggling with the apparatus of the state itself. That is, until very recently, university employers consistently enjoyed the support of federal and state courts in maintaining that graduate students working as teachers were "apprentices" and "primarily students" and denied them the rights of labor, especially the right to bargain collectively. As Randy Martin puts it: academic labor generally and graduate-employee organizers in particular "meet the State head on" in contesting "the claim of the university to be the lawgiver" in defining the conditions of their labor (*Chalk Lines*, 4–5). A consistent problem for the graduate-employee union movement has been the degree to which the interlocking ideologemes of "youth," "study," and "apprenticeship" are underwritten by federal and state law, so that a typical doctoral degree holder in the humanities, completing her degree at age thirty-seven, and having taught near full-time for as much as ten or twelve years—having paid tax on her earnings and acquired debt of $20,000 to $70,000 or perhaps far more (a special kind of debt at an interest rate higher than home mortgages, and unlike the debt of credit-card holders and businesspeople, unforgivable in bankruptcy)—must now begin to seek a new career.[6]

In recognizing that their work is, in fact, labor, graduate employees have been able to get beyond the fetish of "the economy," "the market," and "the law" that bedevils second-wave knowledge. Graduate employees understand that all of these forces do not transpire in a distant field of titans but, instead, occur in the arena of everyday struggle with the employer for control of the workplace. For the graduate employee, it has not been a question of forecasting the economy or learning the limits established by the law but, rather, of making the law responsive to their understanding. Despite setbacks in state courts and before the National Labor Relations Board in the 1970s, and the extraordinary, sustained, and frequently illegal opposition by university employers, graduate-employee unionists throughout the 1990s continuously won victories writing their knowledge ("we work") into law. Just as importantly, they introduced that principle into the consciousness of individuals comprising the political apparatus in many of the largest "education states" in the country. Because the National Labor Relations Act specifically excludes government employees from its protections, the circumstances of workers at publicly funded universities—including tenure-stream faculty, nonacademic workers, and student employees—are addressed primarily by state laws.

The organization of graduate-employee unions at public universities has therefore depended on an arduous legal and political campaign conducted on a state-by-state basis. Despite great variety in state labor law and political climate, there are significant commonalities in successful campaigns to force public universities to the bargaining table. In order to win recognition, organizers have commonly had to initiate decades-long campaigns of litigation in public employee relations boards (PERBs) and appellate courts, or even appeal to state legislators to draft new laws. Inspired and often supported by the movement to unionize tenure-stream faculty, graduate employees in public universities began to unionize in the 1960s, beginning with a successful campaign at the University of Wisconsin.[7]

More typical efforts took longer, often over decades and dozens of graduate-employee "generations," as at the University of California, where graduate employees formed locals affiliated with the AFT in the early and mid 1970s, but failed to win recognition or negotiate a first contract for the next quarter century. In a 1980s resurgence, many of the California locals switched to the United Auto Workers and won a "temporary" recognition in 1989, until a hostile PERB ruled in favor of the university's appeal. The road to a first University of California contract in May 2000 required a series of legal victories in the 1990s. These included favorable PERB interpretation of state laws providing bargaining rights to other higher education employees and multiple successful appellate lawsuits.

One core lesson is that these repeated legal victories were not sufficient in themselves. Even after a series of decisive opinions in administrative and appellate courts, the UC campus administration refused to bargain until the union acted politically, engaging in awareness-raising job actions and appealing to state legislators and the public for assistance. Spurred by the mobilization and will to direct action by the graduate employee locals, and the concern of the electorate for stability and labor peace on campus, the California legislature threatened to shut down university appropriations until the administration complied with state law. This threat finally forced six UC campuses to the bargaining table, resulting in a first contract in May 2000.

Entering its fifth decade, the movement to unionize graduate employees in publicly funded universities has learned that "the law" is a field of political struggle, deeply dependent on the vagaries of the political party that controls appointments to the PERB in each state at any given time. In consequence, they have learned the importance of educating lawmakers and the public served by those lawmakers. Even with the electorate and the legislature on their side, graduate employees have come to understand the astonishing persistence, arrogance, ingenuity, and determination of their employers. The will of public-university employers to defy lawmakers and flout the intentions of labor law rivals the most ruthless union busting of any commercial enterprise (generally hiring, at public expense, the same corporate law firms to guide them).

For example, home to some of the most vigorously oppositional labor and management cultures in the United States, Illinois has a labor-relations board that is dedicated exclusively to education labor, the Illinois Education Labor Relations Board (IELRB). As in California and elsewhere, initial organizing in Illinois began in the 1970s but did not gain significant momentum until the University of Illinois at Urbana-Champaign (UIUC) graduate employees affiliated with the AFT. Losing its first round before the IELRB, in 1996, the graduate-employee organization chose to hold a union election anyway. As yet without substantial legal status, the solid 2–1 vote in favor of unionization supported the determination of the organizers to contest both the IELRB ruling and the statute on which it was based. The UI-Chicago graduate employees joined the struggle, and activists on both campuses worked together to generate the interest of pro-union state legislators and the support of other Illinois educator unions, especially the Illinois Federation of Teachers, the AFT affiliate representing K–12 educators statewide.

The university fought the union hard. Guided by a well-known anti-union law firm, the administration intimidated graduate employees by subpoenaing the records of those graduate employees who had filed affidavits regarding working conditions, then notifying their advisors (and potential recommenders) of the legal proceedings. Independent election monitors reported the circulation of rumors among international graduate employees, specifically targeting Asian students, that a union victory would mean cutbacks in their ranks. When graduate employees won the IELRB ruling on administrative appeal, and again before the State Supreme Court, the University of Illinois still refused to bargain. The graduate employees wrote a bill, passed by the state legislature in March 2000, guaranteeing them bargaining rights. The university continued to stonewall, bringing an action before the original labor board (which remained hostile to graduate employees) that resulted in the fanciful delineation of a bargaining unit that would have excluded 90 percent of graduate employees.

The UIUC and UIC unions continued to work with friendly state legislators and the Illinois Federation of Teachers (IFT). In 2003, new card-check legislation conferred automatic recognition of unions upon state-board certification. And in July 2004, the state senate passed the graduate employee bargaining-rights bill. By the time their bill became law, however, UIUC grad employees had already ratified their first contract. Part of their success was political: as in California, the unions' successful appeal to the public and legislature swiftly eroded the administration's capacity to burn public money on corporate lawyers in increasingly desperate and underhanded efforts to postpone bargaining.

Another significant factor was the graduate employees' decision to engage in direct action. In 2001, they held a series of walkouts; in March 2002, they occupied the UIUC campus administration building. As reported to Nelson and Watt by participants, the occupation was an expression of militant determination to compel recognition: "It's our building now. You get your office back after the union is recognized" (*Office Hours,* 142). Carefully planned and executed, the occupation was timed to coincide with a Board of Trustees meeting and the presence of news media, and the administration gave in before the day was out. Surveying other graduate-employee and contingent-faculty direct actions in California and New York, Nelson and Watt conclude that the will to creatively disrupt university business as usual holds important lessons for the entire campus community, including "rethinking" the professional culture of the tenured professoriate: "We need as faculty members to rethink our relation to ambition, achievement, competition and careerism" (*Office Hours,* 163).

The necessity for continuous organizing and mobilization for action is a lesson that the longest-running graduate-employee unions have fully absorbed over the years. The institutional history of the union at the University of Michigan, for instance, features a thirty-year string of near-continuous job actions, featuring at least one in every successful contract cycle. These began with a series of strike votes during 1970–1974 that forced the university into recognizing the union, despite difficulties with the state public-employee relations board over the shape of the bargaining unit. With recognition, the union had to strike in February and March 1975 to force the university to bargain seriously toward a first contract and then, even after contract ratification, was forced to continue the strike to gain assurance that there would be no reprisals. In 1976, in the midst of negotiating a second contract, the university attempted to backtrack and make the case that graduate employees were not real workers and therefore "could not commit unfair labor practice" in relation to them. Losing at every stage in Michigan administrative hearings and appellate courts, the administration nonetheless protracted its appeal process for five years and was not compelled to sign the 1976 contract until 1981. Winning continuous courtroom victories over five years but without significant contract gains and with its organization in decay, the experience of this litigated contract cycle caused Michigan graduate employees to shift to a "grassroots" steward-ship model of collecting the dues in face-to-face encounters every semes-ter in 1983. Building solidarity through continuous organizing became a central commitment. Yearly rallies on economic issues commenced, and contract negotiations involved strike authorizations, walkouts, or work stoppages in 1987, 1991, 1993, 1996, 1999, and 2002. The result is one of the strongest graduate-employee contracts in the nation.

By 2007, employing militancy, inventive direct action, canny alliance, the principle of continuous organizing, and the will to make both law and lawmakers respect their workplace realities, U.S. graduate employ-ees had forced public university employers to the bargaining table in all of the largest education states: California, New York, Florida, Michi-gan, Oregon, New Jersey, Pennsylvania, Illinois, Massachusetts, Iowa, Kansas, Wisconsin, Washington, and even the smaller Rhode Island. During this period, graduate employees formed unions at publicly funded universities in Indiana, Ohio, Maryland, and Virginia, though these have yet to succeed in compelling recognition from the employer.

Occupying the national news in the 1990s and well into the subse-quent decade was the efforts of graduate students in private universities, especially Yale and, subsequently, NYU. These experiences have also demonstrated the need for the "continuous organizing" model, direct action, strong alliances with other unions and constituencies, and close relationships with communities. Perhaps most importantly, the NYU ex-periences have underlined another key feature that private university or-ganizers share with their publicly funded colleagues: the overtly political nature of the struggle.

Spurred by the victories of their publicly employed counterparts, unionization efforts among graduate employees at private universities sharply accelerated throughout the 1990s. In this decade, efforts began or renewed themselves on as many as two dozen privately funded cam-puses and resulted in nationally affiliated unions at Brandeis, Columbia, Rensselaer Polytechnic Institute, Brown, Yale, and elsewhere. Notably, two groups succeeded in forcing recognition and compelling the em-ployer to negotiate: NYU and Temple (one of the largest "state-related" universities resulting from activist restructuring: it receives public fund-ing but is under independent control).

The culmination of these efforts appeared in the form of an elo-quently composed decision by NLRB Regional Director Daniel Silverman on April 3, 2000, finding that NYU teaching assistants were in fact employees "within the meaning of the [National Labor Relations] Act." Silverman dispensed quickly with such outright prevarications on the part of the administration as the claim that the services performed by graduate employees are "simply part of their education" and that NYU "runs the graduate teaching program for the benefit of the graduate students and not to facilitate its teaching of undergraduates." He brushed off the NYU attorneys' efforts to claim as irrelevant the massive evidence pertaining to collective bargaining in public higher education while attempting to claim relevant precedent in cases involving the Arkansas Lighthouse for the Blind and Goodwill Industries of Denver (i.e., suggesting that the workplace experience of private-university graduate employees had more in common with this "rehabilitation setting" than public universities). He concluded that NYU's expressions of concern about the potential impact of collective bargaining on academic freedom was "essentially a rejection of the appropriateness of graduate students speaking with a common voice."

Most significant from a legal and rhetorical point of view, Silverman's decision set aside NYU's claims that students couldn't simultaneously be considered employees. This point may seem obvious to an average reader. Of course, persons occupying the category students can also occupy the category employees, just as "senior citizens," "women," "wine lovers," and "Red Sox fans" can be all of those things without giving up their rights as employees. However, in the early and mid 1970s, a tenuous thread in NLRB case law had emerged in connection with exactly this claim—just as it had, during the same period, in a number of state boards, where it has consistently been eventually overturned in court rulings sought by graduate employees. Even though the claim that graduate employees are "primarily students" or that the purpose of their work was "primarily educational" had been set aside in the majority of state-court rulings by this time, the NLRB hearing fulfilled Caesar's fantasy for all private-university employers: because the board covered all private universities nationally, all present and potentially future organizing on private campuses presented itself at the hearing with just one neck (instead of the many-headed hydra offered by the state-law-governed public university campaigns). The administrations of private universities across the country swarmed in support of the effort to breathe life into this particular legal fiction.

Pursuing recent NLRB precedent in postgraduate medical education,

Silverman rejected all of the arguments attempting to exclude graduate employee "from the statutory definition of employee on the sole basis that they are also students." Instead, he applied the common-law (and commonsense) meaning of the term "employee," observing that since 1995 the NLRB had held that "a broad and literal interpretation of the word 'employee' is consistent with the legislative history and with the Act's stated purpose of 'encouraging and protecting the collective bargaining process.'" In this context, after an exhaustive and painstaking survey of NYU's own documents and practices in the employment of graduate students, Silverman found that by every reasonable test these students were also workers:

> The graduate assistants perform services under the control and direction of the Employer, in exchange for compensation. The Employer has specific expectations of graduate assistants that are often spelled out in departmental or program handbooks, by job descriptions, or by NYU representatives. NYU representatives supervise the work of graduate assistants. The Employer provides the supplies and the place of work for the graduate assistants. In the case of TAs, NYU provides extensive training as to the nature of the services to be provided, including training on the application of NYU policies to the undergraduates. As for their compensation, graduate assistants' stipends are treated like any other personnel salary in that they are processed through the payroll department and distributed in biweekly checks. The IRS treats the stipends as taxable income or "salary for services rendered." Graduate assistants must complete certain forms, such as the INS I-9 form, which are required of employees, but which are not required of other graduate students. Finally, graduate assistants are subject to removal or transfer. Based on the foregoing, it is clear that the graduate assistants sought by the Petitioner meet the statutory definition of employee under Section 2 (2) of the Act.

On Halloween of the same year, the NLRB unanimously upheld Silverman's ruling and ordered the administration to hold elections. Even a board member who had dissented in the precedent-setting case (involving residents and interns at Boston Medical Center) joined this ruling. This member felt in the previous case, for policy reasons, that collective bargaining would harm certain "educational relationships" such as the necessary period of postgraduate medical training. But he felt the

NYU case "clearly demonstrates" a contrasting situation, in which "the graduate students involved herein do not perform their services as a necessary and fundamental part of their studies. Thus, I regard [them] as employees who should have the right to bargain collectively."

In the days after Halloween 2000, two things happened. First, the NLRB ruling resulted in the prompt election of UAW as the bargaining agent for a large group of NYU graduate employees. They negotiated an extremely favorable first contract at that institution, one of the best graduate-employee contracts ever negotiated. Grad employees at Temple organized a first contract and subsequently a second and third. Organizing on private campuses across the country shot into high gear.

Second, George Bush was awarded the presidency of the United States by decision of the U.S. Supreme Court. In consequence, three Republicans were appointed to the NLRB, constituting a majority over the two Democrats, one of whom (Wilma Liebman) had served during Bill Clinton's presidency and had served in the original review of the NYU case. Over 90 percent of NLRB cases are decided unanimously, but the remaining 10 percent are "high impact" debates that are generally decided along political party lines, so that shifting partisan majorities can result in radical reversals in NLRB interpretations of labor law (Runkel). In the first six years of domination by Bush appointees, the NLRB overturned a series of key advances made by labor during the Clinton administration, including restrictions on threatening speech by employers, the rights of workers employed by temp agencies to organize, and the rights of all workers to representation in disciplinary hearings.

As professional unionists and commentators digested this political reality, the drive to organize private universities began to sputter, anticipating the likelihood that university employers would take the political recomposition of the board as an opportunity to revisit NYU. The board quickly indicated its intention to do so in the case of Brown University. Once more, graduate-employee labor relations at all private universities presented itself with one neck. This was perhaps a final opportunity. If the administrations could not win in a Bush-appointed venue, they were unlikely to win anywhere. Accordingly, Harvard, Massachusetts Institute of Technology, Stanford, George Washington University, Tufts, the University of Pennsylvania, the University of Southern California, Washington University of St. Louis, and Yale filed a joint brief, joining forces with such company as the National Right to Work Legal Defense Foundation and the trustees of Boston University.

In a decision that the dissenting members characterized, scathingly, as "woefully out of touch with today's contemporary academic reality, based on an image of the university that was already outdated [in] the 1970s," the new Republican majority had little to say about the circumstances of graduate employees at Brown. Instead, they openly employed the case as an opportunity to reconsider NYU, baldly concluding that "NYU was wrongly decided and should be overruled." In an unusually impassioned dissent (republished here as appendix B), the minority excoriated the "choice" of the Republican nominees both as bad law and a fundamental error, "in seeing the academic world as somehow removed from the economic realm that labor law addresses." As law, the Republican majority relies on a handful of cases from the 1970s, none of which concerned graduate employees as teachers, and which it construes, somewhat fancifully, as supporting the view, rebutted in a dozen other legal venues, that persons who are "primarily students" can't also be "employees"[8]

As the dissent notes and the majority openly confesses, the majority opinion is founded not in law but in ideology. The ideological arrogance of the majority can be most charitably described as an unusually broad application of the board's discretion, intruding on policy-making powers. Essentially, they imposed their partisan, theoretical, and a priori judgment that collective bargaining is somehow "incompatible" with "the nature and mission of the university." Ignoring substantial evidence that collective bargaining in public higher education has not harmed academic freedom or education, including two empirical studies, the Republican appointees speculate, entirely without foundation and against all of the available evidence, including at NYU itself, that collective bargaining might have different consequences on privately funded campuses. They conclude with a frank, paternalistic, and ideological acknowledgment of the wide latitude in which they've indulged: "Although under a variety of state laws, some states permit collective bargaining at public universities, we choose to interpret and apply a single federal law differently to the large numbers of private universities under our jurisdiction" (Battista, 11).

Implicit in the understanding "we work" and the corollary understanding that the consciousness of work has to be materialized in law, social policy, and workplace practice, are a set of important realizations:

1. *We are not "overproducing Ph.D.s"; we are underproducing jobs.* There is plenty of work in higher education for everyone who wants to

do it. The problem is that this enormous quantity of work no longer comes in the bundle of tenure, dignity, scholarship, and a living wage that we call "a job." The concrete aura of the claim that degree holders are "overproduced" conceals the necessary understanding that, in fact, there is a huge shortage of degree holders. If degree holders were doing the teaching, there would be far too few of them. Graduate employees understand that labor markets are socially structured: with a single stroke (by, say, restoring the 1972 proportion of tenurable to nontenurable faculty in a major state, such as New York or California), all of the "surplus" degree holders in many disciplines could be immediately employed. Even a modest "reconversion" plan designed to re-create tenurable jobs out of part-time piecework would swiftly generate a real shortage of degreed persons. The intervening official knowledge, informed by liberal economic determinism, works to conceal the operation of a policy universe (social, legal, institutional) that shapes academic working conditions—a policy universe that organized graduate employees and contingent faculty understand they can and must transform.

2. *Cheap teaching is not a victimless crime.* Graduate employees understand that the system of cheap teaching hurts everyone, not just the persons who teach cheaply. The cheapness of their labor holds down salaries in the ladder ranks: professorial salaries have stagnated against per capita gains since 1970 and have stagnated most in the disciplines that rely primarily on graduate employee labor. The cheapness and disorganization of flexible labor supports speedup throughout the system: assistant and associate professors teach more, serve more, and publish more in return for lower compensation than any previous generation of faculty. You have to look pretty hard to find avenues of employment where sixty-year-old persons who have distinguished themselves at their work get paid less than college faculty. In the most casualized disciplines, such as English, this means that a sixty-year-old distinguished scholar with a national reputation and three books (and three children in college) earns a salary similar to that of junior faculty in many other disciplines. She earns about as much as either a good accountant with two or three years of experience or a twenty-five-year-old district attorney. At the end of a career covered with distinction, she earns about half of what moderately accomplished professionals in law and medicine earn at the beginning of their careers. She frequently earns less than a secondary-school teacher, civil servant, factory employee, or bartender with the same term of service. In many ways, she also has less control

over her work and fewer rights to due process, despite the fantasies of unfirable tenured faculty. And cheap teaching hasn't only reduced salaries: it has diminished the dignity, research support, and academic freedom of the tenured, as well as their morale and their capacity to govern the academy.

The system of graduate education has also radically altered the experience of general education for nearly all undergraduate students. Ask any thirty-seven-year-old graduate employee, with her ten or more years of service and just beginning to peak in her pedagogical and scholarly powers, yet soon to be replaced by a twenty-two-year-old master's degree candidate: Is this a system that teaches well? And she will answer: Heck, no, it is just a system that teaches cheaply. Accomplishing its marvelous cheapness by allocating an ever-larger section of the curriculum to flexible instructors who typically have between zero and four years of teaching experience, or who have brought their graduate studies to early termination, the system of disposable faculty continuously replaces its *most* experienced and accomplished teachers with persons who are *less* accomplished and *less* experienced.

In English departments, it is now typical for students to take nearly all first-year, many lower-division, and some advanced topics courses from nondegreed persons who are imperfectly attuned to disciplinary knowledge and who may or may not have an active research agenda or a future in the profession. The whole zone of general education—that is, the education that most people who go to college have in common with each other—has been radically evacuated. The proletarianized teachers who will be the only experience that most students have of a language department are commonly deprived of such necessities as offices, telephones, and photocopying privileges—much less the protections of due process that guarantee academic freedom. It is usual practice for administrations to simply dispense with the services of flexible teachers who exercise academic freedom: those who teach controversial material, of course, but also those who generate student complaints by teaching difficult material. Flexible teachers cannot afford to provide an obstacle to the advancing administrative ideal of an ultimately education-free transfer of cash for course credits. Most citizens wouldn't dream of employing an accountant without an office or a telephone—or go to a lawyer who practiced avocationally—but they regularly send their children for writing and liberal arts instruction to a person working out of the trunk of her car.

To paraphrase Emma Goldman: Cheap teaching is a social crime and failure. This is true even if the injuries to all persons who teach are excluded from the equation. Even the persons who seemingly benefit from the labor savings—students and the public they serve and also become —are substantially injured. Nor is it just a matter of teaching. The whole complex of research production is diminished by the elimination of tenurable faculty positions. Casualization systematically replaces the scholarly activity of the professoriate with new management tasks, and it profoundly degrades the undergraduate educational experience, producing such "efficiencies" as a reduced variety of course offerings, reduced access to faculty doing active scholarship in their field, and the regular replacement of experienced professionals with students and avocational labor.

3. *Casualization is an issue of racial, gendered, and class justice.* Frequently, the cheap teachers are people who can afford to teach with little or no compensation, as idealized in such manifestations of mass corporate culture as the financial-services commercial illustrating the corporate employee taking a plush early retirement so he can "afford" to realize his "dream" of being a teacher.

What does it mean that increasingly only people "who can afford to teach" are entering higher education as a profession? Surely one reason the neoliberal second-wave knowledge took such hold of the academy during the 1980s and 1990s is the degree to which academic casualization has increasingly closed the profession to people who rely on waged work to live—and replaced them with individuals for whom teaching figures as a secondary income.

If it typically requires family support to become a teacher, how do factors such as class and the racialized wealth gap affect the composition of the professoriate? Today's graduate-employee unionists are at least half women, and they understand that casualization is a feminist issue. The CGEU *Casual Nation* report headlines the fact that women take about 40 percent of the doctorates, but they represent about 58 percent of the full-time temporary instructors and only 25 percent of senior professors. There is a sharp generational break: women who joined the faculty during 1985–1992 were much less likely to join the faculty as members of the ladder ranks than were women who joined the faculty in earlier cohorts. Despite a plentiful "surplus" of women holding the doctorate, junior faculty women are substantially more likely to work in poorer-paying and less-satisfying higher education sectors than junior-faculty men. The NSOPF *New Entrants* analysis shows that fewer than half of the women who began full-time work during 1985–1992 held the Ph.D.: women were about as likely to hold the M.A. (44.2 percent) as the Ph.D. (48.4. percent), whereas male "new entrants" overwhelmingly hold the Ph.D. (71.0 percent) (Finkelstein et al.). The only fields in which women have achieved near parity in numbers with male faculty in the upper ranks are the most ill-paid fields, primarily language, literature, and writing instruction.

The sectors in which women outnumber men in the academy are uniformly the worst paid, frequently involving lessened autonomy—as in writing instruction, where the largely female staff is generally not rewarded for research, usually excluded from governance and even union representation, and frequently barred even from such basic expressions of academic discretion as choosing course texts, syllabus, requirements, and pedagogy (see chapter 5).

4. *Late capitalism doesn't just happen to the university; the university makes late capitalism happen.* The flexible faculty are just one dimension of an informationalized higher ed—the transformation of the university into an efficient and thoroughly accountable environment through which streaming education can be made available in the way that information is delivered: just in time, on demand, in spasms synchronized to the work rhythm of student labor on the shop floor. The university has not only casualized its own labor force; it continuously operates as a kind of fusion reactor for casualization more generally, directly serving the casual economy by supplying it with flexible student labor (that is, by providing flex workers with the identity of "student"), normalizing and generalizing the experience of casual work. The casualization of the higher education teacher has been accompanied by the wholesale reinventing of what it means to be an undergraduate: the identity of "student" has been disarticulated from the concept and possibility of leisure and vigorously rearticulated to contingent labor. In the twenty-first century, "being a student" names a way of work. The graduate employee understands that the gen-x and millenial structure of feeling proceeds from the generational register of the economic order, insofar as casualization colonizes the experience and possibilities of "youth," cheerfully extending the term of youth and youthful "enjoyment" into the fourth decade of life—because youth now delimits a term of availability for superexploitation.

This knowledge of the graduate employee conditions the political subjectivity of antagonism to the actually existing system of academic labor. Everyone with an interest in transforming that system will inevitably attempt to share into, or even ventriloquize, that knowledge. The one or two attempts to ventriloquize that knowledge have resulted in classic cases of incorporation, reinstalling the neoliberal fetish of "the market" and "the economy"—as when the *Final Report of the MLA Committee on Professional Employment* (December 1997) struggled visibly to deploy the graduate-employee critique of the "job-market" heuristic, developing the compromise language of "job system" (GSC "labor system" + MLA "job market" = "job system"), only to fail to deliver any analysis at the level of system.[9]

Refraining from attributing the critique to the graduate caucus in its own midst and failing even to mention either the graduate-employee union movement or faculty unionism more generally—and conspicuously leaving Cary Nelson, Michael Bérubé, and others from its bibliography —the CPE report attempts to "sound like" the GEU/GSO critique while obscuring the political reality and general experience of faculty unionism: about 44 percent of all faculty (two of three faculty members on publicly funded campuses) are unionized (Rhoades 9–10). In this ventriloquism and disappearing act, the CPE ultimately reinstalls the "imperative" of the "realities of the job market" (6) and offers the same set of "solutions" that David Orr offered in 1970: supply-side balancing of "the market," alternate careers, more teacher training, "buyer beware" labels on admission letters, and so on. Any analysis at the level of system suggests that all of these "solutions" actually contribute to the well-being of casualization—especially the fantasy of "alternate" careers, which enables administrations to flush away the degree-holding waste product. These official disciplinary "solutions" all proceed out of the primary ventriloquism of the Clinton era, "I feel your pain" (see, for instance, Sandra Gilbert's performance in "Bob's Jobs"), but which vigorously reinstalls the market logic that produced that pain in the first place.

Toward a Dictatorship of the Flexible

Basically, I just want to say to your President, the Board, that the stories I've heard tonight baffle me. [voice breaking] I have a personal story, but I'm not going to share it with you because you've heard enough personal stories. I had no idea this problem was an issue. I talked about it with my (student council) president. She had no idea. We students rely on teachers. We rely on them being there. We rely on their service —and they provide it! I've had part-time teachers, many part-time teachers. I'm in a professional/technical program, and they give you service. They put in more hours than they ever get paid for. Twelve—thousand—dollars makes me sick! Oh—my—gosh.

I—I didn't even know how to react to that. Teachers going from one campus to the other? Four and five different colleges? What is this country coming to? Where is this school—I know it's not just at PCC, I know it's across the nation—but it starts at one school. We can, we can start a trend for other schools. We can make a difference. I mean—[applause] Just think about, think about everything you've heard tonight, because—it made a difference to me. (Serrou)

ADMINISTRATOR: Please allow me to introduce myself, I'm a man of wealth and taste. I go by many names. Doctor, Boss, Sir, Chairman, Gentleman, Scholar, Dean, Pillar of the Community, Cheap Bastard, but you can call me the Administrator. (Camhi)

Moving from the discourse of "I feel your pain" to the collective recognition that our problems are mutual ultimately means acknowledging the intellectual and political leadership of the union movements of the casualized, of graduate employees and former graduate employees working part-time and nontenurably in subprofessorial conditions.

Acting at the level of system means acting as graduate employees have acted—writing their knowledge into law and policy at every level of social organization, from the campus and community to state and federal statute, and developing linkages to labor on a global scale. This means that everyone else implicated in the system of academic work will benefit from "acting with" the casual employee (rather than "sounding like" them while "acting with" administration). Against the dominative totality of higher ed marketization—the flexible dictatorship of university administration—the possibility of antagonism at the same level of systemic totality is emergent in the GEU and contingent-faculty movements. Acting with the movement of the contingent, we are privileging the perspective of the graduate employee (as incipient degree holder) and former graduate employee working contingently, and doing so in the belief that accomplishing the particular agenda of the contingent will address the problems that are general to the system (but feel "specific" to other locations). That is, in re-creating jobs out of the piecework done by the contingent workforce, we address with one stroke the problems experienced by everyone else: tenure-stream faculty benefit because eliminating cheap teaching raises the price of experienced teaching and reinstalls the value of research in pedagogy; undergraduates benefit by receiving experienced, secure faculty (who "do knowledge" rather than "provide information") in the first two years, when they are most vulnerable; other movement activists benefit from a more diverse and demarketized professoriate; the public, taxpayers, and employers receive a more literate, accomplished, thoughtful, and civically oriented citizenry—the embodied and political subjects of education, not the reactive "meatware" of information capitalism.

We of the academic system would in a way, then, be submitting to a "dictatorship of the flexible," saying instead of "I feel your pain" something more like this: "Oh, heck, now I realize that your problems are intimately related to my own difficulties. *Solving your problem is solving my problem.*" To the extent that the system of academic labor is a system interlocking in a plane with other systems, it seems plausible that a dictatorship of the knowledge proletariat could be articulated to the proletarian struggles elaborating themselves elsewhere. (The GEU movement, for instance, might be the basis for an important evolution in the undergraduate movement against sweatshops, which in my view would acquire even greater vitality by becoming conscious of the North American student's own status as flexible labor.) The articulation of the GEU movement to other proletarian movements could take place on a more horizontal plane, the shared consciousness of contingency. But the articulation of the GEU movement within "the knowledge class" itself *would* take place in a hierarchical relation—a revived apprenticeship, if you will—except that this apprenticeship would reverse the traditional relationship. In my view, we can only have a workers' movement in the academy when the professoriate (and their unions and institutions) are willing to politically and intellectually indenture themselves to the graduate employee.

The surge in graduate-employee organizing in the 1990s was accompanied by a growing interest in the major academic unions in organizing contingent faculty, who have become the majority workforce. Part of a growing interest in organizing contingent workforces globally, the effort involves challenges that are unique to contingency (difficulties in communication, lower salaries that mean lower dues, etc.), but also special opportunities: there are far fewer legal barriers to unionization. As a result, a string of contingent faculty union successes emerged in the past decade.

The plays, films, testimony, and propaganda of contingent faculty are components of a faculty culture in transition. They are active contributions to a culture war with management, each event an element in the struggle over the meaning of the language that structures our working lives—terms like "faculty," "fairness," "part-time," and "quality." On a Washington State campus, activists sold full-time and part-time cookies, with the part-time cookies identical to full-time cookies—except that they cost at least 50 percent less. In California, COCAL activists dressed as "freeway fliers" disrupted public spaces and distributed "scholar dollars," valued illustratively at the 37 cents paid contingent faculty for the same work performed by the tenured (Nelson, "Contingent Faculty"). One of the street theater pieces performed at Oregon's Portland Community College with the intention of "organizing the community" as well as the workforce is the simple device of asking real adjunct faculty to schedule their office hours at an outdoor trash can (labeled "AD-JUNKED FACULTY OFFICE"), sometimes involving the instructor wearing a sign "AD-JUNKED FACULTY" and the wearing of sandwich boards by willing "STUDENTS" as well. (Guerrilla theater appears to be an established feature of the union culture in Portland, where union janitors protested their intended replacement by convict labor by performing their jobs in black-and-white striped uniforms on the steps of county buildings, and where 100 protestors dressed as bananas occupied a Safeway grocery store to dramatize the efforts by Del Monte to break one of its unions in Guatemala [McIntosh, "Skit Protests"].)

Also scripted for the Portland Community College events, Joe Camhi's *Screw U.* introduces an archetypal administrator, costumed in business suit and horns, employing quotations from the Rolling Stones' "Sympathy for the Devil." Camhi's managerial fiend engages in a classic *Modern Times*–style illustration of managerial speedup of the work process. The administrator permits negligible time to prepare for class and respond to student work, barking "hurry!" and "shift gears!" at a hapless contingent faculty member who has a more thoughtful (and moderately slower-paced) idea of "quality" in the educational process. The curricular demands that "total-quality" management place on an overstressed contingent faculty quickly push the meaning of "academic specialty" into the realm of the absurd. Camhi's administrator continuously interrupts the adjunct's lecture with a sequence of syllabi for a dozen classes with eight different specializations. "How many damned classes am I teaching?" the "part-time" adjunct finally explodes in protest. "How many classes do full-time faculty teach?" The truth of the administrator's answer—that "full-time" faculty often teach just two or three classes—is an extraordinary moment in the skit, one that defamiliarizes the part-time/full-time distinction even for those who "know" why part-time teaching can mean much more than a full-time load. It's an absurd moment in the narrow, technical sense of literary absurdity— the dizzying contingency of the adjunct's existence, structured by language and policy that are continuously available to radical evacuation by administration, becomes, for a moment, a window into the common condition, fast capitalism's permanently temporary structure of feeling.

The confrontational dimension of Camhi's skit—naming the administration as the horned devil—is a common thread in the organizing culture of contingent faculty. Julie Ivey's song parody, "We Are Teachers!" rewrites Helen Reddy's "I Am Woman" by way of The Who with an emphasis on collective defiance: "Hear us roar. . . . No one's ever gonna make us beg or crawl again!" And the image of faculty "begging" and "crawling" before administration has its effect, not just on the faculty but on students for whom the notion of faculty as authority is a core belief. Among the most compelling of the contingent-faculty productions are the images penned by John Kloss, adjunct instructor at several California campuses, and editorial cartoonist for the *Sacramento News and Review.* A member of the California Federation of Teachers (CFT), Kloss has gone on record noting the union's failure to fully address the concerns of its contingent membership. His images for COCAL/Campus Equity Week display a command of diverse graphic styles, sometimes recalling elements of the Industrial Workers of the World (IWW) graphic tradition. This is particularly the case with his "107 Campuses —An Amazing Circus!" which features a huge and menacing tiger encompassing 85 percent of the horizontal visual field. Labeled "2/3 of Instructors are PART-TIME!" the snarling cat leaps through a flaming hoop labeled "FINANCIAL EXPLOITATION," but arches its head and shoulders in the direction of the ringmaster, who bears on hat and cape the legend "THE CHANCELLOR."

Recalling the Wobblies' use of the black cat symbol for direct action against the employer in the workplace (especially sabotage), Kloss's

tiger unmistakably voices the militant strain of contingent faculty culture. The cat is an agent—trained to perform management's tricks, but whose training has eroded to the margins of compliance—a powerful agent on the cusp of realizing that bones labeled "summer classes" and tins of cat food (suggesting the contingent faculty domestic food budget) are hardly sufficient inducements to continued obedience.

Kloss's other militant images are equally striking. His "It's Alive!" features a version of Frankenstein's monster in academic robes, square-headed under a mortarboard, labeled "30,000 Part-Time Faculty" (i.e., of the California community college system), coming to life and snapping its chains while electricity courses through the air. It is a quintessentially romantic trope: the monstrous agency of the contingent awaits only the coming-to-life of militant self-consciousness and also recalls numerous IWW images of the sleeping giant awakening to agency.

Drawn in a deceptively innocuous style different from much of his other work, it takes a minute to realize that Kloss's "Part-Time Instructor/Full-Time Activist!" bears perhaps the most overtly militant message of all, as it features a clean-cut student in robes and mortarboard this time, with his clenched fist emerging from the frame, bearing a "class ring" with the legend "CLASH OF 2000." Less busy than Kloss's other work, this sketch draws together the "CLASH" with just two other typographic elements, a diploma case labeled "PAY EQUITY" and the ubiquitous "37 cents" logo (from the "scholar dollar"). Here, as elsewhere, the target of contingent faculty culture is the culture of academia itself, and the oppressive, silencing, norms of "collegiality," ubiquitous faith in meritocracy, and so on: the "CLASH OF 2000" is as much a clash with the beliefs and institutions of the tenure stream faculty as it is with the administration.

The project of creating a contingent faculty culture involves transforming the contingent faculty culture that is already there. Kloss's "Misadventures of a Freeway Flier" targets the self-conception of the contingent faculty by showing the "freeway flier" as a chicken who is the victim of his own beliefs: "I'm s-o-o Smart! I teach at 5 caw-caw-cawlleges!" crows one of Kloss's fliers, pulling open academic robes to show a joke superhero's logo ("PT," for part-time). Above a landscape littered with the "flier's" broken-down car (labeled "OFFICE") and the state capitol, from which snores ensue, Kloss's editorial comment is written in the sky: "Yes . . . It's the loyal fowl that saves the day for college deans but loses his shirt at the end of the Month!"

Graduating from guerrilla performer to guerrilla filmmaker, Santa Monica College contingent faculty activist Linda Janakos created *Teachers on Wheels* to illustrate the fourteen-hour workdays of the full-time part-timers and to build militance in the community. One of her film's more memorable shots shows the 45,000 petitions that had been painstakingly collected and presented to then-governor Gray Davis, now dumped in a state capitol trash can (American Federation of Teachers). One of the core techniques of contributors to an activist culture for

contingent faculty is rewriting the given tropes of identity, most of which are pejorative: the "invisible" faculty (Gappa and Leslie), "freeway fliers," a "lost generation" (Heller), who figure in the *Chronicle of Higher Education* and the *Washington Post* as victims of history. That is, if the contingent faculty are indeed invisible, despite their status as the overwhelming majority of the faculty workforce, increasingly the contingent faculty are seizing—and recolonizing the meaning of—the tropes of invisibility, victimhood, and loss to become visible, to become agents in history, and to make gains, as in Michael Dubson's collection of contingent faculty experiences, *Ghosts in the Classroom,* and in such widely read weblogs as "Invisible Adjunct." As Dubson writes of his experience of collecting "adjunct horror stories," even in the context of his own project—which is an attempt to tap into "the power of adjuncts sharing their stories with each other, bonding by offering support and solidarity, creating a text that we can use to cry over or fight with" —the project of coming to consciousness is a continuously renewed challenge. As he was editing the stories comprising his book, he says, "I kept thinking, 'These poor people. These poor people.' But these people were me" (Dubson, "Address"). In connection with the release of Dubson's book at COCAL IV in San Jose, faculty dressed as ghosts haunted the campus.

Do these skits, cartoons, films, weblogs, moments of witness, and guerrilla theater pieces "work"? What do we mean by that question? Their effectiveness has to be seen in the context of building a culture of opposition—of "naming the enemy," raising the consciousness of those who work, and reaching the sensibilities of those potentially in alliance, such as students, parents, legislators, and tenure-stream faculty. At Oregon's Portland Community College, where Camhi's administrator-as-devil skit was performed, student and community consciousness was abruptly and permanently raised, as the unmistakably shocked tones of the recorded testimony from Melanie Serrou and other students indicates. Serrou: "Twelve—thousand—dollars makes me sick! Oh—my—gosh. I—I didn't even know how to react to that. Teachers going from one campus to the other? Four and five different colleges? What is this country coming to?" In the aftermath of this realization, Serrou went to work as a legislative assistant for the union.

The militant strain of contingent faculty culture is having an effect on the culture of the tenured and their unions. Historically, the relationship between contingent faculty and the unions of tenure-stream faculty serving directly as their bargaining agents is checkered; often enough, the unions of the tenured have collaborated with management in the creation of multiple tiers of employment (Tirelli; Hoeller, "Treat Fairly"). For many of the same reasons, some graduate employees have historically elected to work with representatives outside of the three unions that together represent nearly all organized tenure-stream faculty (AFT, NEA, and AAUP), instead working with representation as diverse as the Communication Workers of America (CWA), the American Federation of State, County and Municipal Employees (AFSCME), the Service Employees International Union (SEIU), and, notably, UAW. But that is changing.

Now the major bargaining agents in higher education are increasingly eager to organize the contingent—because they are the majority of faculty and because there are far fewer legal barriers than is the case with graduate employees or tenure-stream faculty on private campuses. Nonetheless, a major part of the shifting priority is due to the agency of the contingent themselves, in authoring an activist culture that has pervaded the higher education establishment; the disciplinary associations, faculty unions, and senates; and the myriad forms of organization dominated by the tenurable. The sense of the angry and increasingly organized contingent faculty as the specters haunting the academic status quo has been seized as a trope by the major institutions of faculty labor: by 2005, AAUP organizing kits included instructions for campus contingent-faculty "ghost rallies." Steadily over the past several years, the culture and commitments of contingent faculty have pervaded the literature of the major higher ed unions—the articles, analysis, autobiographical accounts, organizing tips, and bargaining strategies of the organized and organizing. Of at least equal import is that the culture of the contingent is reaching the communities served by their campuses with a compelling vision of an other-than-corporate culture informing the university. If any group on the campus is asking the pressing questions of the moment, it is the contingent faculty: as Linda Janakos's skit has it, the university president can make television commercials, but the contingent faculty captures the community by asking the right question: "Oh Equity, Oh Equity, wherefore art thou Equity?"[10]

2

The Informal Economy of the "Information University"

Class struggle is basic to the capitalist mode of production in the region of "mental" labor, just as it is to be found in the realm of physical production. It is basic not because it is a sign of the special quality of mental labor, but because it is simply labor.
—George Caffentzis, "Why Machines Cannot Create Value," 1997

There is the employer's sabotage as well as the worker's sabotage. Employers interfere with the quality of production, they interfere with the quantity of production, they interfere with the supply as well as with the kind of goods *for the purpose of increasing their profit*. But this form of sabotage, capitalist sabotage, is antisocial, for the reason that it is aimed at the benefit of the few at the expense of the many, whereas working-class sabotage is distinctly social, it is aimed at the benefit of the many, at the expense of the few.
—Elizabeth Gurley Flynn, "Sabotage: Its Necessity in the Class War," 1916

There are interesting differences in the social reception of managed health care and the managed university. Most strikingly, the HMO is the object of widespread concern, whereas "student satisfaction" with management-dominated higher education has never been higher, at least according to corporate-university surveys. According to these sources, students in all institution categories are overwhelmingly satisfied with the learning dimensions of their college experience, in many cases reserving their complaints for the quality of food and availability of parking.[1]

Of equal interest is the widespread belief that information technology is driving the transformation in higher education. Much of even the most informed and committed discourse in the field is obsessively focused on information technology as the engine of change. This leads to the likely mistaken concern that the "real issue" with the management revolution in higher education is that all campus-bound activities will be vacated in the metastatic spread of distance education—as in David Noble's widely known formulation of "digital diploma mills" producing the "automation of higher education."

It is important that these two differences in the social reception of the managed university push toward partly conflicting conclusions. On the one hand, the faculty's concern with technology represents the idea that students are willing to accept a disembodied educational experience in a future virtual university of informatic instruction. On the other hand, the student concerns are overwhelmingly attentive to the embodied character of their experience—where to park, what to eat, and so on. Why do the faculty envision students willing to give up the embodied experience of the campus, when, in fact, the students are increasingly attentive to embodied experience? Campus administrators continue to build new stadiums, restaurants, fitness facilities, media rooms, libraries, laboratories, gardens, dormitories, and hotels. Are these huge new building projects, funded by thirty years of faculty downsizing, really about to be turned into ghost towns? In my view, the claim that (future) students will generally accept a disembodied educational experience is at least a partial displacement of the underlying recognition of the extent to which present students have already accepted an embodied experience divorced from "education," not the reverse. While the dystopic image of distance education captures the central strategy of the information university (substituting information delivery for education), that dystopia erroneously maps that strategy onto the future, as if informationalization were something "about to happen" that could be headed off at the pass, if we just cut all the fiber-optic cables.

What does it mean for students and teachers that informationalization has already happened? It means that we have met the Info. U., and it is us—not some future disembodiment but a fully lived present reality.

We've already done a pretty good job of translating education into information delivery over the past thirty years. This substitution has been accomplished by transformation of the academic workplace, not by stringing optic cable.

Informationalization without Information Technology?

"I am very troubled by it," said Tom Hanks. "But it's coming down, man. It's going to happen. And I'm not sure what actors can do about it."

The spectre of the digital actor—a kind of cyberslave who does the producer's bidding without a whimper or salary—has been a figure of terror for the last few years in Hollywood, as early technical experiments proved that it was at least possible to create a computer image that could plausibly replace a human being. (Lyman, "Movie Stars Fear Inroads")

The text that in some ways strikes nearest and in other ways less close to this understanding is the well-known series of articles drafted by David Noble in the late 1990s (subsequently revised and released as a monograph by Monthly Review Press in November 2001). Noble's work in the "Digital Diploma" series has been widely disseminated across the Internet and remains a core analysis of managerial intentions regarding the tenure-stream faculty. It originates in the actual workplace struggle of faculty in California and Canada, and it maps the area of starkest contrast in the technology conversation: at the bargaining table, with the tenure-stream faculty mostly "against technology" and the administration mostly "for technology." This conflict is at least partially chimerical: the faculty and the administration aren't primarily struggling over technology but, rather, what they think "it" will do—something they agree on, and regarding which they're quite possibly both wrong. The faculty and administration are fighting over what is essentially a shared vision, a vision of a future created by information technology, of a fully downloadable and teacherless education (at least for some people). The material base of this shared vision is a real struggle over the elimination of the jobs of teachers and scholars. The administration seeks to employ ever-fewer teachers and scholars, and the tenured faculty seek to preserve their own jobs. Occasionally, the tenured faculty will act to preserve a handful of positions for a future professoriate. (One recent California State University contract—through which the California Faculty Association compelled the administration to raise tenure-track hiring by 20 percent annually over the life of the contract in exchange for concessions in their cost of living adjustment—is an eye-opening, and heartening, exception to the rule.)

Technology fuels an enormous fantasy on both sides of this fence. On the administration side, it drives an academic-capitalist fantasy of unlimited accumulation, dollars for credits nearly unmediated by faculty labor—as Noble says, an "automated" wealth creation. This is really a version of one of the oldest fantasies in industrial history, the fantasy of profit without workers. If only the investor could build an entirely mechanized factory! With the push of a button, cars and snowboards and washing machines would come out the other end! The same dream animates academic management: with a mechanized higher ed, a line of tuition payers could be run through automated courses that provide them with the "necessary information," and out the other end would emerge nurses! teachers! engineers! sports psychologists! The professoriate has its own equally fantastic idea: that they are preserving teacher work by taking a stand "against technology."

The shared vision of a fully downloadable education creates the scene of a pseudostruggle, with the depressing consequence that it drains off the energies of the movements seeking to preserve the dignity of academic work. Noble himself acknowledges that the struggle over technology is a surface conflict ("a vehicle and disarming disguise"); beneath the technological transformation, "and camouflaged by it," is the major transformation represented by the commodification of higher education. Noble narrates the commodification process as a two-stage affair. Phase one begins about 1980 with the commodification of research ("the systematic conversion of intellectual activity into intellectual capital and, hence, intellectual property"), converting the university into a purveyor in the commercial marketplace of the products of mental labor. Phase two (and this is the chief point at which I vary with his analysis) is what he describes as the more recent corresponding corporate colonization of teaching, the "commoditization of the education function of the university."[2]

Several useful insights flow out of the commodification heuristic as applied by Noble. These include, especially, the understanding that universities are increasingly in open partnership with software, hardware, and courseware vendors in the conversion of student learning activity into a profit center. Additionally, in an area also importantly discussed by Stanley Aronowitz and Dan Schiller (*Digital Capitalism*), this partnership extends beyond the education vendors into the corporate world more generally, with the university eager to provide corporate training and retraining services ("lifelong learning"), an activity for which the rubric of "higher education" serves largely as a kind of academic-capitalist's flag of convenience. In a searing indictment of the growing "mission differentation" of postsecondary institutions (providing tiered learning horizons corresponding closely to the class fractions of their constituencies), Aronowitz argues that most college students receive "higher training" and not higher learning and that, overall, "there is little that would qualify as higher learning in the United States" (xvii).

The primary way in which Noble makes use of the "commodification of teaching" lens is to relate faculty labor to "the historic plight of other skilled workers." For the professoriate as well as cabinetmakers, technological change is an opportunity for management to impose reductions in worker autonomy—so that for academic administration, the ultimate goal of technological deployment is to "discipline, deskill and displace" the skilled faculty workforce, just as in any other labor circumstance. (This is a point on which Gary Rhoades's work has been definitive.) For the most part, again, this approach is enormously helpful, to a real extent because it generates an accurate description of administrative intentions regarding technology. Furthermore, because—as Harry Braverman and the Italian autonomists have been at pains to demonstrate—mental labor is in fact labor (despite the folk-academic sense of exceptionalism), Noble's series of observations paralleling skilled academic work with other forms of skilled work largely ring true.[3] Management dissemination of technology has been used to surveil, punish, regiment, censor, and control faculty; to direct how they allocate time and effort; to cement administrative control over the curriculum; and to impose supplemental duties, including technological self-education and continuous availability to students and administration via email. In some cases, technology has even displaced living labor entirely with automated learning programs tended by software maintenance and courseware sales personnel.

Nonetheless, any discussion of "technologization" is going to leave us room to say more about what is "informationalized" about the information university. Noble is right that the administration's motive in attempting to get faculty to convert their courses to courseware is ultimately to dispense with faculty altogether. He compares the plight of the tenure-stream faculty to the plight of the machinist Rudy Hertz in Kurt Vonnegut's *Player Piano*: "They buy him a beer. They capture his skills on tape. Then they fire him." But does dispensing with the "skilled academic labor" of the tenured faculty result in the *workerless* academic environment that Noble pictures? Not at all: there are more academic workers than ever before. Noble gives, or plays to, the impression that the information university is a fully "lights-out" knowledge factory, an entire virtual u. on a bank of hard drives facelessly dispensing information to students across the globe. This science-fiction vista of an automated higher education completely captures administrative ambition (i.e., for academic capital to emancipate itself from academic labor, realizing value magically in a workerless scheme of dollars for credits completely unmediated by teaching). It equally captures the anxiety of the tenure-stream faculty regarding the systematic imperative that is relentlessly driving toward the elimination of their positions.

Nonetheless, it risks missing the underlying reality: dispensing with the skilled professoriate is accompanied by the installation of a vast cadre of differently skilled workers—graduate students, part-time faculty, technology specialists, writing consultants, and so forth. Similarly, replacing Tom Hanks with a "digital actor" doesn't result in a workerless artistic production but, instead, involves a battalion of talents that are differently but perhaps not "less" skilled: programmers, choreographers, caricaturists, physical anthropologists, animators, scene painters, photographers, voice artists, continuity experts, caterers, writers, and so forth.

In trying to understand what is "informationalized" about the information university, we need to shift our focus to the consciousness and circumstances of the new group of education workers called into being by this transformation of the work process. This transformation cannot be exclusively a question of delivering labor, teacher labor or any other kind, in a commodity form. It is, after all, a general feature of all capitalisms that workers are required to "sell their labor" in order to live. Rather, informationalization is about delivering labor *in the mode of information*.

A word about informationalization and the material world is probably in order. Generally speaking, informationalization does not mean that we cease to have or handle things, or that we have and handle virtual objects "instead of" the material world (as in Negroponte's formulation that we move bits "instead of" atoms). Rather, it means that we continue to have and handle material objects (more and more of them, at least in the thing-rich daily life of the Northern Hemisphere) but that we have and handle these objects in what Mark Poster calls "the mode of information," which means that we manipulate objects *as if* they were data. It's not that we don't have car parts, novels, and armored divisions—only now we expect those things to be available to us in a manner approximating the way in which information is available to us. A fully informationalized fuel injector makes fuel available in the way that electronically mediated data is available—on demand, just in time. When you're not thinking of your fuel injector, it's off your desktop. When you need to think about it, the informationalized fuel injector lets you know. When it does manifest itself, it gives the illusion of a startling transparency—you have in the fuel injector's manifestation the sense that you have everything you need to know about fuel injectors: how they work, fair prices for them here and in the next state, and so on. Informationalization means that artifacts are available on an informatic logic: on demand, just in time, and fully catalogued; they should feel transparent and be networked, and so forth.

Informationalization creates data streams alongside, crossing, and enfolding atomic motion, but in most cases it doesn't replace atomic motion. To the contrary, informationalization is a constant pressure accelerating and multiplying atomic motion toward the ideal speed of the bitstream and toward the ideal efficiency of capturing (as profit) the action of every fingertip, eyeball, and synaptic pulse. This is in part why Tiziana Terranova argues for getting beyond the debates about who constitutes a "knowledge class" and "concentrating instead on 'labor' " (41). In this context, "labor" refers to Maurizio Lazzarato's notion of "immaterial labor," those activities of the eyes, hands, speech organs, and synapses of a "mass intellectuality"—channel-changing, verbal invention, mouse-clicking, fandom, opinion-formation and opinion-sharing, and so on—that are "not normally recognized" as labor, but which can be described as "knowledge work" yet one divorced from "the concept of creativity as an expression of 'individuality' or as the patrimony of the 'superior' classes, and which are instead collectively performed by a creative social subjectivity (133–134, 145–146).

Terranova's understanding that the production of Internet culture absorbs "massive amounts" of such labor, only some of which is "hypercompensated by the capricious logic of venture capitalism" (48), can be partially mapped onto our understanding of higher education and the labor power it composes. For one thing, it is quite clear that much of the "free labor" that goes into creating higher education culture, such as the work of playing basketball, cheerleading, blowing a horn in the marching band, attending the game—even checking the box scores—

can be harvested by university capital as surplus value. The university valorizes the uncompensated labor of the editor of the student newspaper and its "interns" and "service learners," together with the "work-study" efforts of its student dining-hall workers, just as easily as it valorizes the radically undercompensated labor of the faculty and graduate students editing a scholarly journal, or its janitors and librarians. Another lesson of the Italian autonomy involves the question of leadership. It seems equally evident that any movement likely to transform academic capitalism at the level of structure will have to unfold in the consciousness and muscles of an insurrectionary mass intellectuality of all of the fractions performing this uncompensated and undercompensated labor, and it can hardly flow from one segment alone or from one segment "leading" another.

So what does it mean to labor "in the mode of information?" Above all, it means to deliver one's labor "just in time" and "on demand," to work "flexibly." As Manuel Castells observes, the informational transformation relies even more on just-in-time labor than on just-in-time supplies (289). One doesn't have to be employed part time to be forced to work in this fashion—one can have a full-time job and experience contingency. (As many as one-third of even the most economically privileged quartile of the workforce, four-year college graduates, report involuntary unemployment of several months or more in the years after graduation, while moving between what is usually a string of full-time jobs, often without benefits or seniority protections.) Nor does laboring in the mode of information necessarily imply "being an information worker" but, instead, the application to information workers of the management controls developed for the industrial workplace. In many respects, this can be viewed as the extension of the process of scientific management to all forms of labor, as Braverman observed in his study of the rationalization of office work (293–358), even the work of management itself (as in, for example, Bill Vaughn's "I Was an Adjunct Administrator"). Constrained to manifest itself as data, labor appears when needed on the management desktop—fully trained, "ready to go out of the box," and so forth—and after appearing upon administrative command, labor in this form should ideally instantly *disappear.*

When the task is completed, labor organized on the informatic principle goes off-line, off the clock, and, most important, off the balance sheets. This labor is required to present itself to management scrutiny as "independent" and "self-motivated," even "joyful"—that is, able to provide herself with health care, pension plan, day care, employment to fill in the down time, and eagerly willing to keep herself "up to speed" on developments transpiring in the corporate frame even though not receiving wages from the corporation. Above all, contingent labor should present the affect of enjoyment: he must seem transparently glad to work, as in the knowledge worker's mantra: "I love what I'm doing!" Andrew Ross has already described the way that universities, digital industry, and other employers of "mental labor" have succeeded in interpellating intellectual workers more generally with the "bohemian" ideology that previously was reserved for artistic occupations: large new sectors of intellectual labor have proved willing to accept not merely the exploitation of wage slavery but the superexploitation of the artist, in part because the characteristics of casual employment (long and irregular hours, debt subsidy, moonlighting, the substitution of reputation for a wage, casual workplace ethos, etc.) can so easily be associated with the popular understanding of normative rewards for "creative" endeavor.

As with other forms of consumerist enjoyment, flex-timers generally pay for the chance to work—buying subscriptions to keep up, writing tuition checks, donating time to internships and unpaid training, flying themselves to professional development opportunities—in all respects shouldering the expense of maintaining themselves in constant readiness for their right to work to be activated by the management keystroke. Contrary to the fantasy of the sedentary knowledge worker who telecommutes and never leaves home, the actual flex-timer is in constant motion, driving from workplace to workplace, from training seminar to daycare, grocery store, and gym, maintaining an ever more strenuous existence in order to present the working body required by capital: healthy, childless, trained, and alert, displaying an affect of pride in representing zero drain on the corporation's resources.

Laboring in an informatic mode does not mean laboring with less effort—as if informationalized work was inevitably some form of knowledge teamwork scootering around the snack bar, a bunch of chums dreaming up the quarterly scheduled product innovation. Laboring in an informatic mode means laboring in a way that is effortless for labor management. The relevant perspective is the perspective of the management desktop, from which labor power can be made to appear and disappear with a keystroke. Informationalized labor is always informationalized *for management*—that is, so that management can always have labor available to it "in the mode of information," called up effortlessly, dismissed at will, immediately off the administrative mind once out of sight. Indeed, for labor management to feel so transparent and so effortless, a great deal of additional effort has to be expended (just not by management). For capital to have labor appear and disappear at the speed of the bitstream might, for instance, require concrete labor to drive sixty miles between part-time gigs, gulping fast food on the highway, leaving its children unattended. The informatic mode doesn't eliminate this effort; it just makes that effort disappear from the management calculus. Informationalism cannot present labor in the form of data without offloading the costs of feeding, housing, training, entertaining, reproducing, and clothing labor power onto locations in the system other than the location using that labor power.

To return to the Hollywood producer's fantasy of the "cyberslave" that will "do his bidding without a whimper or a salary," really understanding the informational transformation means acknowledging that Hollywood producers already have an enormous army of cyberslaves who don't complain or ask for a salary: they're called actors. (In *All about Eve*, Bette Davis comments on the cost of a union caterer—presumably a would-be actor—by grumbling that she "could get an actor for less," meaning that she could pay an accomplished actor less to "perform the role" of catering her party than she would have to pay a would-be actor to "be the caterer.") Under the regime of information capitalism, a film producer can often get a human being to act informationally—to leap at his command, even anticipate the snap of his fingers, and then obligingly disappear—at a labor cost to himself of exactly zero, except where restrained by the talent unions. But these living and breathing, unwaged "slaves" of the representational economy aren't fed and housed and educated at no cost—just at no cost to the film producer.

So, in reality, it "takes a village" to present informationalized labor to capital. This form of the work process—flexible, casual, permanently temporary, outsourced, and so on—offloads the care and maintenance of the working body onto society, typically, onto the flex worker's parents or a more traditionally employed partner, as well as onto social institutions. In the United States, these social institutions include the health care provided at the emergency room and the job training provided by higher education. As Clyde Barrow, among others, observes, higher education's continuously enlarging contributions to personnel "training and the provision of a scientific-technical infrastructure" have historically been the two areas in which the "costs of private production" under advanced capitalism have been most successfully displaced onto society (8).

The operation of global capital somewhat cushions the care of American and European flex workers by providing cheap consumer goods produced by contingent labor in the Asian factories, so that, without the assistance of a parent or traditionally employed partner, American and European flex workers commonly cannot afford to buy real property (a home) or services (health care, legal services, day care, etc.) at local prices. Nonetheless, they may be otherwise rich in possessions fabricated by Asian labor (compact discs, computer hardware, clothing, assembly-required furniture). The most substantial expenditures made by the American flex worker in particular are commonly the debt-funded car and tuition payments that for many of them figure as the prerequisite for entering the flex-time economy in the first place.

The research of Saskia Sassen and others has been helpful for understanding the relationship between sites of high technological sophistication, especially cities of the advanced economy, and the enormous growth of low-wage, low-profit economic activity in those sites (a fact that confounds most information-society propagandists). Some of this work is formally casual or contingent (legal part-time or term work). Some of it is legal full-time, but with extremely low degrees of worker security and on-the-job protection (Sassen observes that under globalization, firms migrate not to where labor is cheapest but to where labor can be most easily controlled, including to the urban centers of advanced economies with large migrant populations). And much of this low-profit, low-wage work is informal.

As Sassen observes, the informal sector is not easy to define and, while akin to elements of the "underground economy" (i.e., dealers in illegal goods and services such as drugs and prostitution, and financial services associated with tax evasion), the "informal economy" encompasses activities that would otherwise be legal (garment manufacture, child care, gardening, home renovation) but are performed in illicit circumstances, either by being performed outside of or in an unclear regulatory environment, or by persons working illegally (such as underage or undocumented workers). This group includes an extremely disparate collation of workers: high-school babysitters, sweatshop labor, neighborhood day care providers, construction day laborers, farm hands, and gypsy cab drivers, among many others. The informal sector has grown swiftly and unexpectedly in the United States since 1980, and Sassen has argued forcefully that this expansion is structurally related to the characteristics of the "formal economy" itself. In her work on immigrant workers in urban centers, for example, she observes that the rapid expansion of the informal sector of advanced economies is neither accidental nor the consequence of failings or inabilities of third world economies, from which cheap labor migrates to the first world. Instead, in her view, the informal sector is "the structured outcome of current trends in advanced economies" (*Informalization*, 4–5; see also *Mobility*, 7–9, 151–170).

This means that immigration and other "external" factors don't "cause" sectors of advanced economies to become informal; advanced economies require the emergence of informality within themselves, resulting from "the structural characteristics of advanced capitalism" and the "flexibility-maximizing strategies by individuals and firms" in that system (*Informalization*, 19). Samir Radwan redacts Sassen's observation as follows: "If the informal economy did not exist, the formal economy would have to invent it" (Sassen, *Informalization*, 2). The processes of rendering-informal are for Sassen the low-cost equivalent of the expensive, arduous, and politically charged activities of formal deregulation (those that transpire in high-profit sectors of the economy) and a corresponding shadow or de facto deregulation that rests on the backs of "low-profit firms and low-wage workers" (19). These insights might be brought to bear on the present discussion by saying, "It takes a high-tech city (or at least a college) to deliver informationalized labor to capital."

Certainly, any understanding of the relationship between the murkily "informal" and the deceptively transparent "informational" in the advanced economies requires a great deal of further research and theorization. Even limited research questions such as "What role might the information university play in helping the formal economy to 'invent' the relations sustaining the informal economy?" beg book-length empirical studies of their own. But I do think we might make at least some theoretical progress by asking ourselves what can be gained by seeing colleges and universities as a version of these low-profit firms, operating not in a fully informal fashion but, to a certain degree, in a less-than-formal fashion—that is, in an environment of underregulation or one in which the regulatory status of its workers is less than clear.

In terms of university accumulation, the emphasis has been to look at the activities of the top 100 research universities in the United States, and in the light of deregulation of patent law, for instance, see the activities of these institutions as the bellwether of the university's emergence as at least potentially a high-profit, high-wage information industry. (And this line of approach has appeared reasonable, in connection with such visible developments as the university's emergence as a competitor with entertainment capital to provide sports and other programming to media outlets.) With Bill Readings, many have been inclined to view the university as a transnational bureaucratic corporation, in a deregulated environment that is increasingly becoming a global purveyor of educational services and research commodities.

But this construction of the informational transformation within academic capitalism is hardly typical of the other 4,000-plus U.S. institutions of higher education. Strict attention to the expenditure of labor time in these other locations gives a radically different picture of the information university than the fantasy of a workbench for faculty information entrepreneurs or a gateway to the information society for students.

What would happen if we asked, pursuing Sassen, to what degree is the university's role in the advanced economies of the *informational* society structurally related to the relative *informality* of its employment relation? In raising this question, I am not at this time making an analogy between university workers and day laborers or migrant workers (though such analogies have been made, with greater and lesser degrees of applicability), and I am not pointing to the financial relations between universities and garment sweatshops (such as those opposed by United States against Sweatshops [USAS] and other student protest organizations). Nor am I addressing the university's exploitation of its staff, as documented in the recent Harvard and Johns Hopkins living wage campaigns, for example (Harvey, 126–129), though these connections can and must be made as a matter of analysis and workplace organization. For purposes of this particular effort, I am pointing primarily to the actual legal and social confusion regarding the workplace status of the most visible and even traditional members of the academic workforce, the professoriate itself, together with graduate and undergraduate students.

Perhaps the most obvious legal confusion surrounds the status of the graduate employee, many of whom have engaged in legal battles to win recognition that they are indeed workers, in some cases succeeding after decades of struggle, as in California and Illinois, and in other cases continuing the effort as this book goes to press, as at Yale and NYU. Increasingly over the past thirty or thirty-five years, the designation "graduate student" has served as a vector for the university's cultivation of a semiformal employment relation. The regulatory confusion has created a situation advantageous to the employer, in which graduate employees have all of the responsibilities of labor—including a teaching load heavier than many of their professors, commonly an employment contract, supervision, job training, a taxable wage, and so on. At the same time, they enjoy fewer protections than the regular workforce. For instance, graduate employees are generally ineligible for unemployment benefits, and unlike regular workers they can be compelled to pay tuition for their on-the-job training; shoulder job-related expenses, including the production of course-related materials; supplement a subliving wage with unforgivable debt; and engage in various forms of unpaid labor (in keeping with various ideologies of "apprenticeship," "mentoring," and "professionalism," even though for most the term of mentoring and apprenticeship will not lead to professional employment). Nor can a graduate employee who doesn't like his or her working conditions quit the employer and go to an alternative employer in the usual fashion: students who are unable to live on their stipends cannot easily move to a higher-paying program, and those who are not economically situated to take on debt to finish their degrees on the gamble of winning a professorial job are likely to quit rather than change programs.

This is not to say that justifications cannot be offered for at least some of the unusual circumstances of graduate employee labor. It is only to observe that the regulatory circumstances are indeed "special" enough for universities to fight to keep the regulatory specialness of the "student" designation, including spending lavishly on union-busting law firms.

Correspondingly, many graduate employees find the regulatory "specialness" of this designation so disempowering that some are willing to struggle during the whole term of their graduate careers to escape from the "specialness" and win the rights of labor, including collective bargaining. Whether one supports graduate employee unionism or not, it is simply an observable fact that significant numbers of graduate employees are eager to enter circumstances resembling the more regulated environment of other workers.

For most of the past quarter century, the faculty also have worked in a contested and murky regulation environment. This is obviously the case with term workers and part-time faculty, some of whom, for example, have sued the state of Washington for retirement benefits. But the move to substitute flexible labor for faculty labor also transformed the role of the remaining tenure-stream faculty, who acquired additional supervisory duties in relation to the new graduate students and other flex workers. The 1980 Supreme Court decision in *NLRB v. Yeshiva* (444 U.S. 672) created difficulties for faculty at private universities seeking to unionize because the court viewed the activities of tenure-stream faculty at that institution as in certain respects managerial. As discussed in chapter 3, the 5–4 decision was certainly bad law, and its widespread application to other private university faculty wildly exceeds the intended scope of an already dubious judgment. (Justice Brennan's scathing response to the one-vote majority is included as appendix A.) The case's usefulness to a core tactic of the Reagan-Bush era's class war— the quest for new "exclusions" to labor rights under the NLRA—has kept *Yeshiva* central, in health care as well as education. The law's usefulness to management is not in clarification but obfuscation. In consequence of *Yeshiva* and related decisions, faculty and other workers with any responsibilities that can be creatively represented as "managerial" (such as nurses) occupy a legally "special" place in the labor process. It is now an overt managerial strategy to ensure that as many employees as possible participate in "managerial" tasks, in order to lend substance to their defense of any challenge to *Yeshiva* and similar regulatory mystifications of the employer-employee relationship. Here again, regardless of where one might stand on debating these issues, it's clear that this regulatory ambiguity strongly motivates most employers to conserve the special relationship. Correspondingly, it motivates many employees to seek regulatory clarity.

Of course, if it is at all useful to theorize the university as a semiformal employer, discussing the conversion of graduate education to labor in the mode of information and the increasing managerialism of the faculty is only to have scratched the surface. To go on, we must investigate the ways in which the Info. U. has transformed undergraduate experience in the quest for new wage workers, and then we must critically examine the forms of semiformal work to which the undergraduate has been increasingly dedicated over the same period of time.

To return to the three forms of labor commonly employed by low-wage, low-profit firms (casual, full-time but pragmatically contingent, and informal), it is clear that, since the late 1960s, higher education has expanded its reliance on the casual, full-time contingent and the semi-formal labor of students, while also winning new "informalities" in its relationship with the professoriate. This deformalization can be understood in the murkiness of the faculty role in the labor process caused by an increased dedication of professorial labor time to the work of management. It is also evident in the everyday withdrawal of support for research-related expenses. In my discipline, many faculty even at schools where research is required for tenure, pay most of their research and conference travel expenses out of their salaries, salaries that are in most cases already far lower than those with other "professional" degrees. There are, of course, other sectors of higher education (sci-tech, finance) that can be analyzed in relation to high-profit, high-wage dimensions of information capitalism. Even at the handful of top research universities where such analysis is appropriate, however, the financial return on research dollars is notoriously low (when considered as a capitalist investment rather than a social good).

But the evidence of the other, larger trends with which I am concerned appears to suggest that the university's role in information capitalism in many respects is a role understandable in connection with the sort of low-wage, low-profit firms of interest to Sassen, where pressure toward informality is highest, and where workforces are chosen not merely for their cheapness but for ease of managerial control. As Sassen observes, "it is also their powerlessness which makes them profitable" (*Mobility*, 40), a powerlessness that emerges not only from the deskilling observed by Noble, and the industrialization of office work observed by Braverman, but also, especially in the low-cost, low-wage firm, from a "system of control" that is "immediate and personal," in which employers can respond to worker dissatisfaction and complaints simply "by firing them" (42). The observation that low-wage, low-profit firms are driven (by competition) toward informalization of the workplace (hiring undocumented workers or evading other regulations), and derive competitive advantages from increased control over the worker, would seem to have at least some parallel importance for understanding transformations in the academic labor process.

This would lead us to ask in what ways the informatic logic of the university's labor process—its dedication to the casual, full-time, contingent, and semiformal processes of labor "in the mode of information"—contributes to an increasing powerlessness of faculty, students, and the citizens who emerge from the higher education experience.

Management's Dashboard: William Massy's "Virtual U"

> Who among us hasn't longed to be in charge for just one day? Oh, the things we would change! Virtual U gives you that chance—the chance to be a university president and run the show. (Massy et al., *Virtual U* "Strategy Guide")

> Escaping the regulatory apparatus of the formal economy enhances the economic opportunities of such firms. (Sassen, "Informalization," 11)

While it is highly questionable that many professors have been fired as a consequence of having "their skills captured on tape," we are nonetheless witnessing the disappearance of the professoriate. The teacherless classroom is no future possibility. Instead, it's the most pressing feature of contemporary academic reality. By the year 2000, it was difficult to find any sector of higher education institutions in North America where the tenure-stream faculty taught more than 30 percent of course sections —even in the Ivy League (Coalition of Graduate Employee Unions). The elimination over three decades, chiefly by attrition and retirement incentives, didn't reduce the amount of teacher work being performed; it just handed teacher work to term workers who serve as administered labor and not collegially. In some departments of public institutions, as little as 10 percent of the teaching is done by professorial faculty. With occasional exceptions, most of this cadre of students and former students serving as term workers figure as the ideal type of labor power "in the informatic mode"—they can be called up by the dean or program administrator even after the semester has begun, and they can be dismissed at will; they have few rights to due process; they are frequently grateful to "have the chance to do what they love"; like Wal-Mart employees, most rely on parents or a traditionally employed partner for shelter and access to health care, day care, and so on. Of the rest, many are willing to finance their own, sometimes continuous, training with as much as $100,000 of debt. Surely this transformation of the academic work process, the substitution by attrition of contingent labor for faculty labor, is the core feature of educational informatics—a perfected system for recruiting, delivering, and ideologically reproducing an all-but-self-funding cadre of low-cost but highly trained "just-in-time" labor power. Little wonder that every other transnational corporation wants to emulate the campus. By nearly any measure, the university represents the leading edge of labor in the informational mode.

William Massy's *Virtual U* is a "computer simulation of university management in game form" (Sawyer, 28). Designed by a former Stanford vice president with a $1 million grant from the Sloan Foundation, the game models the range of powers, attitudes, and commitments of university administration. In short, it provides a window into one of the more widespread versions of administrative consciousness and world-view—the ideal administrator in the world of resource allocation theory, cybernetic leadership, and revenue center management. The use of such simulations, models, and games is widespread in bureaucratic, professional, service, and manufacturing training environments. The serious gaming trend has seen the emergence of games designed to promote environmental awareness, armed forces recruitment, white supremacy, religious tolerance, better eating habits, approaches to living with chronic diseases, and so on. Wherever there is real-world rhetorical and practical purpose, institutions and activist organizations have commissioned games to propagandize, train, inform, and recruit. Both the U.S. armed forces and Hezbollah recruit through downloadable PC-based games. Even public budgeting has resulted in an at least two gaming simulations designed to influence voters by shaping attitudes toward spending, in New York City and the Massachusetts state legislature.

Massy's game is a budgeting simulation. It draws on two prominent strains of thought in contemporary university management. One is the "cybernetic systems" model of university leadership developed by Robert Birnbaum (*How Colleges Work*) and resource allocation theory, specifically the principles of revenue center management (RCM), of which Massy is a leading proponent. The other is the Hong Kong design team selected by Massy and the Sloan Foundation, Hong Kong's Trevor Chan. Massy and the Sloan Foundation specifically selected Chan for his prior success with the PC game *Capitalism* ("The Ultimate Strategy Game of Money, Power, and Wealth," reviewed by *PC Gamer* as "good enough to make a convert out of Karl Marx himself"). Massy and Sloane felt Chan's game represented a "good match" with their "similar" vision of management strategy, and the code underlying Chan's *Capitalism 2* serves as the base for many of the modules in Massy's game.

There is only one viewpoint possible in Massy's *Virtual U*. Players can choose to be the president of several different kinds of institutions, but presidency is the only possible relationship to the campus. One cannot choose to play Massy's budget game as a student, faculty member, taxpayer, employer, parent, alumnus, or nonacademic staff. The reasons for this design decision are abundantly clear and profoundly ideological. To the audience Massy addresses, only administrators are "decision makers." Only the presidency offers a viewpoint from which to "view the whole institution." As a result, every other standpoint in the game has reality only insofar as it represents a "challenge" to presidential leadership.

Faculty, students, staff, and all other constituents are treated in the game as "inputs" to the managerial perspective. The players have the power to "adjust the mix" of tenure-track and nontenurable faculty, as part of their overall powers to "allocate resources as they see fit." The ease with which nontenurable faculty can be dismissed is accurately modeled. Storing hundreds of faculty "performance profiles," the simulation permits university presidents to troll through the records—including photographs—of faculty in all ranks in every department. As in real life, presidents may terminate the employment of the nontenurable with a keystroke—advancing a great variety of their presidential policy goals with relative ease. What is actually being taught here? Players have to fire adjunct faculty while looking at their photographs. One thing that's being taught is the exercise of power in the face of sentiment: players quickly learn that you can't have an omelet without breaking eggs.

By contrast, the tenured faculty are represented as a much more difficult "leadership challenge." They cannot be easily dismissed—so many leadership priorities could be swiftly reached if only all of the funds tied up in tenurable faculty were released! But the tenured have to be offered expensive retirement packages to free money for other "strategic purposes." And as in so many other ways, the simulated faculty are represented as acting irrationally in response to retirement incentives.

While the tenured faculty may represent a headache for the player-president, they do not represent any real opposition in the world of the game. There are no unions. In fact, as bored game players frequently reported, the game is almost impossible for the player-president to "lose," because no one else has any meaningful power. This is particularly significant because it successfully models the virtually unchallengeable legal-political-financial-cultural supremacy that underwrites contempo-rary management domination. The only question is: How much victory can one administrator stomach over ten years?

Admittedly, Massy's ambition is to train a leadership cadre in the habits of benevolence. Underlying the game's approach to the relation-ship of administrators to faculty is Birnbaum's "cybernetic systems" model, which synthesizes much of the new organization and manage-ment theory of the 1980s into a moderately more faculty-friendly form. Birnbaum's model amounts to a "left wing" of the university manage-ment discourse, but the extent to which this is a "left" wing is highly relative. On the one hand, Birnbaum genuinely feels that education re-quires a different kind of organizational management than business cor-porations. Within limits, he defends the sometimes anarchic and unpre-dictable nature of "loosely coupled" academic organizations, through which administrative subunits retain conflicting missions and identities that are at least partially independent of organizational mission. Birn-baum correctly notes that the corporate wing of the leadership dis-course decries his moderately more faculty-friendly posture as "as a slick way to describe waste, inefficiency, or indecisive leadership and as a convenient rationale for the crawling pace of organizational change" (How Colleges Work, 39). Recalling the current popular trope for fac-ulty managers of "herding cats," he sums up his own view of "effective leadership" by quoting Clark Kerr's ambition to keep the institution's "lawlessness within reasonable bounds" (196). The book with which he launched his retirement was an effort to debunk three decades of "man-agement fads" in higher education, including total-quality management (TQM) and Massy's own RCM.

On the other hand, Birnbaum, together with many in his discipline, is the author of an approving portrait of management's strategic deploy-ment of faculty committees and faculty institutions as the "garbage cans" of governance. Drawing on a trope circulated by Michael Cohen and James March in 1986 and enthusiastically adopted by the lead-ership discourse a decade earlier, Birnbaum notes the utility to leader-ship of establishing "permanent structural garbage cans such as the ac-ademic senate" ("Latent Organization," 233) He observes that task forces, committees, and other receptacles of faculty garbage are "highly visible, they confer status on those participating, and they are instru-mentally unimportant to the institution" (How Colleges Work, 171).

Their real function is to "act like buffers or 'energy sinks' that absorb problems, solutions, and participants like a sponge and prevent them from sloshing around and disturbing arenas in which people wish to act" (165). As in Massy's model, for Birnbaum the term "people" ultimately means administrative "decision-makers." "People" should keep the faculty garbage *away* from decision arenas" (165; emphasis in the original). Serving as coeditor of the ASHE (Association for the Study of Higher Education) reader on organization and governance in higher education throughout the 1990s, Birnbaum's views on the "cybernetics of academic organization" were widely influential, at least among those who were committed to models of university governance as leadership by strong management qua benevolent indulgence of one's "followers."

Essentially, the cybernetic model is about managing feedback loops in an awareness of systematic interconnectedness. Viewing management as a "social exchange," Birnbaum emphasizes the extent to which management enters a preexisting environment "in which there are many 'givens' that restrict to a great extent what can be done," and that while it is possible for a president to transform a "Neil Simon comedy . . . into Shakespeare," it requires incrementalism and the willingness to provide others with at least the sense of agency, so that, as Birnbaum cynically notes, "In future years, they can reminisce about how *they* transformed themselves" (*How Colleges Work,* 228; emphasis in the original). He concludes that leaders have to listen to the organizational environment—or more accurately, *monitor it*—and cannot simply command: "Leaders are as dependent on followers as followers are on leaders," and "Presidents should encourage dissensus" (23, 216). This promotion of dissent is not to encourage organizational democracy; it's to provide more accurate information to "decision arenas" and reduce "leader error" in the larger service of more effectively inducing changes in the behavior and value of organization members.

At its core, the cybernetic management model isn't about enabling *speech* per se on the part of nonleadership constituencies; it's about harvesting information. While faculty or student speech can be a source of information, speech isn't the only or even the primary mode through which presidential "data are collected" (Birnbaum, *How Colleges Work,* 218). (Hence the "assessment movement" that is currently sweeping administrations across the country.) By contrast, Birnbaum often models the administrator as a speaker, often a very creative one—the author, director, or impresario of organizational saga and myth—with the power to "interpret organizational meaning." Rather than "inducing the alienation that may arise from giving orders," presidents should "try to get people to pay attention to matters of interest to the administrator" (207). This isn't about faculty democracy; it's about the usefulness to administrations wishing to create "organizational change" of a *sense* of democracy. Where propaganda and the creation of organizational myth or mission fails, leadership can always induce "organizational learning" with funding. Over time, units that fulfill institutional mission receive funding increases; units that don't, lose funding: "the subunit 'learns' through trial and error in a process akin to natural selection" (191).

Both Massy and the Sloane Foundation are explicit in their intention to promote a managerial model of systems theory in *Virtual U*. As in Birnbaum's vision, the arc of the game is fundamentally incremental. Player-presidents get results slowly over time by tinkering with the environment in which other constituencies act, rewarding certain behaviors and punishing others, primarily with funding: "Many of the decisions don't produce explicit reactions, but instead initiate trends and behaviors that evolve toward a desired result by the manager" (Sawyer, 35). If Birnbaum might be called an "organizational Darwinist," Massy is a managerial Malthus. In his essay, "Lessons from Health Care," Massy praises the system of managed care for insurers' capacity to intervene in the doctor-patient relationship. Because an insurer's "denial of payment triggers organizational learning," hospitals, clinics, and practices "will be less likely to perform the procedure again in similar circumstances" (191).

The same principle, of feeding those who collaborate with management's vision of institutional mission and starving out the opposition, governs every dimension of Massy's management training game. The game's organizing concept is the representation over a ten-year period of the consequences of presidential adjustments in annual budgeting. As Massy's collaborator at the Sloan Foundation has it, money is the yarn that knits this vision together: "Every decision translates, directly or indirectly, into revenue or expense. In considering how to convey the university as a system, we concluded that there was no better way than the annual budgeting process. The way the player, or the president, finally sees the whole institution synoptically is through financial flows"

(Ausubel, 4). Primarily employed in education schools (Columbia, NYU, Kansas, etc.) as a teaching aid in graduate classes in educational leadership, the game's scenarios are generally introduced with a version of the driving fiscal imperative: "Your task . . . is to maintain steady revenue, at minimum, and preferably grow revenue and spend it in ways that advance the institution."

The game is meant to bring forth a particular administrative subjectivity. One dimension of the administrative personality it successfully evokes is information overload. The managerial desktop is full of data. But each datum represents a competing claim on resources. These resources can be translated into livelihoods and potential good deeds or, as Massy has it, "the diversity of intrinsic values that abounds within any higher education institution" (*Resource Allocation,* 5). The overall effect is of fatigue, including moral fatigue: "Each group argues for its view in terms of high principles, often reinforced by the fact that success also furthers self-interest" (5). The reduction of reality to revenue flows becomes a solution for the chief feelings of the administrative standpoint, information overload and something that might be called "value fatigue." As one USC administrator quipped to David Kirp, "if you don't have a vision, RCM becomes your vision." The game teaches a very specific set of feelings and values to potential future administrators. It teaches the utility of maintaining a large disposable faculty both for meeting financial targets and for quick restructuring to meet new presidential priorities. It teaches what I call a "management theory of agency" (see chapter 4), in which managerial decisions appear to drive history.

It even teaches what can be called a "management theory of value," in which the labor of "decision makers" (à la George W. Bush, "I'm the decider!"), and not the strenuous efforts of a vast workforce, appears to be responsible for the accumulation of private and public good in the university labor process. As one community college president using the game puts it to his students at Columbia University: "Senior administrators are the engines that push an institution forward—and like a big train, the larger the institution the more engines must be strung together to drive the institution forward" (Hankin). In the down-is-up world of education administration, it becomes possible for a group of NYU students playing Massy's game to conclude that the game's "Improve Teaching" scenario would be best served by a massive acceleration in the hiring of adjunct lecturers. Ultimately, the game teaches these future administrators the pedagogy that Paul Lauter sees is already immanent in the institutions that it models:

> Universities teach by what they are. When a great university with an $11 billion endowment helps impoverish an already indigent city by using outsourcing to push down dining hall wages, it teaches who counts, and who decides in today's urban world. When a great university stiffs its retirees at $7450 a year while setting up its CEO for a $42,000 a month pension, it teaches who is important and who is not. When the American city in which a great university carries out its medical research has a higher infant mortality rate than Costa Rica, lessons about priorities are being delivered. When 60–70% of the teaching hours at a great university—and at many not at all great universities—are carried out by a transient faculty, many of them paid below the poverty line and provided with no benefits, offices, or job security, a redefinition of teaching as a "service industry" is being implemented. ("Content," 54)

The Academy's "Two Worlds" of Living Labor

There are really two distinct worlds of faculty experience being modeled in *Virtual U*. There is the world of the tenured faculty who must be more ponderously influenced, involving a fairly strenuous effort by administrators. Relatively speaking, it takes a lot of administrator sweat and frustration to surmount the obstacles represented by the tenured— who ultimately must be provided their retirement incentives to get out of the way, and who require the constant creation of new forums (or garbage receptacles) for their opinions. Subject to the Malthusian financial discipline and organizational mythmaking of the leadership cadre, as extensively theorized by Birnbaum, Massy, and others, the first world of the tenure stream is certainly no picnic for most faculty occupying it.

Nonetheless, the second world that the game models for the "other" faculty, our nontenurable majority, is very different. These folks can be dismissed quickly and cleanly. Despite representing the majority of the faculty, they require a minimal fraction of management time and attention. The extensive use of them permits game players to advance most dimensions of the institutional mission with greater speed. And in this dimension of the game play, the premium on management's capacity to swiftly "adjust the mix" of labor to its own changing sense of "mission," is where we find Massy and the Sloane Foundation's vision of the future.

At a University of Pennsylvania meeting full of administrators, game engineers, and potential users of the game, Sloane project director Jesse Ausubel described his own background in modeling systems used for real-time command and control of complex energy-industry operations (such as an oil refinery). Somewhat wistfully, he observed that the current release of *Virtual U* is for "teaching and learning, not real-time operational control." However, he continued: "It would not surprise me if some of the people in this meeting help advance the state of the art in university simulation, *so that in 10 years, we have models that serve for control, for decisive management. For the present, and it is a huge step forward, we have a game*" (3; emphasis added). In the future, the Sloane Foundation promises us, all labor will act informationally, in the interests of real-time control by a yet more decisive management. There'll be no more noodling around with even the trappings of faculty democracy.

What needs to be added to the commodification critique represented so well by Noble's analysis is a systematic accounting for the core transformation represented by casualization. To be sure, this analysis is pushing toward exactly the right pressure point—informationalization as a matter of the workplace—and yet by focusing on the question of transmitting course content over a distance, the commodification critique incompletely addresses the experience of living labor, especially the majority of academic labor represented by flex workers.

Another way of saying this is to observe that Noble has hold of what is incontestably the likeliest agent for resisting and controlling that transformation, and for articulating the labor of the North American academy to global proletarian movements—the faculty union—but then goes on to share in the thirty-year disappointing failure of academic unions to confront casualization. As I've written previously in *Social Text*, this is a story that deserves to be told in the key of Shakespearean tragedy, where one's virtues are equally one's flaws (Lear's fondness, Hamlet's phlegm). Since 1970, the academy has become one of the most unionized sectors of the North American workforce, and yet it's been a unionization inattentive to management's stunningly successful installation of a casualized second tier of labor. While 44 percent of all fulltime faculty and nearly 63 percent of public-institution full-timers are unionized (in comparison with about 12 percent of the workforce at large and 36 percent of public-sector employees [Bureau of Labor Statistics]), consciousness regarding what to do about the contingent workers of the second tier has been slow to develop in faculty unions.

What is inescapably and enduringly important about Noble's work in this series is its grounding in workplace struggle. It is only unionists like Noble who have mobilized any significant opposition to any dimension of the informational transformation and who are capable of sustaining the necessary vision articulated by an organized faculty, as at the University of Washington. Such faculty insist that education can't be reduced to "the downloading of information" and is an "intersubjective and social process" (Noble, *Digital Diploma Mills,* 53). Nonetheless, the rhetorical and mistaken portrait of informationalization as the "firing of professors" and a lights-out knowledge factory rather than the substitution of nonfaculty labor for faculty labor needs to be thoroughly confronted and reconsidered by faculty unionists, as well as by other persons situated in the academic-industrial complex.

Why does it matter? For one thing, the idea that academic informationalization can be equated with "the future" and "distance education" leads Noble to suggest in part III of the series that the battle's been won, even before it was properly started. For instance, in the aftermath of some 1998 consolidation and retrenchment among online vendors, he writes that the "juggernaut" of instructional technology "appears to have stalled" and that "faculty and students have finally become alert to the administrative agendas and commercial con-games behind this seeming technological revolution." Would that it were so! Noble comes to this conclusion (in November 1998) with his "Part III," just eight months after issuing a call in part II (in March 1998) to defend faculty intellectual property rights in "the coming battle." Few people seriously engaged in critical information studies would necessarily jump to the conclusion that defense of faculty IP rights can serve as a core strategy for combating informationalism,[4] but the real issue is the sudden swiftness with which Noble's informatic struggle seems to have opened and closed. If academic informationalization isn't just another Hundred Days' War, then what is it? These chronological problems result from the decision to employ a "commodification-of-instruction" heuristic to the exclusion of a heuristic featuring the casualization-of-instruction. By naming the move to technology as the key measure of informatic instructional delivery, Noble dates instructional transformation as a recent phenomenon, one that follows the 1980s commodification of research, one that is only happening "now" and which can be averted, even one that by 1998 may already have been averted.

But if casualization and not technologization is understood as the key measure of informatic instruction, we see a far more plausible chronology beginning much earlier—in the 1960s, first observed circa 1968, and continuously unfolding in a process of steady implementation, current commitment, and with no end in sight. Noble's history of university informatics essentially recapitulates the two-century transition in manufacturing modes of production (from artisanal production to industrialization to post-Fordism) but compresses that narrative into just two decades, as if university knowledge work were primarily artisanal before 1980 and primarily industrialized thereafter. This is already problematic: university knowledge work may remain artisanal in certain sectors, but it was also in many other sectors enormously industrialized—especially in the sciences—much earlier. Rather than viewing this transformation as relatively smooth and uniform, it might be better to follow Paolo Virno, for example, who sees informationalization not as determining a single "compulsory mode of production" but as supporting a radically uneven terrain of work practice, preserving a "myriad" of "distinct" productive modes, serving as an umbrella "under which is represented the entire history of labor" in synchronic form, "as if at a world's fair" (18–19). (Indeed, this was also Marx's observation in *Capital,* that many modes of production exist side by side.) Stitching Virno's understanding together with the "taxonomy of teacher work" offered by Stanley Aronowitz in the *The Jobless Future,* we recognize a plausible portrait of our own academy, in which some researchers work in entrepreneurial and corporate modes of production and others produce artisanally, but these pockets of entrepreneurial, industrial, and artisanal practice are inescapably conditioned by the umbrella presence of the contingent labor of graduate students and former graduate students working on a subfaculty basis.

One good way to make sense of the commodification of teaching narrative, then, is to approach it as a narrative about the informationalization of academic labor by the sector of academic labor that has been least informationalized. That is: while the tenured faculty (what remains of it) are increasingly becoming what Gary Rhoades terms "managed professionals"—increasingly subordinated to the corporate values, ease of command, and bottom line of the management desktop—the degree to which this informational transformation of the tenure stream has been accomplished is limited. Despite challenges to the Yeshiva decision, many of the cases handled by the NLRB demonstrate the degree to which the faculty function can be read before the law as that of "professional managers" (who can be denied the right to bargain collectively) rather than as "managed professionals."

The degree to which the tenured now present their labor to management in "the mode of information" presents only a narrow ledge of understanding regarding the fully informationalized working reality of contingent academic labor. As tenurable faculty labor moves toward increasing subordination to management, lower pay, and so forth—toward proletarianization—it is possible that they will come to better understand that the degradation of their own work is systematically related to the superdegradation of the contingent workers teaching in the same classrooms. But insofar as there is now, and will likely remain, a large gap between the work experience of the flexible and the tenured, we might be pressed to conclude that what remains of "artisanal" faculty practice since 1970, at least in part, has been preserved by the compliance of the tenured with management's development of a second tier of labor.

Certainly, that sense of faculty complicity drives much of the graduate-employee labor discourse—the discourse of the most vocal segment of those subjected to the informatic logic of higher education. Graduate students rightly feel that their mentors, frequently the direct supervisors of their work, owe them something more structurally significant than moth-eaten advice about "how to do well" in the job search. One reason that graduate employees are so vocal is because they view the transformation of graduate education (accomplished by the three-decade conversion of the university to a center of capital accumulation) as a profound form of "employer sabotage." In the course of reimagining the graduate student as a source of informationalized labor, the academy has increasingly evacuated the professional-certification component of the doctoral degree. Although the degree has a key role in the way professionals maintain a monopoly on professional labor, now that work formerly done by persons *holding* the degree is done by persons *studying* for the degree, the degree itself no longer represents entrance into the profession.

In pushing beyond the perspective of the least informationalized (professorial) sector to the most informationalized (graduate-employee and adjunct) sector of faculty work, we have multiplied the informatic constituency threefold or fourfold. So one way of going on with an analysis of the "information university" is to press at the understanding that it is not workerless but filled with workers, most of whom will never be so lucky as to have the problems of the tenured.

Another way of going on from here might be to use the steady increase of a superexploited labor pool to press quite hard at the shared fantasy by the tenured faculty and the administration regarding technology as a magical source of accumulation in the information university. For example, as Tessa Morris-Suzuki and others have shown, the general failure of the capitalist fantasy that automated production can create value largely continues to hold under information capitalism (Suzuki, "Capitalism," "Robots and Capitalism"; Schiller; Caffentzis). When only a few information capitalists have deployed a particular "labor-saving" technology, the rate of profit rises; but as technological deployment evens out, the rate of profit falls sharply. Because the profit comes from the uneven deployment of technology, and not technology per se, the falling profits associated with increasing technological equilibrium lead even information capitalists back to the fundamental source of value: the exploitation of living labor.

This insight helps explain why neither distance learning nor the earlier "courseware" of correspondence-based degrees of the 1920s and 1930s ever materialized into the threat imagined by bricks-and-mortar education providers. First adopters of a technology purporting to provide education as information download rake in large profits, because they appear to provide "the same" service for less. But if Donald Trump can automate a few textbooks and tests and throw in a cheap call center and call it a "university," it's a game that nearly any modest capitalist can join. (As the explosion of unregulated, underregulated, and deregulated higher education providers in such locations as China and India clearly demonstrates.) As education is stripped down to the provision of information in a larger market share, price competition in that sector intensifies and the rate of profit plummets.

The possibility of accumulation in U.S. higher education, public or private, will in general continue to depend on putting large numbers of people to work—even if those people aren't teachers. As the spending of U.S. administrators on dormitories and fitness centers demonstrates, higher education providers can and increasingly do compete with each other by the provision of noneducation and paraeducation services that involve the labor of personal trainers, janitors, cooks, counselors, nurses, marketing specialists, and so forth. They also compete by offering valuable noneducation intangibles such as prestige and social, career, or cultural capital, many of which are accepted as markers of education quality but have no intrinsic relation to actual learning (as the promoters of for-profit education and others in the assessment movement are quick to point out). The production of prestige and career capital also requires a workforce—including "star faculty," as well as all the workers in public relations, communications, admissions, alumni relations, the big college sports complexes, and so forth. In large part, the rate of accumulation in this arrangement depends on the degree to which competing managers can hold down the wages of the large workforces required to provide competitive levels of service and prestige.

In university terms, the superexploited informatic labor of its ever-growing contingent workforce (and not "information technology") is a major source of the value that the university accumulates as capital. In the higher education teaching force, nearly all of this contingent labor has passed through the system of graduate education, which suggests that graduate students and former graduate students must become visible as doubly exploited: first, in the superexploitation of laboring contingently; second in a silent exploitation in that their "education" no longer leads to employment but is itself that employment. When education is continuously evacuated by increasing quantities of "teacher training" and other duties, something that counts as "graduate education" is stolen from them and something else is substituted—something that contributes to the university's direct accumulation.

So it seems worthwhile at this juncture to insist that the higher ed commodification critique be more rigorously articulated to the standpoint, circumstances, and experience of living labor. In looking at commodified education from a materialist point of view, one key point must be that the production of education in the commodity form necessarily implies the creation of *both* a commodity *and* surplus value. The predominant line of thought tends toward addressing the characteristics of the education commodity while ignoring the intrinsically related and equally important radical increase in the university's collection of surplus value, an increase drawn in most institutional circumstances primarily from the labor of women and young people (students, both graduate and undergraduate).[5] Emphasizing the degradation of the "educational and research product" in commodity form can have the effect of obscuring an underlying reality that in some ways can be more directly described as a measurable increase in exploitation.

The point here is not that the commodity form and the standpoint of living labor are rival or mutually exclusive starting points for an analysis of education capitalism.[6] The issue is that analyses of the commodity form that address only "the degradation of the education and research product" (i.e., tend toward the adoption of a consumer standpoint) fall short of addressing education capitalism as a system that relies on the exploitive extraction of labor for the creation of surplus value. If Paul Smith is right that "the commodity is still the hieroglyph" and remains "a privileged place" for analysis, I think it is equally worth emphasizing, with Smith himself, and ultimately with David Noble as well, that "if this commodity could speak, part of what it would proffer is a memory of the process of the extraction of labor and the production of surplus value" (Smith, 57).

Indeed, when the commodity in question is casualized labor, it does speak, and has been speaking. The question is whether we're willing to listen.

Which is to say that our motivation for opposing the commodification of education can never be only the degree to which commodified education is "better or worse" than noncommodified education but the inextricably associated question of the degree to which commodification represents the increased exploitation of living labor.

New Student Movements, Mental Labor, and Class Struggle

> And trust me, it's a lot more fun reading a book about youth in the workplace than actually experiencing it. (Giammarise)

One way of getting into the undergraduate experience is to ask how teaching in the mode of information affects their learning: that is, if it sucks to be a disposable teacher, what does it mean to be *taught by* this "sayonara faculty," the soon-to-be-disposed-of cheap teachers laboring in the informatic mode? After all, this is a system that takes its most experienced teachers—graduate students who have taught eight years or more—and fires them, replacing them with brand new "teachers" who have no experience at all. The experienced teachers then go to work "in industry," while every year thousands of inexperienced first-year graduate students walk into freshman classrooms with nervous grins on their faces. We could begin by asking whether it is a form of "employer sabotage" when by far the majority of college teaching is done by persons who will never hold a Ph.D. or do not have an active research agenda, and many of whose scholarly ambitions may have terminated in a sense of frustration, failure, or disappointment. Or we might try to get at the structure of feeling that sustains these college teachers and ask what convictions and behaviors are being transmitted to undergraduates in their first two years by persons whose experience in graduate school has taught them to love lifelong learning more than wages, who do not expect their employer to provide benefits, who are grateful to work at the university, who do not generally have or expect any meaningful control over the workplace, who may feel that they "deserve" their fate at $16,000 per year, and so forth. It is not at all uncommon for a person who believes herself to have "failed on the academic job market" to base her pedagogy on "what you need to do to get a job."

But perhaps the undergraduate student's experience is not simply tied to the experience of graduate students and former graduate students along this binary of "teacher and student"; perhaps the undergraduate experience is very much like the graduate experience, on a vector of likeness, "student and student." After all, the "young people" who teach contingently (twenty-one to thirty-eight years old; by the early 1990s, the NCES reports that the average age of the recipient of an academic first full-time job was thirty-nine) are in most cases near to the age of the young people being taught by them (average age of the U.S. college student is more than twenty-six and a half years old; nearly half of all undergraduates are over twenty-five).

The undergraduate's always-lengthening "time in school" is increasingly a term of service as a worker, commonly a flex worker. The majority of college students work while in school; one-third work a full-time equivalent (thirty-five hours or more), often, however, without the benefits associated with full-time employment. As discussed in chapter 4, many work directly for the university; in many other cases, the university "assists private employers" in finding student labor, creating corporate-university partnerships founded on uniting "scholarships" with the university's assistance in finding students to work cheaply and without complaint, even taking advantage of the "special" educational relationship to increase the compliance and dependency of their workforce.

To a meaningful degree, the university's role regarding the employment prospects of youth is no longer merely that of a space of socially supported leisure consequent on the "warehousing" of "surplus labor" for future full-time employment. Instead, the university's role is now to accumulate value extracted from student labor in several ways: as direct employer, as purveyor of the temp services of enrolled students to nearby corporations, and also, eventually (in no particular hurry), to provide some degree-holding graduates trained and socialized to deliver their labor in the mode of information. Once we recognize that the categories of "student" and "worker" increasingly overlap, we start to have a way to add to our already developed understanding of education as an ideological apparatus vis-à-vis students (i.e., what Samuel Bowles and Herbert Gintis term "the people production process" [53]). In the context of massive student employment, we cannot restrict analysis to the ideological questions of curriculum and the content of knowledge production (though these questions are vital) or even the direct repression of teacher labor in the industrialization of knowledge production. Once we feature the labor of the student centrally, it is possible to make different sorts of inquiries and have different hypotheses.

For instance, why shouldn't we expect to find the organic intellectuals of academic informationalism in the student body (and not among the professoriate), for the simple reason that it is really the students, graduate and undergraduate, who labor informationally? While so many of the professoriate are willing to see themselves as "information vendors," and use their unions to defend "their" intellectual property rights, it is not clear that this position makes them intellectuals organic to information work. (To the contrary, it seems that the professoriate has tended more toward providing intellectuals organic to information capitalism—the defense of intellectual property rights by tenured faculty is more like the artisan-capitalist Duncan Phyfe than Paolo Freire.)

In this connection, we might devote more consideration to questions raised by the emergence of the student anti-sweatshop movement; among other things, this movement is obviously a sabotage of the corporate university's regime of accumulation. And rather than see this phenomenon as evidence of professorial intellectual leadership ("at last, the young people are listening to us again") or the resurgence of an earlier movement culture, what would happen if we saw this intellectual activity as emerging from the increasingly contingent material experience of the North American "youth" formation? And if this intellectual activity—this will to sabotage—is, indeed, at least partially symptomatic, perhaps we can ask this question: Is not the focus on the sweatshop an indicator of a student movement that also wants to be a labor movement? In addition to forging an alliance "between students and labor," what would a movement based on the self-consciousness of students *as* labor look like? If the anti-sweatshop movement were to recognize its symptom as such, what would it do next? It is already a subjectivity articulated to proletarian struggle elsewhere on the planet, albeit mediated by a notion that the struggle is "for" others and "really" over there. How much more of its potential might the anti-sweatshop movement realize if it incorporated an activism against the flexible dominion of the university managers more locally?

A movement based on the recognition that, under information capitalism, the term "student" names a category of worker returns to certain compelling questions: What is education for? What is the difference between knowing and acquiring information? We might even ask: What would an information socialism look like, especially when we understand that the dissemination of information technology and "access to higher education" will not automatically produce it? Over the past thirty years, the expansion of the higher education franchise has incorporated a steadily larger segment of the U.S. population, but evidently this has had the overall effect of increasing economic inequalities. NCES data strongly suggest that the increased "access" to education between 1970 and the present has widened the earnings gap between the more and less educated, not by increasing the earnings of the educated (which have declined) but by slashing the incomes of the less educated even more ("Condition of Education 2000," table 23-1).[7] One way, therefore, of reading the incorporation of larger class fractions into "higher education" is to suggest either that it has produced new economic penalties for staying out of the education regime or that the place of the university in the informational transformation is substantial enough to help economically organize the lives of even that minority who have no direct connection to it.[8]

A student-labor movement might provide a standpoint from which to explode the fantasies that emanate from attempting to resolve the contradictions of capitalism with providing "access to capital." Regardless of whether information is construed as economic or cultural capital, it seems clear that providing student laborers with "access to information capital" is no substitute for actual education. As Henry Adams wrote, "Nothing in education is so astonishing as the amount of ignorance it accumulates in the form of inert facts." Obviously, anything that counts as "actual education" will involve devoting labor time to study, to "leisure activities" such as sport and listening to concertos, and not submitting to the in-formatting of vocational instruction. But information capitalism's hostility to the devotion of student labor time to study and to leisure is not merely a consumer ripoff (information download as ersatz education) but the class struggle itself—an organized "employer sabotage" of worker consciousness; a programmatic obsolescence by the credit hour; substituting the lifelong drudgery of perpetual training for leisure, enjoyment, and free mental activity. The struggle over higher education is not a struggle over the "distribution of cultural capital" but a struggle to contain, divide, and divert the subject of social transformation.

If we are in a moment where information is the ideal commodity, characterized by a form of the work process in which the student is the most characteristic worker, should we not expect the demand of the student to emerge organically as the foundational demand of labor at this time? If we accepted the not-capitalism specific to the student as our own not-capitalism, a more general and generalizable not-capitalism, wouldn't it look something like a refusal to work in the informatic mode? This would naturally be a variant on the demands of the Italian autonomy: rather than working without income, it would be to have an income without work. And in making such a demand, are we not making the demand of the student simply to be allowed to be a student? To have years to study, to do mental labor outside of the regime of accumulation? And in opposing a lifetime of study, sport, enjoyment, and leisure to the regime of "lifelong training," we might find the authentic demand of the flexible: under a socialist informatics, laboring in the mode of information will invite persons to that joy in their muscular and synaptic efforts that capital commands them to ape.

3

The Faculty Organize, But
Management Enjoys Solidarity

> The salary of an annual appointee at the start should be low,—
> about the amount needed by a young unmarried man for
> comfortable support in the university's city or village. . . . He
> should receive, as assistant professor, a salary which will enable
> him to support a wife and two or three children comfortably. . . .
> Approaching forty years of age [and] ready for a full professorship
> [the salary] may easily be four times the sum which the young man
> received at his first annual appointment.
>
> —Charles Eliot, *University Administration*, 1908

> Teaching here is like being in a bad marriage that looks good to
> outsiders. I'm the wife whose husband slaps her around but who,
> nonetheless, smiles gamely, maintaining the relationship "for the
> sake of the kids."
>
> —"Lucy Snowe" (pseud.), "lecturer in English at a
> major research university in the East," 2004

Charles Eliot's *University Administration* portrait of faculty
life radiates a confident paternalism that remains viable in many ways
today. Despite sporadic press coverage of the term faculty and graduate
employees who do 75 percent of the teaching in higher education, the
public image of the professoriate remains that of Stanley Aronowitz's
"last good job in America": tweedy eggheads effortlessly interpellated
in a system of rational, meritocratic reward, administered on a generous scale by a trusteeship of honorable men. Indeed, for faculty in certain overwhelmingly male-dominated disciplines, Eliot's picture is accurate enough. In engineering or business at a research institution, the
phenomenon of a generously compensated young male wage earner on

track to a quadruple family wage (say, $140,000) by the age of forty is quite common.

For most others, and especially the majority of women faculty, like "Lucy Snowe" working off the tenure track in the feminized liberal arts, the wages are similar to those of the women who stitched and laundered Eliot's shirt. (The author's use of the educator-heroine of Charlotte Brontë's *Villette* refers to the condition of nineteenth-century schoolteachers, who often compared their compensation unfavorably to that of needleworkers, whose circumstances were then, as now, a byword for extreme exploitation.) In every region of the United States, women faculty teach for as little as a few hundred dollars per course, frequently earning less than $16,000 for teaching eight courses a year, without benefits. Even in the full-time nontenurable positions, women with doctorates, averaging as much as ten years of post-baccalaureate study, commonly earn under $30,000, often without benefits.[1]

A chief component of Snowe's oppression is the very idea that this arrangement is fair or rational, the inevitable—and impersonal—consequence of some such guarantor of the public good as a "market" in the wages of women (and the men who do such "women's work" as writing instruction in higher education). She characterizes her injuries in the terms employed by survivors of domestic violence with the intention of underscoring the systematic solidarity of the oppressor's logic—the web of beliefs, loyalties, privileges, and institutions composing the patriarchy itself, not just the individual abuser. She is especially attuned to the way the solidarity of the oppressor calls forth the participation of the victim, encompassing such diverse motivations as the opinion of outsiders (feeling the desire to show herself in a situation that "looks good") or caretaker obligations, the fear that exposure of the violent nature of the relationship will harm "the kids." The economic and social violence experienced by most faculty in their working lives, especially the majority of women faculty working in undervalued disciplines and in nontenurable positions, is experienced bodily, like a blow, and is sustained by a network of beliefs and institutions "outside" the relationship between administration and employee.

The patriarchal web includes other women, including many academic and professional women who identify with the feminist movement, in the sort of crypto-machismo of Ann Marcus's adjunct hiring policy at New York University: "We need people we can abuse, exploit and turn loose" (Westheimer). Even leaving out notions that are overtly associated with gender, relevant beliefs shaping the gendered relations of work in higher education include those regarding "the position of the United States in a global economy," the "value" of different kinds of education, "the responsibilities of management," what it means to be "accountable" to the public and who belongs to that public, not to mention such ideological portmanteaux as "quality," "excellence," "merit," "market," "efficiency," and so forth, maintained on these topics and many others by persons in legislatures, professional organizations, social movements, judicial panels, and political parties.

Snowe's vivid rhetoric underscores for us that the solidarity maintaining her oppression is not an abstraction that will wither away upon exposure to the light of good analysis. Knowing that she is oppressed, even knowing that she participates in her own oppression, doesn't of itself transform Snowe's situation, who remains employed on the same campus under the same conditions. There must also be someplace for Snowe to go, an *alternate* solidarity.

In this chapter I look at the self-consciousness of, and relationship between, two of the three waves of thinking about higher education as a workplace since 1945—first, the academic labor movement comprised primarily of tenure-stream faculty and nonteaching campus workers that arose in close connection with teacher unions and public-employee unionism generally; second, close on its heels, the managerial consciousness that presently dominates. Elsewhere in the book, I examine components of the rising third wave—the unionism of graduate employees and other contingent faculty, whose struggle with managerial domination is one of the leading forces shaping employment regulation and education policy today.

It is worth emphasizing that the movements of thought and action here dubbed "waves" are (or were) to a degree hegemonic. That is, as the consciousness of a politically empowered group, they circulate values and ideas about limits and possibilities shared by other groups in advance of debates about particulars. Each in their moment, they led in setting the terms of discussion and framed the world of possibility. For instance, during the 1960s and 1970s, the values and expectations of higher education unionism (as part of a broad wave of movements committed to the expansion of social democracy through economic redistribution, direct action, and the law) yoked the notions of "faculty," "tenure," "freedom of inquiry," and "workplace democracy" to a previously unprecedented degree. Even at the campuses where faculty feeling or the state legal climate did not favor unionism, the best defense against unionism by administrations was granting a large portion of the union agenda—instituting such now-standard reforms as consistent tenure policy and written guarantees of academic freedom, improved salaries and benefits, and securing greater faculty participation in decision making. Of course, to a certain extent, these grants of union goals are simply cynical calculation: "If we do not grant some control, we will lose it all."[2] But to a significant degree, the beliefs were (and are) sincerely held. Many administrators (until very recently, the vast majority) believe something along these lines: "Of course, faculty should have a powerful voice in governance; how could one imagine it differently?" The inability to "imagine differently" is the trace of the union movement's success. In the period in which faculty interests were hegemonic, opposition to unionism often nonetheless involved adopting many of the values and goals of unionists.

It is obvious today that managerial values interpellate the faculty and students as well, framing not just possibilities for action (what can be done) but possibilities for knowing ("this is the world"). In this way, tenured faculty, even unionized tenured faculty, accept the managerial accounts of "necessity" in the exploitation of part-time faculty, graduate students, and the outsourcing of staff. Through the managerial ideology, itself supported by a vast ensemble of reactionary social movement in the 1980s and 1990s, faculty no longer question the claims of "fiscal crisis" while the campus pays millions to basketball coaches but sub-Wal-Mart wages to mathematics faculty and custodians. The knowledge has taken hold everywhere that "markets" are real but "rights" are insubstantial, as if "market-driven" indicated imperatives beyond the human and political, of necessity itself, rather than the lovingly crafted and tirelessly maintained best-case scenario for the quite specific minority interest of wealth. The managerial mind-set is currently widely shared by faculty, including the values, structures, and limits to possibility of, for instance, "continuous quality improvement" and "responsibility centers" and "informal" decision-making (as if the absence of regulation or due process benefited anyone but those with the power to hire, fire, reward, and discipline). Students, too, share the mania for assessment, ranking, pay-as-you-go, revenue maximization, and continuous competition in pursuit of "excellence," even where those values are demonstrably against their own interests.

The extent to which managerial ideology is at least partly hegemonic of faculty generally and even, distressingly, of organized faculty, is a matter of immediate political urgency. To some extent, the vulnerabilities of faculty in this regard flow from their situation as educators. Like others involved in the labor of social reproduction, educators are under particular pressure to embody and transmit the values of power—which seeks through their labor to reproduce itself and the circumstances most favorable to itself. The degree to which schooling can serve anti-egalitarian and anti-democratic purposes, and complicity with capitalist exploitation, is also the degree to which educators can be persuaded to arrangements that are hostile to democracy and equality in their own workplaces.

Some newer vulnerabilities, however, have to do with the situation of U.S. organized labor generally. Educator ideology might make faculty unions especially willing to tolerate a multi-tier workplace, but nearly all American unions have acceded to multiple tiers of employment, defending some of the privileges of enrolled union members while permitting the employer to hire its new workers on a "second tier" of often very different wages, fewer benefits, and so on. Academic unions are complicit with management in worker exploitation in their own way, but they are consistent with American unions in this regard.

This means that higher education is a typical workplace in that "solidarity," like faith and chastity for Augustine, is more of an ongoing project and often-deferred goal than a naturally occurring phenomenon waiting to be discovered.

Collective Bargaining as a "Survivor Project"

The court's perception of the Yeshiva faculty's status is distorted by the rose-colored lens through which it views the governance structure of the modern-day university.

The Court's conclusion that the faculty's professional interests are indistinguishable from those of the administration is bottomed on an idealized model of collegial decisionmaking that is a vestige of the great medieval university. But the university of today bears little resemblance to the "community of scholars" of yesteryear.

Education has become "big business," and the task of operating the university enterprise has been transferred from the faculty to an autonomous administration, which faces the same pressures to cut costs and increase efficiencies that confront any large industrial organization. The past decade of budgetary cutbacks, declining enrollments, reductions in faculty appointments, curtailments of academic programs, and increasing calls for accountability to alumni and other special interest groups has only added to the erosion of the faculty's role in the institution's decisionmaking process.

[Today's decision] threatens to eliminate much of the administration's incentive to resolve its disputes with the faculty through open discussion and mutual agreement.

By its overbroad and unwarranted interpretation of the managerial exclusion, the Court denies the faculty the protections of the NLRA and, in so doing, removes whatever deterrent value the Act's availability may offer against unreasonable administrative conduct. (Justice William Brennan, writing for the four dissenting members of the Supreme Court in *NLRB v. Yeshiva University*, 444 U.S. 672 (1980); included in this volume as appendix A)

We need people we can abuse, exploit, and then turn loose. (Dean Ann Marcus, NYU, on the hiring of term faculty; email submitted in evidence before the NLRB in the *Westheimer* case)

The higher education labor force is enormous. Including clerical, service, and administrative personnel, together with instructors of all kinds, colleges and universities directly employ over 3 million full-time and part-time employees. Hundreds of thousands more are indirectly employed through outsourcing contractors, now used by 95 percent of campuses in such areas as food service, vending, custodial work, and campus bookstores. (While the number of campus administrators soared almost 50 percent between 1993 and 2001, the numbers of clerical, skilled workers, and service and maintenance workers held near steady or declined in the same period, largely due to massive outsourcing [NEA Higher Education Research Center]. By contrast, through the 1970s, expansion in administrative hiring ran "parallel" to increases in numbers of both students and tenurable faculty [Duryea, 11].)

Additional millions of undergraduate students work on campus through work-study programs and other arrangements. Nonteaching employees outnumber teaching employees, and the largest group of persons working on a typical campus are undergraduate students.

In this diverse basket of workers, the group most likely to be unionized is tenure-track faculty (44 percent) (Rhoades). They are closely followed by skilled, service, and maintenance workers (42.8 percent); white-collar staff, including clericals (23.4 percent); and graduate student employees (about 20 percent) [NCES 1994, cited in Ehrenberg et al.; Lafer]. All four groups are much more likely to be unionized than other American workers, of whom currently just 12 percent bargain collectively, including only about 8 percent of those in the private sector.

Among nonteaching employees, union membership has a dramatic influence on wages and benefits. For example, in a 1997–1998 study of 163 institutions of all types, mean salaries were dramatically higher for organized staff: unionized administrative secretaries earned 23 percent more, or an additional $5,000 per year; custodians and groundskeepers earned 35–39 percent more; and painters and heating-cooling workers earned 40–42 percent more, representing as much as an additional $12,000 annually.[3] Undergraduate students and other casual employees are the lowest paid and least likely to be organized, and they are increasingly assigned to duties previously performed by salaried persons.

At present, faculty on over 1,000 college campuses are represented by collective bargaining agreements, especially public institutions: nearly two-thirds of all full-time faculty at public institutions are unionized. Contingent faculty and graduate students often affiliate with the largest staff unions, the American Federation of State, County, and Municipal Employees (AFSCME) and Service Employees International Union (SEIU), as well as the United Auto Workers (UAW; which has scored major victories in the University of California system, as well as the milestone contract with NYU, the first between a private university and its graduate employees). Full-time tenure track faculty, however, are mostly represented by the National Education Association (NEA), the largest independent union in the country, or the American Federation of Teachers (AFT), an affiliate of the AFL-CIO (American Federation of Labor and Congress of Industrial Organizations). A significant minority of campuses feature an independent union, sometimes derived from a faculty senate or else affiliated with the American Association of University Professors's (AAUP's) collective bargaining operation, which is the most popular representation choice among private four-year schools.

While the largest percentage and absolute number of union campuses are among the ranks of community colleges, the total number of organized faculty on four-year campuses is significantly higher: nearly 140,000 faculty on four-year campuses versus about 100,000 at two-year schools. Even observers who have been skeptical of the economic impact of unionization agree that it has reduced wage and benefit inequalities, especially between highly paid and lower-paid disciplines on individual campuses, or between units in multicampus systems—for instance, raising the pay and improving the benefit structure of tenure-track community college faculty in the City University of New York system to greater parity with the four-year campuses. Overall, in excess of 700,000 campus employees are union members, about 250,000 of them faculty. By Gary Rhoades's calculation, 85 percent of faculty in public four-year institutions—exclusive of research universities—are unionized (12).

Despite these impressive numbers, and continuing growth in higher education organizing overall, it is fair to raise the question whether most organized faculty and staff see themselves as belonging to a labor "movement." Clearly, there are a couple of thousand labor organizations on campus today. But do they have the larger sense of belonging, solidarity and commitment that Joe Berry of Chicago COCAL calls "a social collectivity without clear edges, which in its power and motion creates, impacts, supersedes and floods and sometimes raises up organizations and institutions" (17)? Berry, together with other innovative organizers and labor theorists—such as Kate Bronfenbrenner, Robert Hickey, and Dan Clawson—calls for a unionism of the largest possible resemblance to, and relationship with, social movement tactics and values, including organizational democracy, widespread participation, and the intent for a widespread social transformation. From this point of view, movements create institutions, which may survive in the absence of the movement's culture and passion. In the absence of the broad-based democratic "upsurge" that Clawson attributes to the animating force of a movement, however, the things that those institutions and organizations can accomplish remain limited. In Birnbaum's 1983 first edition, the ASHE reader on organization and governance included a chapter on collective bargaining; by Christopher Brown's fifth edition in 2000, the entire chapter had been excised as among topics no longer "relevant or of general scholarly interest" (xi).

Indeed, it may be more accurate to speak of the clustered institutions of full-time faculty and staff as a set of "survivor projects," to use Johanna Brenner's term, rather than a "movement." By characterizing worker associations as survivor projects, Brenner means to capture the diversity of ways "people group together in order to live in capitalist society" (42). She notes that the diversity of forms of association and resistance also represents a very diverse degree of effectiveness, insofar as many forms of worker association involve a high degree of "accommodation" to oppression, as well as "particularistic" and "exclusionary" organizing strategies:

> The skilled disregard the unskilled, the organized disregard the unorganized, the stronger unions disregard the weaker ones—and this happens among workers who share ethnic identity or gender as well as those who do not. . . . Registered nurses have been no more willing to take "less credentialed" hospital workers into their unions than male craftsmen were willing to assimilate the "lesser skilled" women workers into theirs. Unionized women teachers have often made separate contract deals with school administrations and failed to support the demands and organizing of clerical workers and teachers' aides. (45)

By approaching the offenses against solidarity of trade unionism from the perspective of a "survivor project," Brenner is seeking a way to value the successes of institutions whose missions, vision, and practices fall well short of the ideal of worker solidarity against exploitation.

"Managerial Revolution" and Academic Capitalism's Common Culture

> And so, Management Joe, your political pronoun is "we." Your bargaining units are "they." Remember that the strike requires your team to organize a public relations office, generate a steady stream of public announcements of victories, and cackle over the clerical union's inability to mount a decent strike. Never mind if management is faltering, the union triumphing; the Rhetoric of Bull is essential. . . . You who wanted to be provost in order to facilitate discussion of Great Ideas are now to organize a corps of inspectors—your fellow administrators, whatever their titles—to stalk the campus with clipboards every hour on the hour to check that classes are held. Good luck persuading your late 1960s activist-turned-assistant-provost that this is her job. (Dean David Johnson, Gustavus Adolphus College "Response #1" to a clerical unit strike scenario; quoted in Ehrle)

In thinking about academic labor, it is common to talk about the faculty as acting in various organizational groups (disciplines, senates, unions) or to have shared values and traits (academic freedom and a preference for a semiautonomous work process). It is far less common for critical scholarship to approach academic management as a collectivity, except in a largely abstract sense (as the instruments of "corporatization," etc.). Even in the most sociologically informed quarters of the "organization and governance" discourse, the pronounced tendency is for scholars of higher education to approach faculties in groups but to treat "decision-makers" as individuals.

Today, however, a booming "leadership" discourse is aimed at introducing the many tens of thousands of deans, chairs, presidents, and provosts, together with all of their associate deans, associate chairs, vice-presidents, program heads, institute chairs, and so forth, to a common culture. This culture has blossomed since 1980, introducing a new and quite distinct system of values and practices. It completes a radical break with the homelier tone of earlier treatises, over many decades, on the "art of administration," typically compilations of addresses by retired university presidents. In 1978, a volume with that title, and a very late instance of the genre, was fairly typical of the relatively modest discourse. Its overall ambition was to serve as an "amateur's guide" to the mundane challenges of administration. Offering a series of homely how-to's to other amateur administrators (be on time, pay attention to detail), it used the controlling and rather humble metaphor of the administrator as "file clerk" to a largely ungrateful and disdainful faculty (Eble).

One significant precursor to the transition in management thought is the "governance" discourse, especially the material produced by the Carnegie Commission on Higher Education under Clark Kerr, beginning in 1969. As discussed in detail below, this discourse gazed with tremendous apprehension at the New Left social movements and inferred a strong relationship between faculty and student involvement in those movements and the faculty union movement. It is not an exaggeration to say that Kerr and the commission at times shared Daniel Bell's sense that the 1970s campus legitimacy crisis included the need to craft a campus administrative response to the possible success of political revolutionaries (Bell: "One thing we can expect is a force of urban guerrillas" [162]).

Like Bell, Kerr would see both analogies to, and relationships between, the labor movement and radical social movements. This might be called the "solidarity" phase of administrative discourse because administrations quaked with fear at the relative unity displayed by the faculty. For administrators, a solidarity of their own was an urgent goal. Few contributors at this time imagined such eventualities as the 1980 *Yeshiva* decision or Reagan's 1981 assault on the air traffic controllers' union—one stalled unionism on private campuses, and the other inhibited it in the public sector. As sponsored by Kerr, this discourse was designed to make predictions (What would be the future of higher education?) and policy recommendations (What forms of governance would meet that future?). Above all, it is a discourse of reaction—reaction to the perceived revolutionary new faculty power.

In calling for a science to be called "university relations" on the model of industrial relations, Kerr included the problem of managing revolutionary students and organized faculty under the same head. He envisioned revolutionaries and unionists as mutually reinforcing components of the same "new social force" comprised of "students and intellectuals." This force was potentially "more damaging to the existing social fabric" than the radicalism of industrial workers, and to institutions of higher education especially. "The actions of quite small groups are potentially more likely to break the campus asunder. The campus is a hot-house plant that withers before the hot wind of disruption" ("Society," 185). Kerr reassured his audience by pointing to the outcome of the 1968 revolution in France: sometimes, he emphasized with prescience, "it has been the reaction that is triumphant" (181–182).

The 1968 Kerr essay that I've been quoting is interesting because it shows the transition from the older discourse to the new quite explicitly. In it, he is visibly turning away from an older, more egoistic notion of the administrator. He is beginning to embrace a radical new vision of the administrator as member (and often architect) of an administrative community that, in turn, sees itself as the collective architect of the sense of a community "whole." Commenting on an earlier essay in which he defined the role of the university president as equal parts "mediator, initiator, and gladiator" who fights "for academic freedom and institutional autonomy," he eschews the homelier, looser, and more spontaneous former terminology of gladiation, as well as the whole notion of "fighting" (in this case, against the state). Now he is in favor of a cooler, less playful, and more determined terminology that indicated a willingness to collaborate with the state, especially in deflecting "the hot wind" of social change: "I would now use the phrase *campus leader.*" Throughout, he touches on core elements of the Druckeresque leadership discourse, including mission ("responsibility for the coherence, cohesion, integrity, and structure of the institution") and maintaining the control-advantageous "sense of community and the sense of participation throughout" ("Society," 186).

The turn to "leadership" as a trope for governance and the value to management of a "sense of participation" anticipate the key shift in the discourse of higher education administration toward the wholehearted embrace of management theory, circa 1980, especially the Toyotist innovations that succeeded in other enterprises by systematically treating all workers as intellectual workers. In treating auto assembly plant employees as brain workers, Toyota management was systematizing many of the features that white-collar workers, including professionals and college faculty, found desirable about their jobs. These features included a degree of autonomy in the work process and participation in management-level decisions.

Rather than envision the team of management facing the opposing team of labor, Toyota management established teams of area responsibility, which included managers and laborers working together in what was meant to be a quite earnest spirit of cooperation. If Toyota practice sounds a bit like the idea of shared governance, it should: in treating its workers like intellectuals and its unions like "partners in governance," Toyota's goal was to encourage its workers to have a primary identification with the institution that employed them, rather than with other workers, much the way that intellectuals and professionals develop primary loyalties to their firm or their campus.

As it cascaded through the corporate world in the 1980s and 1990s, the cultural dimension of Toyotism involved a panoply of rhetorics, institutions, values, and processes aimed at creating a common culture within the corporation, a common culture "led" by management but "shared" by the workforce. These principles were first circulated in the United States in 1981 and 1982 in a series of popular management texts: *Theory Z, The Art of Japanese Management,* and *Corporate Cultures* (Masland). The modern "intentional communities" of multinational employers are supported by a massive corporate-utopian discourse that deploys the rhetoric of "liberation" (e.g., Tom Peters's *Liberation Management*) and "revolution," with the intention of convincing workers and taxpayers that redistribution is occurring downward, while it is in fact occurring upward; that worker democracy consists of "dialogue" with management organizations rather than independent associations of their own; and that mass firings represent opportunities to exercise creativity and spontaneity for the "free agents" thus created. This pie-in-the-sky, down-is-up, snake-oil, and free-love discourse is best observed by Thomas Frank, who notes that this literature's real goal was to address the 1970s legitimacy crisis of the multinational corporation and the class who directed them. Nearly every writer in the field, he notes, coopts the rhetoric of social "change," rejects the older Taylorist models of "scientific management" and "elitism," especially of technocrats and intellectuals, and promises a populist utopia of abundance, choice, and participatory democracy. During these decades, the major texts of the management community's "theory industry"

> almost universally insisted that its larger project was liberation, giving a voice to the voiceless, "empowering" the individual, subverting the pretensions of the mighty, and striking mortal blows against hierarchies of all kinds. Even as the lot of the worker deteriorated, [the management class] was announcing that democracy was thriving in the nation's factories and office buildings. Captains of industry were they no longer: Now they were the majestic bearers of the popular will, the emancipators of the common man. (*One Market*, 178)

Of course, as in Japan, this discourse didn't succeed without the direct cooperation of the state (in helping to crush more militant social forces that might intrude from "outside") and, especially, the unwavering enthusiasm of the corporate media, which continues to report as fact management theory's self-described contributions to economic and political democracy.

The revolution in academic management, and the accompanying discourse, is simultaneously new and familiar, in some ways slightly in advance of Toyotist management cultures in the multinationals but trailing them in other ways. The widespread adoption of "Japanese" management techniques in corporate organizations precipitated a crisis in research into the organizational behavior of education institutions that "raged" between 1980 and 1985 (Peterson). The new, "cultural" wing of research drew on such traditions as Burton Clark's 1973 vision of viewing the university as a unique culture held together by "organizational saga," and Malcolm Baldridge's discussion of the university as more of a "jungle" than a "bureaucracy," but the primary inspiration was the shifting interests of corporate management, not the literature internal to research in higher education or education administration.

In 1981, David Dill observed a chiasmus in the trends of business and academic management. Throughout the 1970s, academic enterprises adopted the management techniques of business: strategic planning, marketing, and a variety of accounting schemas now familiar to most with academic work experience. But trends in corporate administration were "flowing in the other direction"—that is, adopting methods in the "management of meaning" traditional to academic life (262). In academic life, Dill notes, skill at "nurturing the ideologies and belief systems of their organizations" was both untheorized and on the wane, all but "absent": "both the overall strength of academic culture and the skills for managing it have declined" (265).

Observers such as Christopher Newfield and specialists like Roald Campbell et al. have both pointed out that education administration has participated in all the major phases and philosophies of organizational management: scientific management, human resources, bureaucracy, and the current "open systems" model associated in the theoretical literature (not the literature of workplace experience) with cultural rather than directly hierarchical models of control (Campbell et al., 101, 199). Newfield is especially adept at tracing the shared humanistic origins of traditional academic organization and recent trends in management theory. For Newfield, the entwined traditions of corporate and academic management stretch from the corporate organization of medieval colleges and Emerson's social philosophy to the present. This suggests to him a set of rich possibilities for what he terms "corporate" or "managerial humanism," of which "figures like Tom Peters are only the most visible recent incarnations" (215). Many informed observers will agree with Thomas Frank, Saskia Sassen, David Harvey, Donna Haraway, and others that it's hard to reconcile the working conditions produced by this management with the humanist rhetoric of liberation.[4]

To the extent that Toyotism adapts the cultural and ideological methods of socializing and controlling white-collar professionals such as academics, there are innumerable contact points at which "the Toyota way" fits hand in glove with academic work processes. This is especially the case with partial worker autonomy and participation in management, and, of course, the ideological reproduction of minds suitable to the dominant circumstances of production and distribution is a core function of higher education. It is common for the managerial literature, both empirical and theoretical, to be frank about the usefulness of "institutional collegiality" as a management tool: empirically, "it motivates diverse members of the community to participate in strategic initiatives and support a conception of the organizational mission," and again, empirically, through collegiality, individuals are "more willing to make the sacrifices" called for by "financial restraint" (Hardy, 183–184). As Michael Yates points out in an early and important *Workplace* essay on the subject, through faculty senates and other ideological institutions, most academics "have already absorbed" the ideology of labor-management cooperation, but they fail to understand that the underlying motivation for management's eagerness for labor cooperation is the Toyotist conviction that every aspect of work must be controlled— by management, with labor's cooperation—to the greatest degree possible (3).

As the "academic leadership" discourse acquired momentum and influence throughout the 1980s, it offered ever more nakedly utilitarian recommendations regarding the elements of faculty participation in decision-making. For instance, Cohen and March (originators of the faculty-forum-as-garbage-can analogy) contributed such gems in their widely influential 1986 *Leadership in an Organized Anarchy* as the recommendation that administrators should "overload the system" of faculty governance with trivial problems in order to induce "flight" from governance, thus advantaging "the full-time administrator who is left to make the decision in cases of flight" (25).

In addition to its cultural dimension, Toyotism represents a genuinely radical transformation of the work process, which most workers have experienced as profoundly dystopian. The core concept is of continuous reinvention—often called, following W. Edwards Deming, "continuous quality improvement," where "quality" means efficiency, so that managers are *continuously* being asked to improve efficiency: that is, to continuously produce more with lower labor costs. This is otherwise known as "stressing the system" or "kaizen," a philosophy of continuous testing of the limits of worker performance, or "management by stress" (Yates; J. Slaughter; Weissman). Key "stressing" strategies include compelling "teams" and individuals to "act entrepreneurially" and compete with each other for raises or continuing employment, the continuous outsourcing of work elements to lower-cost casual employees, and a pyramid of reward that provides jobs for life to a few while the vast majority are consigned to a permanently temporary existence. To understand the scale at which this philosophy applies today, one only has to think of the relationship between Wal-Mart and its suppliers, who complain of that chain's practice of demanding lower prices in every new contract, intruding under the guise of "partnership" into its supplier firms' accounting, production methods, and employee relations in search of continuously lower prices for itself. Toyotism isn't only a philosophy through which capitalist employers stress their workers, it's an embracing worldview through which large multinationals "continuously stress" and test the limits of smaller capitalists, governments, and the environment itself.[5]

In its academic version, the Toyotist work regime is supported by a triumphalist administrative literature—for example, *Quality Quest in the Academic Process, On Q: Causing Quality in Higher Education, Continuous Quality Improvement in Higher Education,* the *Total Quality Management in Postsecondary Education* newsletter—as well as by a series of active financial and philosophical partnerships with legislators and corporate leadership, such as the multicompany TQM Forum in 1988, as well as IBM's TQM competition in 1991 and its successor TQM University Challenge, funded by Motorola, Milliken, Proctor and Gamble, and Xerox, all of which provided major grants to universities that adopted "quality" initiatives, including prominent public research institutions such as Penn State and University of Wisconsin–Madison. These were followed by the American Society for Quality's Educational Division and the Continuous Quality Improvement Project of the American Association for Higher Education in 1993 (the now-defunct former higher ed division of the National Education Association, which broke away in 1968 over the issue of faculty unionization) (Dew and Nearing, 10).

Certainly, major figures in the discourse of "educational leadership," such as Robert Birnbaum with his critique of "management fads," have tried to distinguish themselves from the "quality" movement. But reviewers from within the educational leadership discourse have emphasized the near-complete continuity of Birnbaum's own approach with "the principles and practices that guide continuous improvement within TQM" (Fife, 470). The vast majority of the literature supports this reviewer in cautioning against following Birnbaum in the substantial conceptual error of

> declaring TQM dead and a fad when, in reality, the values and processes of TQM have remained and matured under new labels, going from Continuous Improvement to Organizational Effectiveness. Evidence of the vitality of what has been called the quality movement can be seen in the activities of such organizations as the National Consortium for Continuous Quality Improvement Network (CQIN), North Central Association's Academic Quality Improvement Project (AQUIP), the Malcolm Baldridge National Quality Award program, and more than 40 state "Baldridge-like" quality award programs. (Fife, 471)

Many observers would conclude that, in fact, the "quality" movement has internationalized and globalized, so that in its current manifestation the "assessment movement" is placed under the rubric of "quality assurance" (Newton).

In all of this literature, the notion of administrators "causing quality" is fundamentally a literature about the stressing (or "continuous improvement") of faculty productivity. A key ambition of leadership is to create a culture that is amenable to the process of stressing and which shares the aims of stressing. Ultimately, managerial "leadership" of institutional culture is a functional concern: "causing quality is easier to accomplish in strong cultures than in weak cultures" (Seymour, 146).

Continuous improvement in faculty productivity, of course, means working harder for lower wages, but it also means that such work is productive for certain kinds of aims and not others. The Scylla of "quality as lower labor cost" is always accompanied by the Charybdis of "responsibility" or "revenue," as in revenue or responsibility center management (RCM), where campus units are placed under a regime "in which resources will flow according to market demand and assessed performance." From the "resource" pillar, teams (now "responsibility centers") are "free" in the sense that they experience "relaxed restrictions" in "how to manage resource trade-offs" and "determine for themselves how to meet the agreed objectives within the available budget" (Massy, 7). That is, while responsibility centers are not free regarding the availability of budget, and are only nominally free in the agreement regarding objectives, they do have new flexibility in managing trade-offs in the goal of "improving quality," such as choosing for themselves whether to increase class sizes or reduce travel funds. RCM does offer the prospect that some of what is robbed from Peter will be paid to Paul: cost savings from some revenue centers can be passed on to other "high-performing" centers, especially those showing a spirit of entrepreneurship, albeit according to management's principles of assessment of independent accomplishment. Leading resource allocation theorist William Massy writes, "If one owned several gold mines, wouldn't it make sense to invest in the one with the highest assay?" (6).

Of course, Massy's syllogism depends on the capitalist assumption that all "values" can be converted into a universal medium of exchange —such as gold—in the first place. Hence the need for empty signifiers— such as Tom Peters's "excellence," notably analyzed in its academic deployment by the late Bill Readings. Employing Readings's analysis of the operation of empty signifiers in the capitalist redefinition of educational mission, one might reply to Massy's loony reduction of all human value to "gold": "Well, if a hiking party includes four people, would it benefit from a distribution plan that gave eight lungs to the fastest runner, and none to everyone else?" Readings's pioneering work on the utility to capital of empty signifiers such as excellence needs to be followed up by a raft of committed research. Especially important will be a thorough analysis and even a moment-by-moment historiography of the continuously shifting but positive and traceable content of such parallel usefully ambiguous signifiers as "quality."

By now, the TQM-RCM continuous "stressing" of academic labor is long institutionalized, not the least by the scene of perpetual retrenchment, in which every year is a year of fiscal crisis, and in which every year sees "new" pressures on wages, workloads, class sizes, benefits, and autonomy. Despite a high unionization rate among both faculty and staff, higher education is a leading example of the Toyotist labor pyramid, with a minority workforce employed for life, "participating" in the management of a majority casualized underclass (albeit one created by the "internal outsourcing" of women, minorities, and student workers rather than a global outsourcing). The faculty workforce often voluntarily competes with each other for funding, raises, course relief, and so forth and tends to view competition—even competition for wage increases lower than the cost of living—as "natural." As Slaughter, Leslie, and Rhoades have contended, the cluster of behaviors they term "academic capitalism" (engaging markets and engaging in market behaviors, such as competition, the defense of property rights, etc.) is not just the product of managerial leadership but, instead, is the result of a complex interaction of agencies—especially state and local government and multinational corporations but including faculty and other academic workers themselves: "We have come to see colleges and universities (and academic managers, professors, and other professionals within them) as actors initiating academic capitalism, not just as players being 'corporatized.'" (12).

Academic Management and the Regulation Environment

> Institutions not only are acted upon by corporations external to them but actively seek to lobby state legislatures in order to change regulations so that colleges and universities have more opportunity to engage in market and marketlike behaviors. (Rhoades and Slaughter, 5)

> The most important single factor that explains the pattern of unionization is the character of state public-employee bargaining laws. (Garbarino, 61)

By emphasizing the agency of higher education participants—even where one's agency is devoted to furthering one's own exploitation—Slaughter and Rhoades are mapping the lines of association that connect agencies of capitalist exploitation within the academy to those without, rejecting the notion that higher education has been "subverted by external actors" without participation in its own fate. They are particularly concerned to avoid what they describe as the "triangle" model of analysis, in which the three points of campus, market, and state are taken as three independent groups with three clear agendas. Instead, they focus on the "blurring of boundaries among markets, states, and higher education" and on the competition between the agendas of organizations and networks that cross those blurred borders, often in a struggle over state resources and state power (such as the law) regarding the ways that higher education will participate in the new economy (8–11).

From this perspective, university managements and the organizations that support them will often seek the backing of the state to economically position campuses and campus workforces in ways that are different from those sought by individual faculty and their organizations. Of particular interest are the ways that university management and corporate management "external" to the institution have collaborated with political actors for the reinterpretation of labor law since 1980. The degree to which university management has been successful at shaping the regulation environment suggests the usefulness of Brenner's "survivor project" frame for viewing the extent to which tenure-stream faculty have collaborated in the exploitation of themselves and others.

Certainly, the institutions of faculty and staff unionism are the survivors of a series of great judicial, executive, and legislative traumas after 1980. In a 5–4 decision that year, the Supreme Court delivered the most profound of the injuries caused by the judiciary branch, holding that the Yeshiva University's "full-time faculty members are managerial employees excluded" from legal protection for collective bargaining activities under the National Labor Relations Act. (At the time, "full-time" implied tenurable, and this decision played a huge part in crafting the very different contemporary reality.) Most responsible scholarly observers are likely to be persuaded by Justice William Brennan, writing for the four dissenting judges, that faculty performance is assessed primarily on their teaching (and presumably in many cases, their research), not on their generally minor "managerial" contributions.

In a forceful, learned, and often acerbic opinion (included in this volume as appendix A), Brennan points out that the legislative intent of the "managerial exclusion" is twofold. First, Congress intended to protect workers from having to include management in their bargaining units. Second, they intended "to ensure that employers would not be deprived of the undivided loyalty of their supervisory foremen." The act's supervisory exemption was subsequently enlarged judicially to include "managerial" employees who were "involved in developing and enforcing employer policy," with the same motivation: "that an employer is entitled to the undivided loyalty of its representatives."

The majority opinion essentially creates a radical reinterpretation of the faculty role in governance. On the grounds that they are "involved in implementing and developing employer policy," the majority held that such involvement *necessarily* implies an inevitable coincidence of faculty interest with the interest of his employer—that is, Yeshiva was entitled to the faculty's "undivided loyalty." As Brennan observed, this was a classic case of judicial activism from the right. It flies in the face of the act's explicit inclusion of "professional employees" as a category of protected workers and the Board's congressionally mandated powers to interpret the meaning of the act. The board's reasonable holding that faculty were professional employees entitled to collective bargaining rights was consistent with legislative intent, state law supporting the unionization of public university faculty, and the history of faculty governance. To overturn the board and substitute its own "distorted" judgment, the five members of the majority had not only to misinterpret centuries of faculty governance but further to hold the patently false position that the board's inclusion of faculty was not "rationally based on articulated facts" and that the board's interpretation was fundamentally "inconsistent" with the act itself, a position at which Justice Brennan, writing for the minority of four, scoffs. As Donna Euben's brief on the decision for AAUP emphasizes, the majority opinion in *Yeshiva* is narrowly written to cover the facts of the individual case. (This is because its rationale for overturning the NLRB is their claim that the board holds the "view that the managerial status of particular faculties may be decided on conclusionary rationales rather than examination of the facts of each case.") While this has left the door open for case-by-case challenges, these have been few.

As Judith DeCew points out, most recent research "supports" the dissenting opinion, "indicating that administrators [not faculty] have continued to control institutions of higher education," and that additional evidence shows that few faculty feel that their generally limited governance activities are "managerial" in nature (47). The subsequent history of *Yeshiva*—most notoriously, in efforts to deny nurses bargaining rights—raises huge questions about the initial decision.

Notably, Justice Stevens, who in a what-were-you-thinking moment signed on to the 1980 *Yeshiva* majority, has since been forced to help struggle to jam this particular management genie back into the bottle. One of the excluded employee cases is particularly troubling, since in it a Supreme Court majority is now willing to treat workers as "supervisors even if they have no subordinates," as Stevens complains. In 2001's *NLRB v. Kentucky River Community Care*, Stevens found himself writing the dissent for a minority of four. Attempting to preserve the bargaining rights of nurses, Stevens now sounds exactly like Brennan two decades earlier:

> Moreover, since Congress has expressly provided that professional employees are entitled to the protection of the Act, there is good reason to resolve the ambiguities consistently with the Board's interpretation. At

the same time that Congress acted to exclude supervisors from the NLRA's protection, it explicitly extended those same protections to professionals, who, by definition, engage in work that involves "the constant exercise of discretion and judgment in its performance." As this Court has acknowledged, the inclusion of professional employees and the exclusion of supervisors necessarily gives rise to some tension in the statutory text. Cf. NLRB v. Yeshiva Univ. Accordingly, if the term "supervisor" is construed too broadly, without regard for the statutory context, then Congress' inclusion of professionals within the Act's protections is effectively nullified.

Extremely interesting in Stevens's opinion is his subsequent citation of the *Yeshiva* majority in support of the *Kentucky River Care* dissent. He cites a single sentence from the majority opinion, but the one that underscores the majority's view that they decided the case on the *uniqueness* of Yeshiva's faculty rather than its typicality: "Only if an employee's activities fall outside of the scope of the duties routinely performed by similarly situated professionals will he be found aligned with management." While reasonable observers will question whether Yeshiva faculty were in fact engaged in activities "outside of the scope" of those routinely performed by other faculty, the real point that Stevens is drawing from the case law is that the Yeshiva faculty was excluded on exceptional grounds, and that the opinion should not be generalized. Essentially, he's citing *Yeshiva* against itself, in exactly the opposite sense that it has been used by opportunistic management. Rather than saying, "*Yeshiva* held that professionals, like nurses, are supervisors," he is saying, "*Yeshiva* proved that the NLRA is ambiguous regarding professional labor and all cases must be judged on their individual merits."

In my view, Stevens is attempting to rewrite his earlier assent to bad law. Specifically, he seems to be trying to contain the damage wrought by his swing vote on *Yeshiva* by, contrary to the majority in *Yeshiva*, emphasizing the primary right of the NLRB to interpret the NLRA, and then citing *Yeshiva* as proof that (a) the NLRA incorporates "tension" between professional inclusion and supervisory exclusion and (b) only professionals acting differently from most others in their circumstances can be dubbed managerial. Unfortunately, Stevens can't put this genie back into the bottle by himself.

The chilling effect of the decision was widespread and instantaneous. In the five years immediately after *Yeshiva*, activist administrations at private colleges refused to bargain with faculty unions more than fifty times ("Yeshiva Watch," quoted in Arnold, 46). By 1989, one-third of the colleges that engaged in collective bargaining pre-*Yeshiva* had succeeded in discontinuing that arrangement (Saltzman, "Legal Regulation," 50). In other cases, hostile administrations succeeded in using Yeshiva to decertify the faculty union entirely. As Gordon Arnold points out, a series of executive decisions in the 1980s, especially Reagan's termination of 11,000 air traffic controllers and the decertification of their union, as well as a series of strategic anti-labor appointments, including to the NLRB itself, also had traumatic consequences for faculty unionism.

As a result, while private-sector organizing came to a "virtual halt," public-sector organizing also slowed dramatically in the "cooled environment for organized labor": between 1986 and 1990, the University of New Hampshire was the only faculty of a four-year institution, public or private, to unionize (Arnold, 46–47). Subject to partisan executive appointment, the federal oversight of private higher education is highly volatile, frequently reversing course in the aftermath of national elections. This volatility can favor faculty, as when a Clinton-era NLRB narrowed the scope of the *Yeshiva* decision, finding that even "where there is substantial indicia of faculty's managerial status," including "effective recommendation in such nonacademic matters as tenure and promotion," does not "require" the board to find any given set of faculty exempt from the protections of the National Labor Relations Act (Saltzman, "Higher Education," 46). But more commonly since 1980, federal oversight of higher education has favored union-busting administrations, as in the recent finding in *Brown* when Bush appointees to the NLRB reversed the historic finding of the Clinton-era board on the employee status of graduate students, adducing no new evidence or precedent, but simply drawing different politically motivated conclusions from the same set of facts about graduate student employment.

The consequences of judicial setbacks such as *Yeshiva* and blows from executive appointees at the NLRB have been much studied. But fully comprehending the situation of academic unionism requires a close look at the encompassing web of state legislation. Labor scholarship during the 1970s often concluded that restrictive labor law had only a "modest impact" on the growth of organized labor because powerful movement-driven politics could compel the creation of new supportive law after the fait accompli of forcing employers to the table. As Gregory

Saltzman points out, during the 1980s a series of substantial studies found instead that "bargaining laws were the key factor" ("Legal Regulation," 45).[6] The legislative environment is a riotous patchwork of fifty states administering labor relations in public higher education, each in a complex of boards and regulations entirely of its own invention. Each state system of higher education confronts wildly varying state laws regarding the workplace rights of its public employees, and even more varying interpretations of the rights of faculty and staff under those laws. In the northeast and in California, public employee bargaining rights typically receive some measure of protection; in the south and west, there are generally no protections; in Texas, Virginia, Alabama, and North Carolina, collective bargaining is prohibited by statute. Where bargaining rights are protected, individual states vary on the relationship between "professional" academic employees and others, on whether full-time faculty and part-time faculty belong in the same bargaining unit, and so on.

Overall, the general trend of lawmaking after 1980 was to accommodate university management, presenting a lattice of hostile regulation through which many of academic labor's "survivor institutions" squeezed but through which the movement often failed to pass.

The Moment of the Movement

The 1960s were marked by student dissent and student organization. The 1970s may equally be marked by faculty dissent and faculty organization. The decade of the student may be followed by the decade of the faculty. The locus of activism is shifting. (Carnegie Commission on Higher Education, 39)

Grousing about the decline of shared governance will only make faculty members more marginal to management decisions than they already are. (Lazerson et al., A72)

The handful of recent books looking at faculty unions describe the movement as stalled or at a virtual halt (Arnold; DeCew). And as Marvin Lazerson and his colleagues at the University of Pennsylvania, the first Ivy League school to adopt TQM principles, acknowledge, the faculty can hardly be "more marginal to management decisions" than they are at present. (Though it's worth noting that the Lazerson rationale for a "leadership" theory of governance—"Like the cities they increasingly resemble, colleges must train and retain competent managers"—neglects the key point that, however imperfect the process, those of us living in cities still *elect* our leaders.) With membership in the AAUP having declined from nearly 90,000 in the early 1970s to 43,000 today, the commitment to workplace democracy in higher education is in disarray. The most widely read critics of the corporate university are themselves administrators, such as the union-busting Derek Bok and David Kirp, who urge a centrist approach to corporatization ("making peace with the marketplace") while trying to preserve some academic values, in some institutions, and limited elements of faculty governance. The relationship of the faculty with social movement commitments to the administration is generally one of collaboration, and at the outer limits of this collaboration, William Tierney uses standpoint theory to argue for faculty support of administrators seeking "high performance in a reengineered organization": "I am gay, politically on the left, White, a tenured faculty member at a research university, a card-carrying member of the AAUP, and a vocal advocate [of improving faculty productivity]" (99).

But the view during the 1970s was very different. Growing from essentially no representation in 1963 to 20 percent of the profession in 1973, the movement looked unstoppable. Opining that "the 1970s may belong to faculty activism as the 1960s did to student activism," the Carnegie Commission under Clark Kerr, himself a labor economist, observed this "volatile situation" with a degree of alarm, noting that "collective bargaining sentiment goes far beyond the organized units of the present time," with a clear majority of faculty in all institution types including Research 1, and of all ages, including those over fifty, favoring both unionization and faculty "militancy" in their own interests. Even among those faculty self-describing as "strongly or moderately conservative" in their political views, 45 percent agreed that collective bargaining was appropriate for higher education. Among those who evaluated their administrations, or the effectiveness of their faculty senates, as only "fair or poor," the majority agreed that a faculty strike would be a "legitimate" tool. Most of the mid 1970s observers of faculty unionism shared the "long-term prognosis" of Frank Kemerer and J. Victor Baldridge for "substantial" growth in unionization (69), and the view of Everett Ladd and Seymour Lipset that unionization and collective bargaining would be the decade's most important "intramural issues" (40–42). The commission concluded that the initiatives and issues originating in the faculty movement for collective bargaining "may be the dominant ones in the near future" (56). In the vast majority of cases, organizing campaigns expressed the core motivation of securing meaningful faculty participation in governance, as well as wages and benefits, with the creation or securing of elements of workplace democracy providing the primary motivation for a sizable fraction of faculty activists.

The radicalization of faculty beliefs regarding bargaining was associated with a degree of radicalization on the question by the most significant professional faculty organizations in the country, notably the National Education Association and the American Association of University Professors. Primarily an advocacy association for schoolteachers until the early 1960s, the NEA transformed itself in half a decade into the largest independent union in the country. Under pressure from the American Federation of Teachers and its urban membership, and as part of a great wave of unionist feeling among public service employees, including civil servants, police officers and fire fighters, the NEA in 1962 reversed its near century-long opposition to unionism, devoting its enormous resources (dues income in that year alone was over $7 million) to a nationwide organizing effort, initially using such euphemisms as "professional negotiation" for collective bargaining and authorizing what it termed "refusals to work" (that is, strikes) to force the employees of teachers to the bargaining table (Hutcheson, 68–69; Garbarino, 96–99; Ladd and Lipsett, 6–7). Where necessary, NEA partnered its emerging locals with the AFT and the emerging might of the new, militant, and half-million strong public employees' union, the American Federation of State, County, and Municipal Employees (AFSCME). While its higher education operation was and remains much smaller than its efforts in the schools, NEA had organized 234 college locals by 1970 (from zero in 1962), achieving rough parity with the AFT. A professional association long dominated by administrators, NEA's movement into organizing was the result of an insurgency of the membership—schoolteachers taking control of the organization with the aim of taking greater control over their working lives.

Its movement into higher education organizing proceeded similarly by initiatives from below, especially by activist junior college faculty. Task forces arranged by the organization in 1962 and 1967 both recommended greater faculty participation in higher education decisionmaking but stopped short of endorsing collective bargaining. Meanwhile, however, several of NEA's local affiliates at community college locals negotiated collective bargaining agreements on their own, and NEA formed a separate division for two-year schools, reflecting their greater militancy. By 1968, NEA had begun assisting four-year schools to organize as well, resulting that year in a schism with its higher education division, the American Association of Higher Education (AAHE), a group that survived as a policy outlet for administrators, eventually disbanding in 2005 (after an undistinguished decade of promoting TQM).

AAUP's decision to serve as the representative for those chapters wishing to engage in collective bargaining unfolded on a similar schedule, evoking similar tensions. A City University of New York (CUNY) chapter recorded the first "display of interest in bargaining" in 1964, and a largely skeptical or adversarial officership was compelled to make substantial shifts of policy in rapid succession, as more and more chapters sought bargaining arrangements with or without the organization's support or approval. While in 1965 a proposal to involve the association in "binding agreements" was voted down (Hutcheson, 73), in 1966 the association acknowledged that local chapters might serve as the bargaining agent in "extraordinary circumstances." In 1968 and 1969, the association permitted chapters to seek collective bargaining arrangements wherever "conditions of effective faculty participation" in governance were absent; by 1971, after a stormy debate, the executive council abandoned any criteria except the preferences of the local chapter, voting 22–11 to acknowledge bargaining as "a major additional way of realizing the Association's goals."[7] One of the problems with AAUP's collective bargaining efforts was the continuing opposition of an influential minority of its membership, including its executive officers, such as University of California–Berkeley labor law professor Sanford Kadish, who presided over an executive committee that enacted the 1971 policy against his opposition (Hutcheson, 70).

Despite the overwhelming support of the membership for the association's work as a bargaining agent, AAUP lost nearly 10,000 members between 1972 and 1973, in large part due to protest resignations over the issue (Ladd and Lipset, 6). In 1974, the election for association president became a referendum when an anti-bargaining candidate entered the race by petition and then won because the pro-bargaining vote split between the two nominated candidates (Hutcheson, 157). Today, the membership of the AAUP has declined almost 50 percent from its 1972 peak. However, most of the recent decline probably represents the increasing minority role of the tenure-stream faculty in the workforce. The issues on which the association is most visible (academic freedom, defense of tenure, the annual survey of tenure-stream salaries) are issues that tenure-stream faculty have failed to preserve as meaningful expectations for the "new majority faculty" of graduate students and the nontenurable.

One of the key differences between higher education organizing and the larger unionization of the public sector during the 1960s was the greater conservatism of the faculty on workplace issues, in contrast to that of firefighters, civil servants, police officers, and schoolteachers. The faculty were also behind in taking the initiative organizationally, tending to follow the law rather than participate in making new law, as was often the case with militant police officers and teachers. The faculties that organized in the late 1960s and throughout the 1970s often did so against the intense and dedicated opposition of other faculty members, sometimes the most influential faculty members on their campuses, in their disciplines, and in the national associations.

During this period, while on the faculty of Harvard's law school, Derek Bok embarked on what was to become a landmark study of the changing face of the American labor movement, *Labor in the American Community,* coauthored with John Dunlop. Far from predicting the savage war on labor of the Reagan-Bush reaction, this study—begun in 1966 and published in 1970—represents a movement led by postal and sanitation workers, enjoying high public approval and forging social movement alliances, and successfully entering new areas of representation, notably the public sector. The chapter on public-employee unionism explores the association of these unionists, from postal workers to municipal clerks, with broader social movements and commitments to community transformation, underscoring that Martin Luther King Jr. was assassinated in Memphis while appearing "in support of the sanitation workers of the city in a strike in which the decisive issue is the right of the union to negotiate" wages and working conditions for public employees. Bok's 1966–1970 conclusions regarding unionization belie his 1988 opposition to an innovative staff union as Harvard president (when his then seventy-four-year-old coauthor Dunlop had to stop him from using Harvard's money to draw out an extended NLRB appeals process). During the 1960s moment of the union movement, Bok concluded that the movement had improved working conditions even in "countless nonunion firms," by forcing up employer standards, shaping the regulation environment, and providing political representation (465). Furthermore, he and Dunlop concluded that collective bargaining improved worker productivity and even resulted in better management (266, 667).

While many aspects of the newly organized sectors of the union movement broadly intersected with 1960s movement culture, faculty opponents of collective bargaining tended to overemphasize the relationship between faculty unionism and the most radical dimensions of the New Left. Perhaps this overemphasis served the rhetorical purpose of reinforcing the exceptionalist view of faculty work and underplaying any possible connection between the work of faculty and others employed in the public interest. For instance, the Carnegie Commission's Ladd and Lipset placed particular emphasis on the "sudden growth of militant egalitarian movements among the intellectually oriented strata" and "liberal-left ideology" within higher education unionism, especially among groups they somewhat arbitrarily choose to describe as a "less professional" faculty. At its core, they attribute the movement to the victory of a spirit of what they dubbed "faculty egalitarianism" over what they describe as a previously triumphant spirit, termed by them "faculty individualism," in close connection with the ensemble of movements through which "the egalitarian pressures of the late 1960s have broken the hold of meritocratic values." Approvingly quoting the anti-unionist sentiments of Christopher Jencks and David Reisman, they portray bargaining as an opportunity for "weak" faculty and "the mass of academe" to "strike back" at "meritocracy" maintained by the "domination of a relatively small group of distinguished scholars" (6, 102–104). In its concluding section, Ladd and Lipset's rhetoric devolves into an Orwellian register, ultimately claiming that the "changes introduced into academe by collective bargaining" threaten the possibility of a future in which "eccentricity and nonconformity can still flourish" and "in which cost-benefit analysis is not the sole basis on which the value of every course or degree program is judged" (107). (Of course, reasonable observers will attribute the regime of "cost-benefit analysis" to pretty much any university constituency other than the faculty.)

The Carnegie Commission's tendency to overemphasize the influence of New Left sensibility to faculty unionists was doubtless in large part due to the personal experience of the commission's chair, Clark Kerr, in the potential for mutual reinforcement between students and faculty in their demands for campus "participatory democracy" (*Uses of the University*, 134). Kerr himself was a well-known labor economist before serving as the chancellor of California's massive university system during the Free Speech rebellions, and like many liberals he broadly shared such goals of unionism as a more just distribution of income. He believed in the progress of humankind and the rationality of historical development, as well as the emergence of a (relatively) classless society, writing in 1957 that the "the painfully evident divergence between worker and capitalist is disappearing," in terms of both power and income, and that "we stand a long way from a society based on two sharply differentiated classes" ("Unions' Effects," 238).

In his scholarship as a labor economist, Clark Kerr adopted a largely dismissive role of unions as a social and economic force, viewing them as subsidiary to the force of industrialization itself, which he saw as trending inevitably toward greater equality and democracy, regardless of political arrangements, even claiming that capitalism and socialism tended toward similar degrees of wage parity ("Unions' Effects," 236–238; "International Comparisons," 266–268).

In particular, Kerr believed that unions were of limited historical importance and had limited historical agency; that while collective bargaining "can raise labor's share, it cannot raise it very much"; and that, to a large extent, union activity "is much ado about very little, that unions are relatively powerless institutions in a market which responds to other, more persuasive forces" ("Unions' Effects," 236). Instead, he believed that "advanced industrialism" and skill differentials shaped wages more than unions or even politics, including revolutionary politics, claiming that "universal tendencies" of advanced industrialism tended to cause very similar wage effects even in such diverse political arrangements as capitalism and socialism. In his 1983 *The Future of Industrial Societies,* Kerr observed that in its advanced stages, the industrialization of a national economy, irrespective of political arrangements, tended toward greater equality of wages ("most people come to live within a distribution range of disposable income of two or two and a half to one"), with the remaining difference explained by "merit and seniority" and skill premiums that are "universally more highly paid . . . even in Mao's China and Castro's Cuba" ("International Comparisons," 266–268). There are many problems with this view, including his data, which are based on industrial workforces (thereby excluding the vastly greater wage inequalities experienced by women and ethnic minorities in service work, as well as professionals, managers, proletarianized white-collar workers, and the huge employment in government service), as well as the consequences of globalization, through which the regime of wage stabilities internal to nation-states was completely upended by the greater freedom of producers to exploit huge international wage differentials.

Most significant for us here is Kerr's view of the inevitability of industrialism's "universal tendencies" toward equality, in the context of which he viewed movement politics, and sometimes unions, as potentially anarchic forces and, concomitantly, viewed well-intentioned, highly educated management as a requisite for stability and the realization of human potential. For Kerr, "history" (i.e., industrialization) is profoundly rational, whereas human beings are quite likely not, including in their most highly organized forms of collective activity, such as unions and protest movements. Even in his earliest work, his portrait of union activity is of an emotional rather than a rational investment. After observing that collective bargaining is "much ado about very little," he explains that unionism nonetheless serves the important social function of assuaging workers' emotional concerns. The relative powerlessness of unions, he writes, could not be known in advance,

> and it is worth knowing. Workers could not be expected to accept the broad allocation of income among distributive shares without having their organizations explore the possibilities of major shifts. The probing of the situation by unions gives the workers a greater assurance of the equity, or at least the inevitability, of the distributional pattern. Thus the pursuit of the employer may be of worth even if he is never caught at all. ("Unions' Effects," 237)

This representation of labor "pursuing" the employer is interestingly feminized, with the contract resulting from bargaining figuring as a kind of marriage that does little to address the essential powerlessness of the worker. Kerr's tone regarding organized labor has the bemused quality of the village fathers observing the "ladies in an uproar" on Sadie Hawkins day or the nobility observing the serfs kicking about a ball representing the head of the king with much the same festival import. For him, unions provide an outlet for the structurally oppressed to vent their frustrations at oppression and come to terms with the "inevitability" of their circumstances.

Regarding academic unions in particular, Kerr's personal views were largely consistent, both with his sentiments regarding unions in general and with the views of the Carnegie Commission. In a chapter composed for the 1983 edition of *The Uses of the University*, Kerr aired the similar view that bargaining had little effect on faculty salaries, further claiming, without adducing any evidence, that "organizations that rely on informal codes and implicit contracts ["as in a 'gentlemen's club' where some things are just not done"] are more effective and more satisfactory to their participants" than those that rely on bargaining and formal arrangements. However, he also wrote that in the "breakdown" of a system of implicit contracts, collective bargaining provided an alternate form of contracting, having at least the bare merit of superiority to "anarchy or chaos" (134, 168–170).

This last sentiment closely parallels the official views of the Carnegie Commission published in the chapter on "Collective Bargaining and Faculty Power" in the "Six Priority Problems" governance statement, where the reality of the New Left looms large. Claiming that "the locus of activism is shifting," the commission clearly envisioned a close correspondence between "student dissent and student organization" in the 1960s and "faculty dissent and faculty organization" to follow: "The decade of the student may be followed by the decade of the faculty." Declining to "take a position on whether faculty members should unionize," the commission nonetheless urged that "faculty members should analyze very carefully whether or not" their best interests are served, instantiating at least seven potentially negative consequences (43). And the commission's orientation is perfectly clear when it admonishes the administrations of instititutions involved in bargaining that they would be "well advised to employ experienced negotiators" (50). Alternately, the commission's profound anxiety about New Left social upheaval leads them to forecast the grim possibility that "collective bargaining will become more clearly preferable to an otherwise more anarchic situation" and that "history may carry higher education beyond its current state of development":

We may be involved in a long-term period of greater social conflict in society and greater tension on campus. If so, it may be better to institutionalize this conflict through collective bargaining than to have it manifest itself with less restraint. Collective bargaining does provide agreed-upon rules of behavior, contractual understandings, and mechanisms

for dispute settlement and grievance handling that help to manage conflict. Collective bargaining also provides a means through which the
public interest in the conduct and performance of the campus can be
brought to bear upon decision making within the campus. Collective
bargaining, thus, is one aspect of the rule of law, if and when a rule of
law is required. (51)

Key to our understanding of the commission's perspective is the sense,
parallel to Kerr's technocratic worldview, that unionism represents a potentially conservative force, serving via contract to impose "the rule of
law" in a situation in which the settled (desirable) "informalities" of
managerial control have been supplanted by (undesirable) informalities dubbed "anarchic" because they are "out of [managerial] control."
Unionism, it is fairly clear, is not otherwise desirable.

Recovering the foreboding with which Kerr and the commission
viewed the movement in its moment is highly instructive. If those who
work in higher education are to have even a fraction of the solidarity
that management shares, one possibility that suggests itself is that academic unions might make real the sort of connections with social movements that Kerr particularly feared. They might also create larger co-
alitions of workers on campus and among other workers in the public interest. These strategies are common among graduate employees
and term faculty, who often have to work either against faculty unions
or within them as insurgencies (Gottfried and Zabel; Hoeller, "Treat
Fairly"; Berry). Especially important to the future of academic unionism
will be a renewed commitment to workplace democracy, which the neglect of term faculty and graduate employee rights has eroded, and to a
critical analysis of workplace inequalities, especially those organized by
gender. One significant and neglected possibility is the commitment of
academic unions to principles of gender equity via analysis of "comparable worth," seeking to rectify imbalances organized by gender between disciplines and job descriptions. In 2005, several major unions
split with the AFL-CIO at least putatively over the issue of organizing,
demanding that a much larger share of union energies go into reaching
new workers and workplaces in new kinds of ways. Perhaps the academic unions should devote more energy to organizing on the model of
movement-building as well: the interorganizational COCAL project receives only a tiny drop of support and token attention from the major
unions. As Kerr and the Carnegie Commission understood all too well,

the trade unions of the faculty can very easily serve to conserve a balance of power favoring the administration.

The era after 1970 was not the first moment of struggle between faculty and administration in higher education. As Christopher Newfield and Clyde Barrow, among others, have each observed, the decades of the late nineteenth and early twentieth centuries saw the successful imposition of Taylorist management practice on aspects of the faculty work process. And from this period also dates the first self-organizing of the faculty, including the founding of the AAUP and the AFT, both presided over by John Dewey at one time. There are elements of historical continuity that need to be drawn out. For instance, Toyotist management theory, while relying on a rhetoric of opposition to Taylorist scientific management (and hierarchical control of the work process), actually intensifies managerial control of the work process, an observation that is especially relevant to the reduced workplace rights of the nontenurable teaching majority.

But the continuities are probably less important than the startling rupture with the earlier consciousness, on both sides. For the faculty to participate in the public employee union movement was an epochal shift toward considering themselves not only as a collective agency in their own economic interests but also as a political force, with the capacity (and the burden) of confronting lawmakers with a vision of what higher education should be and how it might fit into the future envisioned by other political forces and movements. Even the most militant and politically active of faculty unions, at the City University of New York (CUNY) and the State University of New York (SUNY) systems, initially rejected affiliation with "regular unions" and attempted to bargain their first contracts with independent organizations based in the faculty senates, before reversing course and seeking the professional bargaining assistance of the paid staff employed by the militant schoolteachers of the NEA and AFT.

Similarly, the current dominance of management thought drawn from Toyotist lean production is an epochal shift. The older Taylorist production model sought to impose scientific management and maximize efficiency in order to *maximize output* as part of the capitalist utopian imaginary of plenty for all. Aiming to place a Model T in every garage, Taylorist efficiency implied more and better goods for more people to enjoy. By contrast, Toyotist lean production represents an effort to *minimize output to the most profitable level of demand.* In industrial terms, lean production is an attempt to bypass crises of overproduction. We have the industrial capacity to provide food, cell phones, and computers for everyone on the planet, but actually doing so would not maximize profits. The notion of overproduction is relative to profit, not human needs, which, in capitalist economics, are always undersatisfied, so a capitalist is "overproducing" when profits are low, regardless of whether the industrial capacity exists to provide millions of needed goods.

One particularly frank college president, John Harris of Alabama's Samford University, explains that lean production means that higher education, like other enterprises, divides its "customers" into two groups: a "vital few, each of whom is of great importance to us," and another much larger group, "the useful many, each of whom is only of modest importance to us." He elaborates:

> The "Useful Many and Vital Few" in business means a few customers account for a disproportionate number of sales dollars. Is this concept applicable to higher education? The way many institutions support athletes suggests to me that the concept is not foreign to us. Are Honors students the Vital Few? Who are the Useful Many? Do we actually treat all students the same? Each institution has its Vital Few and Useful Many, given its mission, particular constituencies, and cultural ethos. Quality planning requires the identification of the Vital Few and Useful Many and of their needs and expectations in priority order. (10)

In short, a lean institution with quality planning caters to the few and attends only modestly to the needs of the many. Harris describes the few in familiar terms—privileged students, corporate vendors, revenue-producing disciplines, elite institutions. But there's a remarkable silence regarding the many: "Who are they?" Harris asks.

In my view, academic unionism will once again be a movement when it can answer his question.

4

Students Are Already Workers

I know that I haven't updated in about two and a half weeks, but I
have an excuse. UPS is just a tiring job. You see, before, I had an
extra 31 hours to play games, draw things, compose music . . . do
homework. But now, 31+ hours of my life is devoted to UPS.

I hate working there. But I need the money for college, so I
don't have the option of quitting. My job at UPS is a loader. I
check the zip codes on the box, I scan them into the database, and
then I load them into the truck, making a brick wall out of boxes.

— "Kody" (pseud.), high-school blogger in a
UPS "school-to-work" program, 2005

The alarm sounds at 2:00 AM. Together with half a dozen
of her colleagues, the workday has begun for Prof. Susan Erdmann, a
tenure-track assistant professor of English at Jefferson Community College in Louisville, Kentucky. She rises carefully to avoid waking her in-
fant son and husband, who commutes forty miles each way to his own
tenure-track community college job in the neighboring rural county.
She makes coffee, showers, dresses for work. With their combined income of around $60,000 and substantial education debt, they have a
thirty-year mortgage on a tiny home of about 1,000 square feet: galley
kitchen, dining alcove, one bedroom for them and another for their two
sons to share. The front door opens onto a "living room" of a hundred
square feet; entering or leaving the house means passing in between the
couch and television. They feel fortunate to be able to afford any mortgage at all in this historically Catholic neighborhood that was originally
populated by Louisville factory workers. It is winter; the sun will not
rise for hours. She drives to the airport. Overhead, air-freight 747s bar-
rel into the sky, about one plane every minute or so. Surrounded by
the empty school buildings, boarded storefronts, and dilapidated underclass homes of south-central Louisville, the jets launch in post-midnight

salvos. Their engines lack the sophisticated noise-abatement technology required of air traffic in middle-class communities. Every twelve or eighteen months, the city agrees to buy a handful of the valueless residences within earshot.[1]

Turning into the airport complex, Susan never comes near the shuttered passenger terminals. She follows a four-lane private roadway toward the rising jets. After parking, a shuttle bus weaves among blindingly lit aircraft hangars and drops her by the immense corrugated sorting facility that is the United Parcel Service main air hub, where she will begin her faculty duties at 3:00 AM, greeting UPS's undergraduate workforce directly as they come off the sort. "You would have a sense that you were there, lifting packages," Erdmann recalls. "They would come off sweaty, and hot, directly off the line into the class. It was very immediate, and sort of awkward. They'd had no moment of downtime. They hadn't had their cigarette. They had no time to pull themselves together as student-person rather than package-thrower." Unlike her students, Susan and other faculty teaching and advising at the hub are not issued a plastic ID card and door pass. She waits on the windy tarmac for one of her students or colleagues to hear her knocking at the door. Inside, the noise of the sorting facility is, literally, deafening: the shouts, forklift alarms, whistles, and rumble of the sorting machinery actually drown out the noise of the jets rising overhead. "Teaching in the hub was horrible," recalled one of Erdmann's colleagues. "Being in the hub was just hell. I'd work at McDonald's before I'd teach there again. The noise level was just incredible. The classroom was just as noisy as if it didn't have any walls." In addition to the sorting machinery, UPS floor supervisors were constantly "screaming, yelling back and forth, 'Get this done, get that done, where's so and so.'"

Susan is just one of a dozen faculty arriving at the hub after midnight. Some are colleagues from Jefferson Community College and the associated technical institution; others are from the University of Louisville. Their task tonight is to provide on-site advising and registration for some of the nearly 6,000 undergraduate students working for UPS at this facility. About 3,000 of those students work a midnight shift that ends at UPS's convenience—typically 3:00 or 4:00 AM, although the shift is longer during the holiday and other peak shipping seasons.

Nearly all of the third-shift workers are undergraduate students who have signed employment contracts with something called the "Metropolitan College." The name is misleading, since it's not a college at all.

An "enterprise" partnership between UPS, the city of Louisville, and the campuses that employ Susan and her colleagues, Metropolitan College is, in fact, little more than a labor contractor. Supported by public funds, this "college" offers no degrees and does no educating. Its sole function is to entice students to sign contracts that commit them to provide cheap labor in exchange for education benefits at the partner institutions.[2] The arrangement has provided UPS with over 10,000 ultra-low-cost student workers since 1997, the same year that the Teamsters launched a crippling strike against the carrier. The Louisville arrangement is the vanguard of UPS's efforts to convert its part-time payroll, as far as possible, to a "financial aid" package for student workers in partnership with campuses near its sorting and loading facilities. Other low-wage Louisville employers, such as Norton and ResCare have joined on a trial basis.

As a result of carefully planned corporate strategy, between 1997 and 2003, UPS hired undergraduate students to staff more than half of its 130,000 part-time positions (Hammers). Students are currently the majority of all part-timers, and the overwhelming majority on the least desirable shifts. Part of UPS's strategy is that only some student employees receive education benefits. By reserving the education benefits of its "earn and learn" programs to workers who are willing to work undesirable hours, UPS has over the past decade recruited approximately 50,000 part-time workers to its least desirable shifts without raising the pay (in fact, while pushing them to work harder for continually lower pay against inflation) ("Earn and Learn Factsheet"). The largest benefit promises are reserved for students who think they can handle working after midnight every night of the school week.

Between 1998 and 2005, UPS claims to have "assisted" 10,000 students through the Metropolitan College arrangement (Conway). Of the 7,500 part-time employees at UPS's Louisville hub in May 2006, some were welfare-to-work recipients picked up in company buses from the city and even surrounding rural counties. A few hundred were Louisville-area high school students in school-to-work programs. Three-quarters of the part-timers—5,600—were college students (Howington). More than half of the students—about 3,000—were enrolled in Metropolitan College, which, with few exceptions, accepts only those willing to work the night shift. Metropolitan College "enrollment" and "recruitment" activities are entirely driven by UPS's staffing needs. Ditto for scheduling: all of the benefits enjoyed by Metro College students are contingent on showing up at the facility every weeknight of the school year at midnight and performing physically strenuous labor for as long as they are needed.

The consequences of night-shift work are well documented, and the preponderance of available evidence suggests markedly negative effects for the Louisville students. Every instructor to whom I spoke reported excessive fatigue and absenteeism (due to fatigue, but also an extraordinarily high physical injury rate: "They all got hurt," Erdmann reports). Students who signed employment contracts with Metro College showed substantial failure to persist academically. "I would lose students midterm, or they would never complete final assignments," Erdmann said. "They would just stop coming at some point." Erdmann served as chair of a faculty committee that attempted to improve the academic success of students employed by UPS at her institution. The group scheduled special UPS-only sections between 5:00 and 11:00 PM, both on campus and at the hub, and began the ritual of 3:00 AM advising. Since nearly all of the faculty involved taught and served on committees five days a week, their efforts to keep students from dropping out by teaching evenings and advising before dawn resulted in a bizarre twenty-four-hour cycle of work for themselves. The institutions even experimented with ending the fall semester before Thanksgiving for the thousands of UPS employees, in order to keep their finals from conflicting with the holiday shipping rush (and the one season a year when the students could be assured of a shift lasting longer than four hours). Even in the specially scheduled classes and shortened terms, Erdmann recalls classes with dropout rates of 30 to 40 percent. "It was most definitely worse for those with children," she concluded:

> It was a disaster for those with children. Students who had family obligations tended to do poorly. When you had younger, more traditional age students with a very clear and limited goal—and they were often men—if they had a limited goal, such as "I am going to get Microsoft certified," and if they were healthy and young, and physically active, those individuals might be okay.
>
> Whenever you had people with children—you know, people who can't sleep all day, they would get tremendously stressed out. I feel like very few of them actually did well with the program, the ones with family.

Pressed to offer instances of individual students who undisputably benefited from the program, Erdmann described just two individuals, both
at the extreme margins of economic and social life. One was a single
mother who worked multiple jobs and saved some of her wages toward
a down payment on a residential trailer, thus escaping an abusive domestic life. The other was a young man coping with severe mental illness.

Rather than relieving economic pressure, Metropolitan College appears to have increased the economic distress of the majority of participants. According to the company's own fact sheet, those student workers who give up five nights' sleep are typically paid for just fifteen to
twenty hours a week. Since the wage ranges from just $8.50 at the start
to no more than $9.50 for the majority of the most experienced, this
can mean net pay *below* $100 in a week, and averaging out to a little
over $120. The rate of pay bears emphasizing: because the students
must report five nights a week and are commonly let go after just three
hours each night, their take-home pay for sleep deprivation and physically hazardous toil will commonly be less than $25 per shift.

In fact, most UPS part-timers earn little more than $6,000 in a year.
Most have at least one other job, because their typical earnings from
UPS in 2006–2007 would generally have covered little more than the
worker's car payment, insurance, gasoline, and other transportation-
related expenses. "Everyone had another job," Erdmann says. "Even
the high school students had another job. The high school students
were working two jobs. For some people, that meant working Saturday
nights as a waitress, but for others, it was much more extensive. For a
lot of people, it meant that they got up every day and went to work in
the afternoon before going in to classes and UPS in the evening." Every
instructor to whom I spoke confirmed the pressure that the ultralow
wage added to the unreasonable working hours and physical hazards as
a detriment to students' chances for academic persistence. "That was
when they skipped class," affirmed another instructor, "when they were
going to another job. I was just amazed how many of them were going
to another job."

UPS presents a triple threat to students' prospects for academic persistence: sleep deprivation and family-unfriendly scheduling; ultralow
compensation, resulting in secondary and tertiary part-time employment; and a high injury rate. Student employees report being pressured
to skip class. Especially at the end of the fall term, the night sorts can

run four or five hours beyond the anticipated 4:00 AM completion: "Each time I said I was unwilling to miss class for an extended sort, the supe would tell me to 'think long and hard about my priorities,' " reports one student employee. "I got the message."

UPS refuses to provide standard statistics that would permit evaluation of the impact that this triple threat is actually having on the students it employs. None of its partner institutions appears to have responsibly studied the consequences of the program for its students in terms of such major measures as persistence to degree, dropout rate, and so on.

Amazingly, all of the press coverage of the UPS earn and learn programs in general, and the Louisville Metropolitan College arrangement in particular, has been positive. In fact, most of the coverage appears to have been drawn closely from UPS press releases themselves or conducted with students selected for their success stories. Acknowledging that the night shift "took some getting used to," one local newspaper's coverage is typical in quoting a student shrugging off the challenges, "I just schedule my classes for the afternoon" (Howington). Other stories are more meretricious, suggesting that the UPS jobs keep students from partying too much. One quotes a UPS supervisor who suggests that college students "are staying up until dawn anyway" (Karman).

Ironically, UPS has received numerous awards for "corporate citizenship" and was named one of the "best companies for minorities" in connection with the program. It emphasizes recruitment among Latino students, and numerous Hispanic organizations have either endorsed the program or published unedited UPS press releases marketing the program to "nontraditional students, such as retirees and moms re-entering the workforce" (LatinoLA).

"I Dread Work Every Day"

UPS has long pioneered low-cost benefitless employment, abetted by the Teamsters themselves, who under Jimmy Hoffa Sr. signed one of the first contracts in American industry to permit the regular use of part-time employees in 1962. This second tier of employment was massively expanded after the Teamsters agreed to 1982 protocols that raised the wages of full-time workers while freezing those of part-timers. In that year, part-time UPS employees started at $8 an hour, the equivalent in

2007 of about $17 per hour ($34,000 a year). Similarly, in 1982, part-time employees averaged about $10 per hour, the equivalent in 2007 of $22 per hour ($44,000 a year).

Not incidentally, at the 1982 wages, a UPS part-time worker could indeed successfully fund a college education. One employee from the 1970s recalls:

> At the old full and fair rate prior to the 1982 UPS wage reduction, despite soaring volume and profits, a part-time worker in exchange for back-breaking work could afford to rent a room, pay tuition, buy food and clothing, and afford to own and operate a used car. This was a good deal that was profitable to the student and society, as well as profitable to UPS. I went through six years of college that way and am very grateful to the Teamsters for the good pay. I find it a national disgrace that UPS has effectively reduced the pay by nearly 65% adjusted for inflation since 1982 and destroyed a positive job for over a hundred thousand workers and for society as well. There are [UPS] part-time workers living in homeless shelters in Richmond, California, and other parts of the country. ("saintteamo," Brown Café weblog, 2003; punctuation regularized)

As with Wal-Mart and other predatory super low-wage employers, many of UPS's student workers are homeless. At the Louisville hub, "I knew people sleeping in their cars," Erdmann recalled.

After the union's concession to a radically cheaper second tier of employment, 80 percent of all new UPS jobs were created in the "permanent part-time" category. While the pay between part-time and full-time diverged slowly between 1962 and 1982, the differential accelerated rapidly in the 1980s and 1990s. Serving as a UPS driver is still a coveted blue-collar position. From the Reagan years to the present, these full-time Teamsters continued to enjoy raises, job security, due process with respect to their grievances, and substantial benefits, including a pension. But over the same period of time, these and other full-time positions became the minority of employees covered by the contract.

In less than fifteen years, permanent part-timers became the majority of the UPS workforce in the United States. The ratio of permanent part-timers was particularly pronounced at the Louisville main hub, where a high-speed, high-pressure night sort was conducted. As the wages of the part-time majority steadily shrank against inflation, opportunities to join the full-time tier all but disappeared. Today, even the company's human resources recruiters admit that while full-time positions "still exist," it can take "six to seven years or even longer" to get on full-time. A single-digit percentage of the company's part-time employees last that long. Few of those who do persist are actually offered full-time work. During the long night of Reagan-Bush-Clinton reaction, according to employees, the company unilaterally abrogated work rules, including safety limits on package size and weight. Injuries soared to two and a half times the industry average, in especial disproportion among part-time employees in the first year.

As jointly bargained by UPS and the Teamsters, the part-time positions devolved into one of the least desirable forms of work in the country, with one of the highest turnover rates in history. Featuring poor wages, limited benefits, a high injury rate, and unreasonable scheduling, the Teamster-UPS agreement created compensation and working conditions for the part-time majority so abysmal that most rational persons preferred virtually any other form of employment or even not working at all.

Most part-timers departed within weeks of being hired. According to George Poling, director of the Louisville Metropolitan College, the average term of employment for part-time workers on the night sort was just eight weeks. At the Louisville facility, 90 percent of part-time hires quit before serving a year. Across the country in 1996, UPS hired 180,000 part-timers on all shifts, but only 40,000 were still with the company at the year's end. In part as a result of steadily accelerating turnover, UPS agreed in just sixteen days to the most publicized core demand of the 1997 Teamsters strike, the creation of 10,000 new full-time jobs out of some of the new part-time positions.

Overlooked during the press coverage of the Teamsters' apparent victory was the fact that these new "full-time" positions were paid well below the scale of existing full-timers and would earn just 75 percent of the rate of regular full-timers by the end of the contract. This introduced a new, lower-wage tier in the ranks of the full-timers. The lower wages of this group would continue to support the wage increases and benefits of the union's powerful minority constituency, the shrinking core of long-term full-timers. (Readers employed in academic circumstances will recognize this strategy as having been pioneered in their own workplaces, with the institution of nontenurable full-time lectureships as one of the "solutions" that the long-term tenured faculty have accepted to management's expansion of part-time faculty.) It would take three years of foot-dragging through arbitration and federal court before UPS delivered even these watered-down full-time jobs.

Despite credulous ballyhoo about the strike as the decade's exemplar of labor militance and solidarity between full-timers and part-timers, the part-time majority of UPS workers benefited little from the Teamster "victory." The starting wage for part-timers, which had remained at $8 for fifteen years (since 1982) was raised in the 1997 contract a grand total of 50 cents. Ten years later, the Teamster-negotiated starting wage for UPS part-time package handlers working between 11:00 PM and 4:00 AM remains just $8.50, or exactly one raise in a quarter-century. This is a loss against inflation of more than half. In 1982, the $8 per hour starting wage for part-timers was more than twice the minimum wage (of $3.35), and slightly above the national hourly average wage (of $7.72). In 2006, the UPS starting wage was about half of the national average hourly wage of $16.46 for nonsupervisory workers. With the "minimum" wage so low that only half a million Americans earn it, the $8.50 per hour UPS starting wage in 2006 was equal to or lower than what most traditionally "minimum wage" occupations actually earn and lower than the statutory metropolitan living wage established in many major cities. This isn't eight or nine bucks an hour for eight hours a day, 9:00 AM to 5:00 PM. This is eight or nine bucks an hour for showing up five nights a week at midnight and working three and one-half to five hours, depending on the flow of packages for physically demanding, dangerous, night-shift work at the company's convenience.

Moreover, there is at least half an hour, often more, of unpaid commuting around airport security on either side of the paid three hours. The commute each way can total as much as an hour, even for students who live just a mile or two from the facility: "When I was there, you'd have to be in the parking lot by 11:30 at the latest if you wanted the shuttle bus to get you to the gate by 11:40, where you'd then wait to have your ID checked, and then walk through the maze of hub buildings for 500 yards before finding your workspace and clocking in," one recalled. "The point being if I got parked at 11:45, I'd be late and get bawled out. The traffic outside UPS leading into the shift is nightmarish, so you'd really need to leave the house an hour before work to have a shot at getting to the sort station on time." With the unpaid commute, that's five hours of third-shift time, being paid close to the minimum wage for just three hours.

In the past twenty-five years, working conditions at UPS have eroded even faster than the wage. With the union's lack of interest in part-time workers, UPS has increasingly introduced ultrashort shifts, technology-driven speedup, and managerial surveillance of every aspect of the work process, including real-time tracking of errors. Employing constant surveillance by a battalion of "part-time supes," themselves generally students, UPS deploys cameras and manned watchtowers throughout the multilayer sort. "They're always watching you work from tall perches that exist nearly everywhere in the plant," one former student worker recalls; "the perches are ostensibly ladders to other layers of the sort, but the consistent presence of management at the stair landings creates the feeling of almost total surveillance. Even when you can't see them, you know they're in hidden rooms watching you on camera." Nearly all student workers are repeatedly tested by "salting" packages with bad address labels; employees decry the practice as a "particularly nasty" form of continuous stressing of their work environment.

Several current or former UPS employees have begun weblogs to chronicle the high-speed, high-stress nature of their employment. One, writing as "Brown Blood," explained that he'd begun the weblog for "the employees of UPS to express their true feelings about their job in all aspects," noting, "I must apologize now for any foul language that may . . . *will* occur in this community because most of these jobs not only test the limitations of your physical capacity it also shatters all anger management." On the JobVent weblog, UPS workers' rating of the workplace were commonly *below zero*:

> Little did I know that I would spend 4 hours a day in a dark, oven hot dungeon being screamed at by idiotic powertrippers who having given up believing life has some kind of meaning and now want to make themselves feel better by humiliating the only people in their lives that they have any sort of advantage over. All this while you are sweating liters and giving your back life-long injuries. I couldn't help but laugh in disbelief when I received my first paycheck for $120. IF YOU EVEN THINK OF WORKING AT UPS, realize that if you don't want to spend the next ten years of your life being treated like toiletpaper just to become a lousy driver then go work for FedEx, the benefits are as good, the pay is better and you get just a little respect, a friend of mine worked there for 5 days and became a driver. UPS is no less than 7–10 years. Bottom line: UPS SUCKS A BIG ONE!!!!!!!!! I dread work every day.

According to at least one long-term Teamster full-timer, the part-time students working the night sort are driven particularly hard: "They cram eight hours work into five." Agreeing with this characterization of the workload for undergraduate employees, one student worker said, "Around finals time, I'd go for days without sleep. The scary thing is, I'd see the sleepless period coming, know there was nothing I could do about it other than quit school or quit work, and then learn to psych myself up for it."

Most bloggers complained of the pay ("pathetic"), schedule ("random, terrible hours"), injuries ("I was killing myself physically"; "constant muscle pulls/strains, a lot of safety hazards"; "horrible; you'll sweat like a dog in the summer and freeze in the winter—unsafe—watch out for sharp objects and falling boxes"), and supervisory harassment. As a whole, the evaluations were resoundingly negative: "This was the worst job I ever had"; "You can imagine it's bad when the highest UPS scores with me in any category is a minus 2"; "If you're thinking of working here, DON'T DO IT!" Many of the bloggers give a vivid portrait of the nature of the stressful nature of the work. Every error is tracked, and a minimum standard for error-free sorting is one error in 2,500. How often do you make an error while typing? If you're like me, you make several typing errors per page, for an error rate per word of 1 in 60 or so. At UPS, an error of 1 in 500 is considered extremely poor. The student workers are particularly likely to be placed in these high-stress positions. If younger, they are commonly inexperienced at work generally. If older, they have typically suffered substantial economic or personal distress. Either way, those who don't express rage and disappointment, or vote with their feet by quitting, appear likely to internalize management's construction of them as slow-moving failures. Students sometimes contribute to weblogs like "Brown Blood" less to complain than to get coping advice ("Is there a better way of doing this without going miserably slowly? . . . I want to show that I can be competent in some form of employment.")

The work of the loaders intensifies during the holiday rush:

> I hate how UPS is always fucking you over. On a normal day I load 3 trucks and lately it's been a total of about 800–900 packages. . . . They told me I would only have the 4th car one day per week. Well guess what . . . they gave me 4 cars 3 days this week. Today I had a total of over 1600 packages with no help, the bastards. My loads

were shit and my drivers were bitching, but what the hell can I do about it?

I suppose the fact that I've slept less than 5 of the past 55 hours had something to do with my despising work today. But Red Bull helps with that.

I'm so f——ing glad it's a long weekend. ("hitchhiker42")

These notes of stress, fatigue, and powerlessness on the job are nearly uniform throughout the UPS permanent part-timers.

Employee of the Month

Some 70 percent of the workers in the main UPS hub in Louisville are women. The average age is thirty-four, and many are parents. Some of the women work in data entry, but most of the work involves package handling. For every teenage worker, there's another part-timer well into her forties.

The reality of the undergraduate workforce is very different from the representation of teen partiers on a perpetual spring break, as popularized by television (*Girls Gone Wild*), UPS propaganda ("they're staying up until dawn anyway"), and *Time*: "Meet the 'twixters,' [twenty-somethings] who live off their parents, bounce from job to job and hop from mate to mate. They're not lazy—they just won't grow up" (Grossman; for more, see Bartlett).

There are more than 15 million students currently enrolled in higher ed (with an average age of around twenty-six). Tens of millions of persons have recently left higher education, nearly as many without degrees as with them. Like graduate employees, undergraduates now work longer hours in school, spend more years in school, and can take several years to find stable employment after obtaining their degrees. Undergraduates and recent school leavers, whether degree holders or not, now commonly live with their parents well beyond the age of legal adulthood, often into their late twenties. Like graduate employees, undergraduates increasingly find that their period of "study" is, in fact, a period of employment as cheap labor. The production of cheap workers is facilitated by an ever-expanding notion of "youth." A University of Chicago survey conducted in 2003 found that the majority of Americans now think that adulthood begins around twenty-six, an age not coincidentally identical with the average age of the undergraduate student population (Tom Smith).

The popular conception of student life as "delayed adulthood" is reflected in such notions as "thirty is the new twenty" and "forty is the new thirty" (Irvine). The fatuousness of these representations is confounded by looking at the other end of one's employment life. Few people are finding, in terms of employability after downsizing, that "fifty is the new forty": people in their fifties who lose their jobs often find themselves unemployable. What are the economic consequences for a person whose productive career can begin in their middle thirties or later, then end at fifty or sooner? This pattern presents real obstacles for both women and men wishing to raise a family. Yet mass media representations of extended schooling and the associated period of insecure employment are often cheery, suggesting that it's a stroke of good fortune, an extended youth free of such unwelcome responsibilities as home ownership, child-rearing, and visits to health-care providers. In this idealistic media fantasy, more time in higher education means more time to party—construing an extended youth as a prolonged stretch of otherwise empty time unmarked by the accountabilities of adulthood.

Concretely, the apparently empty time of involuntarily extended youth associated with higher education is really quite full. It's full of feelings—the feelings of desperation, betrayal, and anxiety, the sense that Cary Nelson has captured for graduate employees under the heading of *Will Teach for Food*. Writers like Anya Kamenetz and Tamara Draut have captured the similar feelings of upper-middle-class college graduates in books like *Generation Debt* and *Strapped*. Many of the persons Draut and Kamenetz describe will have added graduate school to successful bachelor's degrees at first-tier or second-tier institutions. But little attention has been paid to the role of higher education in organizing the vast majority of the lives it touches—those who don't graduate or those who graduate with community college, vocational, or technical degrees.

"Employee of the Month" ("The Dance That Is My Life") is typical of the more successful students employed by UPS. As she tells it on her weblog, this "mom/stylist," aged thirty, the mother of children aged three and five, is a fan of Christian apocalyptic fiction and a part-time student who hopes to become a teacher. She has an "A" average. She depicts her husband as a substance abuser who provides no contribution to the household finances; during the months covered in her weblog, he moves in and out of the house. Like most students who find a job with UPS, she was already working hard before signing on with Big Brown. While parenting and starting school, she was working three jobs, including office work and hair styling. In the first few weeks, she enjoys the work: "I am digging this job! I get to work out for 4–5 hours a night," plus collect education benefits. Anticipating the 50-cent raise, she writes, "The pay sucks at first but within 90 days I should be ok." She plans to continue working as a stylist, but feels that she can quit her other two job part-time jobs, "with doing hair 3 days a week I will be making just as much as I have been making [with three jobs] and only working about 35–37 hours a week total. Woo Hoo!"

Rather than a partying teen, this typical working undergraduate is a devout thirty year old who is thrilled simply to be able to work a mere full-time equivalent at two different jobs, in addition to schoolwork and solo parenting of two small children.

After the Christmas rush, and still in her first two months of employment, the upbeat blogger notes: "I am getting muscles in my arms and shoulders, my legs are getting a little toned. I do need to lose about 25 lbs so the more muscle thing is a good start. . . . I am getting better at my job now that I am a little stronger and can lift the boxes up to the top shelf." Within six months, by March 2006, she had made "employee of the month" at her facility. In the same month, she had her first work-related injury: a strained ligament from working with heavy packages. On a physician's orders, she was placed on "light duty," dealing with packages weighing one to seven pounds (seven pounds is approximately the weight of a gallon of milk). She had also grown discouraged about her prospects of continuing her education and was considering dropping out of school.

Her family life is increasingly stressed by the UPS job. In order to collect less than thirty bucks a night, she has to leave her children to sleep at her mother's house five nights a week. Now that the holiday rush is past, she finds that, on her UPS salary and even with a second job, she is unable to afford such everyday staples as Easter baskets for her children, which her sister provided. "A guy at work told me about a job at a private school, I applied and had an interview. I hope I get the job. I need to pay bills and the UPS job isn't enough," she concludes:

My kids did have a good Easter, thank you to my sister. We went down to her house and she bought my kids candy, toys, and each kid a movie!! I thought that was above the call of duty. I can't tell you how much I appreciate my family for coming to my aid in my time of need this past year. I know I could get another job and put my kids in day-care all day again and be able to support them better, but I wouldn't be able to go to school. It's hard right now, but I am already a year into school and I will be a teacher in a few years. I can't stop now. Even with this drama going on in my life I have still kept a 3.6 grade point average. I want to finish it. My son still wants me to be a teacher, so I have to show him that with work and perseverance you can accomplish anything despite your circumstances. Facts don't count when it comes to reaching a goal. ("The Dance That Is My Life")

In other words: for UPS to receive one super-cheap worker, that worker's parents have to donate free child care and other family members have to donate cash, time, and goods. Like the vast majority of her coworkers in a UPS earn and learn arrangement, this A student and employee of the month is so sapped by the experience, physically injured, under-compensated, and domestically disarranged that she's on the verge of quitting school.

Despite her qualifications, energy, and commitment, the only thing keeping this UPS worker going is the desire to shore up achievement ideology for her children ("I have to show him that with work and per-severance you can accomplish anything despite your circumstances"), to create a Disney narrative out of their lives when she drops them off to sleep at their grandparents five nights a week, a Disney narrative that will prove that "facts don't count when it comes to reaching a goal."

Supergirl: "My Back Hurts So Fricken Bad"

This five-foot two-inch, 110-pound, twenty-three-year-old undergraduate woman writing under the moniker of "supergirl" has a charming sardonic flair: "America needs no more cheese, ham, huge-ass boxes of summer sausage, holiday popcorn tins, or kringles. . . . I think I've moved enough of these that every man, woman and child should already have one by default. No wonder obesity is an epidemic."

As with most, her daily UPS shift is a second job. After a year, she's ready to quit. She's had one work-related arm surgery: "I really don't want to have another, or worse, risk permanently damaging the nerves in both arms," she writes; "and I sincerely don't think I'm being paid enough to stay there 2 years and blow out both arms unfixably. . . . I know pain and can tolerate it, but I can't even fucking sleep because every position somehow puts pressure on a nerve in my arm that's already got problems and is being pushed to the limits." When I asked another Louisville student employee to comment on "supergirl's" representation of the injury rate, he called the physical toll exacted by the workplace a "key point," adding, "The physical harm this work does will long outlast the span of the job."

She complains of the culture of UPS—of speedup, the pressure to deny injuries and work through them, and the pressure to continue employment through the milestones that dictate education benefits such as loan and tuition remission. Under the rubric "don't make UPS yours," she warns other prospective student employees away:

> My back hurts . . . so fricken bad. It doesn't benefit me to say I hurt because I've noticed that if you hurt of any kind the sort super just asks you to quit (in not so many eloquently and legal to say to an employee words). . . . I lift tons of shit that's got 20–30 pounds on me . . . but as I stand; a girl of 5'2" and a buck ten . . . I can't do that kinda shit everyday. . . . I guess I can be supergirl fast or supergirl strong or a normal mix of either . . . but I can't be both every fucking day. Who can, anyway?

What disturbs her most is the pressure (from family, coworkers, supervisors) to work through her injuries to benefit-earning milestones. She understands the pressures driving everyone else to push her to continue, "but shit why can't I just say I'd like to not be at a job like that?" In any event, she writes, "everyone should know I'll probably just stay there anyhow . . . cause I'm too damn busy to find anything else anyway."

10,000 Students and 300 Degrees

There's little mystery regarding UPS's motivation for the earn and learn programs—not benevolence, but the cheapness and docility of the student workforce. In addition to the ultralow wage, students' dependency on UPS includes loan guarantees and tuition remissions, which are lost or reduced if the student resigns "prematurely" from the program. As a result of its campaign to hire undergraduates, UPS's retention of part-time package handlers has improved markedly, despite speedup and continued stagnation of the wage between 1997 and 2007. Average time of employment for part-timers grew by almost 50 percent, and retention increased by 20 percent, with some of the most dramatic improvements in the Louisville main hub. This tuition benefit is tax-deductible and taxpayer-subsidized. It's a good deal for UPS, which shares the cost of the tuition benefit with partner schools and communities and saves millions in payroll tax (by providing "tuition benefits" instead of higher wages), while holding down the part-time wage overall. All earn and learn students must apply for federal and state financial aid. Many of its workers attend community colleges, where tuition is often just a few hundred dollars. Many students are subjected to a bait and switch: attracted to the program by the promise of tuition benefits at the University of Louisville (currently over $6,000 a year), program participants are instead steered toward enrollment in the community colleges—a decision that doesn't reflect their academic needs, but as Metropolitan College director Poling admits, exclusively the desire of the state and UPS to contain costs. Studying on a part-time basis, as most in the program do, a student seeking a B.A. can therefore remain in a community college for three or four years before earning the credits enabling transfer to a four-year school. One student pointed out that trying to schedule around the UPS jobs was a "lot harder than it sounds," and for many it was "downright impossible to do this and get the degree in any reasonable period of years." Students who attend inexpensive schools or qualify for high levels of tuition relief (as is often the case in the economically disadvantaged groups targeted by UPS recruiters) substantially reduce UPS's costs. Undergraduate students also represent lower group health insurance costs.

Another way in which students reduce UPS's cost is by quitting before they become eligible for benefits, by taking an incomplete, or failing a class. No benefits are paid for failed or incomplete classes. Students who drop out of school but continue to work for UPS also significantly lower UPS's cost.

To put UPS's costs in perspective, look at these figures. In a decade, it has spent no more than $80 million on tuition and student loan redemption in over fifty hubs. By contrast, its 2006 deal with the state of Kentucky—for a 5,000-job expansion of just one hub—involved $50 million in state support over ten years. Company officials are fairly frank about UPS's dependency on cheap student labor, supported by massive taxpayer giveaways. "It would have been nearly impossible to find an additional 5,000 workers [for the expansion] without the resources of Metropolitan College," a public relations vice president told the Louisville business press (Karman and Adams). It has expanded earn and learn programs to fifty other metropolitan centers, to Canada, and to for-profit education vendors such as DeVry.

It's a lot less clear whether this is a good deal for students. "We've solved employee retention," Poling admits, "but we've got to work more on academic retention." Of the 10,000 students Poling's program claims to have "assisted" with their higher education since 1997, in a fall 2006 interview, he was able to produce evidence of just under 300 degrees earned: 111 associate's and 181 bachelor's degrees. Since both UPS and Metropolitan College refuse to provide public accountability for the academic persistence of undergraduate workers, it's hard to estimate what these numbers mean in comparison with more responsible and conventional education and financial aid circumstances. The most favorable construction of the evidence available for Metropolitan College shows an average entry of slightly more than 1,000 student workers annually. Based on two and one-half years of data after six years of program operation, according to Poling, the program between 2003 and 2006 showed approximate annual degree production of about 40 associates' and 75 bachelor's degrees. This approximates to a 12 percent rate of persistence to any kind of degree.

UPS's student employees in the Metropolitan College program are more likely to be retained as UPS employees than they are to be retained as college students. In May 2006, of the 3,000 or so Metropolitan College "students" working at UPS, only 1,263 were actually taking classes that semester. This means that during the spring term, almost 60 percent of the student workers in UPS's employ were not in school; "another 1700 or so," in Poling's words, "took the semester off" (Howington).

Of the minority actually taking classes, at least a quarter failed to complete the semester. UPS pays a bonus for completing semesters "unsuccessfully" (with withdrawals or failing grades) as well as "successfully." Counting the bonuses paid in recent years for "unsuccessful" semesters together with the successful ones, Poling suggested that during terms in which between 1,200 and 1,700 student workers were enrolled, between 900 and 1,100 students would complete at least one class. These numbers appear to hang roughly together. If in any given year, the majority of UPS night-shift workers are "taking the semester off," and 25 percent or more of those actually enrolled fail to complete even one class in the semester, this seems consistent with an eventual overall persistence to degree of 12 percent.

In plain fact, it would seem that UPS counts on its student workers failing or dropping out. Because of the high rate of failed classes, withdrawals, and dropping out, UPS ends up paying only a modest fraction of the education benefits it offers. If each of the 48,000 students who had passed through its earn and learn program as of 2005 collected the full UPS share of tuition benefits over a five-year period, it would have cost the company over $720 million. In fact, it spent just 10 percent of that total—$72 million—on tuition remission, or an average of only $1,500 per student (the equivalent of just one semester's maximum tuition benefit per participant). Similarly, the loan remission benefit (theoretically as much as $8,000 after four years of employment) would total almost $384 million. But as of 2005, UPS has had so far to pay off just $21 million, an average of just $438 per student worker, well under 10 percent of its liability if all of its student workers actually persisted to completion of a four-year degree (UPS, "Fact Sheet").

In the absence of meaningful accountability by UPS and its partners, we can only raise questions about this arrangement, not answer them. Since the program has been in operation for ten years, there are plenty of data. These are questions that can be answered. And these are questions that parents, students, partner institutions, and host communities should demand be answered. Many of these are similar in form to questions I posed to UPS through its press representative and which it refused to answer:

1. On average, how long do student workers remain employed with UPS?
2. What percentage of student workers exiting UPS's "earn and learn" programs remain enrolled in school?
3. What percentage of UPS student workers have additional employment?
4. What percentage of current or former UPS student workers earn associates' degree within three years and bachelor's degrees within six years?

144 | *Students Are Already Workers*

5. Do these percentages vary by shift worked?
6. What is the total and average amount of loans taken by earn and learn students? How much of those loans have been paid off by UPS?
7. What is the grade-point average of students enrolled in UPS programs?
8. UPS advertises that students can earn up to $25,000 in tuition and loan benefits. What is the average tuition and loan benefit actually paid per student?

One of the major unanswered questions is this one: Why haven't the partner institutions asked UPS for these answers already? Don't they have a responsibility to ask whether their students are being well served by these arrangements? If a promise to fund a citizen's higher education actually results in reduced likelihood of educational success, shouldn't the institution, the state, and the city revise or discontinue the arrangement?

One reason the University of Louisville hasn't asked these questions is because, in connection with its willingness to contract its students out to UPS, it collects tuition revenue and other subsidies, and the Metropolitan College partnership contributes heavily to new building plans across the campus, most notably erecting a series of new dormitories to house the UPS student workforce recruited from all over the state. Nor has it wanted to draw attention to the success rate of its own students. When the Metropolitan College program began in 1997–1998, the University of Louisville's six-year graduation rate was under 30 percent. This compares unfavorably with the institutions in its own benchmarking. The six-year graduation rate for Mississippi State is 58 percent; Florida State is 65 percent, and North Carolina State–Raleigh is 66 percent. A six-year graduation rate of around 30 percent means that if 2,000 undergraduates enter as first-year students, *close to 1,400 will not have graduated six years later.*

That figure is almost twice the number at many comparable institutions. Over ten years, a gap this size in academic persistence means that many thousands of individuals are not receiving degrees, in contrast to students in benchmark institutions. Over the past ten years, that graduation rate has crawled up to 33 percent, but even the improved number places the University of Louisville dead last among its own benchmark institutions, and dead last among thirty-eight comparator institutions generated by the IPEDS (Integrated Postsecondary Education Data System) database. Louisville and the state of Kentucky consistently rank near the bottom of educational attainments by a variety of indicators. Since the educational success rate of students at the institution and surrounding community was already so low, the success rates of UPS students flies under the radar.

One dean of students with whom I spoke claimed not to have studied the UPS students' success rate but shrugged off concerns with the impression that their attainments were "probably roughly comparable" to the low rate of other Louisville students. Using the measure of "year-to-year persistence," Poling was willing to compare his Metropolitan College student workers to other Louisville students, but not when it came to comparing persistence to degree.

Good for UPS and Who Else?

One of the reasons few hard questions have been asked of arrangements like Metropolitan College is that the superexploitation of undergraduate workers is not just a matter of UPS's individual dependency but a system of profound codependency, extending through the web of local, national, and even global economic relations.

As John McPhee's *New Yorker* profile of the Louisville hub makes clear, working for UPS at the Louisville main hub is really working for a lot of companies. A short distance from the sorting facility, UPS maintains millions of square feet of warehouse facilities, where its employees fill orders from online vendors for books, computers, underwear, and jet engine parts. When a Toshiba laptop breaks, Toshiba sends the repair order to UPS, who directs a driver to pick up the machine; from the local hub, it is flown in a UPS jet to an industrial park abutting the Louisville airport, where eighty UPS computer technicians repair Toshiba computers with Toshiba parts, returning the machines to their owners in about seventy-two hours. UPS is a major outsourcing contractor for fulfillment of products sold across the globe: the entire inventory of companies like Jockey is kept in UPS facilities in Louisville and handled exclusively by UPS employees from the point of manufacture to the consumer or retail outlet.

So the "good deal" that UPS is getting from the state and working students of Kentucky is also a good deal for all of the companies with which it has outsourcing contracts and, ultimately, for all of its customers. Shipping from the Louisville Worldport is faster and cheaper than ever before. It's a good deal for the full-time Teamsters, who no longer have to feel pressure to negotiate better for a significant fraction of UPS's new employees.

Chris Sternberg, senior vice president of corporate communications at Papa John's International, is frank about the multilayered economic advantages of the Metropolitan College arrangement for local businesses:

> Anytime new jobs are added to the Louisville economy, we are happy both from a community standpoint as well as for our business. When you have more people employed and the economy is thriving, we'll sell more pizzas. We are obviously pleased with the announcement. From an employment standpoint, many of our part-time workers also work part time at UPS, where they may work a four-hour shift at UPS and another four-hour shift at Papa John's. It's worked very well, and we like that shared employment arrangement. (quoted in Karman and Adams)

The local businesses associated with student consumption—such as pizza, fast food, banks, and auto dealers—benefit directly from this employment pattern: feeding workers, processing their loans and paychecks, and so on. The chairman of the largest auto group in Louisville was thrilled—student workers buy cars in order to commute between school and work. The local newspaper estimated that the 5,000-job expansion could mean as much as $750 million annually to the local economy.

But as Sternberg makes clear, for certain businesses relying on service workers, the UPS arrangement provided a double benefit by drawing a super-cheap workforce that needed to supplement its four hours after midnight at UPS with another four hours before midnight in a pizza shop.

Internal Outsourcing and 10 Million "Students Who Work"

As it turns out, UPS is just one of thousands of employers large and small whose business plans revolve centrally around the availability of a workforce who primarily consider themselves something other than workers.

To the extent that one function of education is people production, the question of subjectivity is unavoidable: What sort of consciousness is being framed by this experience? In the case of Louisville educators and UPS, the most common subjectivity produced appears to be that of failure—of persons who fail to persist, and therefore end up believing that they deserve their fate. "They all blame themselves," confirmed every instructor with whom I spoke regarding UPS student workers. "The only ones who didn't blame themselves were some of the high school students," said Susan Erdmann. "Some of them blamed UPS, rightly so." In general, student workers view themselves through a classic lens of modernity, as someone who is really someone and something very different than their embodied self at work: I am not a package handler; I am a student working as a package handler for a while.

Very little work of any kind has been done on the question of undergraduate labor. Of particular interest is Laura Bartlett's *Working Lives of College Students* website, featuring the original compositions of scores of student workers regarding their experience. Even in its early stages, Bartlett's site is a rich resource for understanding the experience of undergraduates who work. The essays feature the complexity of student consciousness regarding their working lives. Some emphasize positive dimensions, such as the student who acquired her educational sense of purpose from her part-time job assisting the disabled. Others attempt to make a virtue of necessity, hoping that working while studying will teach them "time management and multi-tasking" or to "build life-long coping skills"; one added the afterthought that, "hopefully, I will survive!" ("Work, Meet Education"; "School-Work Connection"). More widespread was a sense of exploitation, sounded in the common notes of "stress" and the running analogy to "imprisonment" in several contributions. Some wrote of physical injury and mental anguish, even in light-duty service and office positions, or wrote of repeated indignities, sexual harassment, and bullying: "I am treated as if I am subhuman" ("Wonderful World of Work"). One made precise calculations of the huge gap between the costs of education and the wages earned from the university and other employers (tuition, books and fees at an Ohio State campus consuming nearly the whole of a forty-hour week's wages, leaving just $6 a week for housing, transportation, food, clothing, entertainment, medical expenses, and the like). Some described the need for simultaneous multiple part-time jobs in addition to loans and grants.

Most of the contributors viewed their work as something very different from the "real" work they hoped to land after graduation. After describing her work-related injuries in a pretzel concession at an Ohio Wal-Mart as akin to imprisonment and torture, for instance, one of the contributors concludes by observing, "Someday, this little pretzel shop will be just something I did once upon a time just to get through college" ("Rude Awakening").

We could go any number of ways from here. For instance, we could ask what are the consequences of separating one's consciousness from "being" the pretzel baker or package handler? One terribly important answer is that persons who were unable to recognize their own humanity in pretzel baking or package handling are perhaps less likely to acknowledge the humanity of others who handle packages, or clean toilets, or paint walls, or operate cash registers. I'll return to this point before concluding.

Over 70 percent of U.S. high school grads enter college, 67 percent in the fall immediately after high school. Fewer than half of these complete a four-year degree. Those who do average far more than four years to do it. About 40 percent of those with a baccalaureate go on to graduate school. This professionalization of everything—the provision of degrees for so many different kinds of work—is one form in which higher education acts opportunistically. That is: it attracts more customers for credit hours with the (increasingly hollow) promise of the kinds of security nostalgicallyassociated with the classical professions of law, medicine, education, and so forth.

There is a social bargain with youth-qua-student that goes something like this: "Accept contingency now, in exchange for an escape from it later." The university's role in this bargain is crucial: it provides the core promise of escaping into a future, without which their "temporary" employment would otherwise require larger enticements. The campus brokers the deal: give us, our vendors, and our employing partners what we want (tuition, fees, and a fair chunk of labor time over several years), and you can escape the life you're living now.

Higher education is an industry, like others in the service economy, that is "structurally and substantially" reliant on youth labor (Tannock). Campuses of all kinds are critically dependent on a vast undergraduate workforce, who (as is in the fast-food industry) are desirable not just because they are poorly paid but because they are disposable and "more easily controlled" (Schlosser). This is true regardless of whether campus workers are unionized or whether the school is located in a state with a relatively labor-friendly legislative environment. For an example of a school that has campus unions and a more responsible legal climate, we might take SUNY Oswego, Jerry Seinfeld's alma mater. Oswego is a fairly modest employer of student labor, directly employing 2,000 undergraduates as part-time workers, or a bit more than a quarter of the student population. Nonetheless, students are overwhelmingly the largest sector of the workforce on campus, substantially outnumbering all other employment groups combined; taking full-time and part-time together, the campus only employs 1,500 nonstudent employees. Measured by full-time employee equivalent, it appears that student workers provide as much as half the labor time expended on campus (SUNY Oswego, "Fast Facts").

At Oswego and nationally, student labor time is expended in work that mirrors similar low-wage benefitless positions in the service economy at large: food service, day care, janitorial work, building security, interior painting and carpentry, parking enforcement, laundry service, administrative assistance, warehouse restocking, and so on (SUNY Oswego, "Student Employment"). These activities are far more typical than the tutorial, library, community service, and internship activities that provide the public image of student work. (The nature of the work in "internship" and "community service" positions is another story, but is itself commonly similar service-economy activity such as data entry, document reproduction, and so forth.)

Student employment offices function as temp agencies or outsourcing contractors for local businesses and campus units. At a typical public campus, the student employment office has hundreds of positions advertised by off-campus employers, generally entirely without benefits or unemployment insurance, with a wage in the vicinity of $6 or $7 per hour (sometimes more and often less). The off-campus work includes farm labor, satellite installation, short-order cooking, commission sales, forklift operation, and personal care in nursing homes, as well as clerking in banks, malls, and insurance offices. Public universities will sometimes provide cheap workers for nearby elite private universities (which often place limits on the number of hours that their own undergraduates can work). The federal government employs cheap student labor in general office work and, for instance, as receptionists for the Social

Security Administration, in positions that formerly provided full-time employment for a citizen with reasonable wages and benefits. Student workers often replace full-time unionized staff.

Sometimes the temp-agency function is quite frank: at the University of Illinois–Chicago, for instance, the student employment office maintains a separate Student Temporary Service exclusively for the purpose of providing near-minimum-wage day labor on a just-in-time basis to any location on the campus. That frank admission by UIC that they're running a temp agency may seem quite up to date and cutting edge, but it is, in fact, quite old school of them. The real cutting edge is Monster-TRAK, a subsidiary of the online job service Monster.com, which has standardized an interface with hundreds of public campuses. Initially providing on-campus interview services for graduates, the all too suggestively named Monster.com has moved into the lucrative business of managing undergraduate temp labor for hundreds of campuses, including federal work-study positions on major public campuses (Cal Tech, University of Virginia, University of Wisconsin). At all of these campuses, students cannot get work—even work-study positions funded with public money and which represent themselves as a citizenship entitlement, that is, "financial aid"—without registering with this private corporation, obtaining a password from them, and entering a nationwide temp agency, a world of work that is password protected and shielded from public view.

In the United States, only 20 percent of undergraduates do not work at all. About 50 percent of all undergraduates work an average of twenty-five hours per week. The remaining 30 percent work full-time, more than full-time, or at multiple jobs approximating the equivalent of full-time, averaging thirty-nine hours a week. This means that about 10 or 12 million undergraduates are in the workforce at any given moment. Indeed, if you're a U.S. citizen under age twenty-five, you are more likely to be working if you are a student than if you are not. Over 3 million persons aged twenty to twenty-four are unemployed. Being a student isn't just a way of getting a future job—it's a way of getting a job right now.

Here's something to think about. The main demographic fault line employed by the National Center for Education Statistics is a fairly reasonable sounding division of the school-work continuum into two groups, Students Who Work and Workers Who Study. This sounds very clean, scientific, even empirical. In fact, however, those divisions involve no empirical criteria. They're entirely subjective, based on the self-reporting of subjects who are given just two choices for self-description: "I consider myself a student who works," or "I consider myself a worker who studies." There are patterns within that self-reporting, but they aren't clear-cut at all: a huge fraction of persons describing themselves as "students who work" work full-time or more, and likewise a large proportion of those self-reporting as "workers who study" work part-time and go to school on a full-time basis (NCES, *Profile of Undergraduates*; NCES, *Work First, Study Second*).

My point is not that self-reporting of this kind is a somewhat questionable primary organization of a core national database, though it is, in my opinion. My point is that these researchers resorted to the gambit of subject self-reporting as a primary organization because in the current relationship between schooling and work, including the regulation environment, there isn't any clear way of "distinguishing" between students and workers.

This isn't just a problem for investigators with the NCES; it's also a problem for the most thoughtful analysts of labor, social justice, and the social function of higher education. Although I'm going to use an essay by Barbara Ehrenreich as an example, let me emphasize that I am not criticizing her but suggesting the pervasiveness of the intellectual and emotional hurdle represented by the legal, cognitive, and affective label of "student."

In fall 2004, Ehrenreich penned a column for the *Progressive* called "Class Struggle 101." It's about the exploitation of the higher education workforce, and it does an excellent job of making the necessary parallels to the wages, hypocrisy, and union-busting of Wal-Mart, while pointing out the good things that Harvard and Stanford undergraduates have done in support of what she calls "campus blue-collar workers." Throughout this piece, she uniformly identifies students and workers as two mutually exclusive groups, generally assigning social and political agency to "the students" and helplessness to "the workers." This is well intentioned but clearly not accurate, even on privileged campuses. At her Harvard example, for instance, labor militancy has a lot to do with the culture disseminated and maintained by one of the most noteworthy staff unions in the country, mainly comprised of, and wholly organized by, women. Similarly, at Yale, it was the militant "blue-collar" and "pink-collar" unions with a $100,000 grant that put the union of students on its feet. It is difficult, in other words, to do the usual thing in left theory or in labor studies and write about an "alliance between students and labor," when we haven't made sense of the fact that students *are* labor. As one of Laura Bartlett's student contributors observes, "Work, Meet Education, Your New Roommate."

In short, I believe the left is correct in assigning a powerful agency to the undergraduate population but at least partly for the wrong reasons—that is, while they do have a degree of agency as students and credit-hour consumers, they also have a powerful and enduring agency *as labor.*

The Social Meaning of Student Labor

According to one observer, in 1964, all of the expenses associated with a public university education, including food, clothing, and housing could be had by working a minimum-wage job an average of twenty-two hours a week throughout the year. (This might mean working fifteen hours a week while studying and forty hours a week during summers.) Today, the same expenses from a low-wage job require fifty-five hours a week fifty-two weeks a year.

At a private university, those figures in 1964 were thirty-six minimum-wage hours per week, which was relatively manageable for a married couple or a family of modest means and would have been possible even for a single person working the lowest possible wage for twenty hours a week during the school year and some overtime on vacations. Today, it would cost 136 hours per week for fifty-two weeks a year to "work your way through" a private university (Mortenson). In 2006, each year of private education amounted to the annual after-tax earnings of nearly four lowest-wage workers working overtime.

Employing misleading accounting that separates budgets for building, fixed capital expenses, sports programs, and the like from "instructional unit" budgets, higher education administration often suggests that faculty wages are the cause of rising tuition, rather than irresponsible investment in technology, failed commercial ventures, lavish new buildings, corporate welfare, and so on. The plain fact is that many college administrations are on fixed-capital spending sprees with dollars squeezed from cheap faculty and student labor: over the past thirty years, the price of student and faculty labor has been driven downward massively at exactly the same time that costs have soared.

For the 80 percent of students who are trying to work their way through, higher education and its promise of a future is increasingly a form of indenture, involving some combination of debt, overwork, and underinsurance. It means the pervasive shortchanging of health, family obligations, and, ironically, the curtailment even of learning and self-culture. More and more students are reaching the limits of endurance with the work that they do while enrolled. One major consequence of this shift of the costs of education away from society to students, including especially the costs of education as direct training for the workforce, is a regime of indebtedness, producing docile financialized subjectivities (Martin, *Financialization of Daily Life*) in what Jeff Williams has dubbed "the pedagogy of debt." The horizon of the work regime fully contains the possibilities of student ambition and activity, including the conception of the future.

Overstressed student workers commonly approach their position from a consumer frame of analysis. They are socialized and even legally obliged to do so, while being disabled by various means, including employment law, from thinking otherwise. To a certain extent, the issue *is* that student workers are underpaid and ripped off as consumers. In terms of their college "purchase," they are paying much more, about triple, and not getting more: the wage of the average person with a four-year degree or better is about the same today as in 1970, though for a far greater percentage, it takes the additional effort of graduate school to get that wage. From the consumer perspective, the bargain has gotten worse for purchasers of credit hours, because there are many more years at low wages and fewer years at higher wages, plus there are reductions in benefits, a debt load, and historically unprecedented insecurity in those working "full-time" jobs.

But the systematically fascinating, and from the perspective of social justice far more significant, difference is that the U.S. worker with only a high school education or "some college" is paid astonishingly less than they were in 1970, when the "college bonus" was only 30 to 40 percent of the average high-school-educated worker's salary. Now, the "going to college" bonus is more than 100 percent of the high-school-educated worker's salary, except that this "bonus" represents exclusively a massive reduction in the wage of the high school educated and is in no part an actual "raise" in the wages of the college educated.[3]

So while it is true and important that higher education is much less of a good deal than it used to be, we also have to think about the role higher education plays in justifying the working circumstances of those who can't make the college bargain. Whether one is inclined to accept higher education as an unspecial and seamless path—school to work—or alternatively as something "special," without any necessary or obvious relation to work, it can be considered straightforwardly as a distribution issue. That is: Who should enjoy the "specialness," whether that specialness is college as self-culture or college as a relatively larger and safer paycheck? On what terms? Who pays for it? What kinds and just how much specialness should the campus distribute? Why should the public fund a second-class and third-class specialness for some working lives, and provide the majority of working lives none at all? Wouldn't it be a straighter—not to mention far more just—path to dignity, security, health, and a meaningful degree of self-determination, even for the most highly educated, if we simply agreed to provide these things for everyone, regardless of their degree of education? Why should education be a competitive scramble to provide yourself with health care?

And here we've run up against the classic question of education and democracy: Can we really expect right education to create equality? Or do we need to *make equality* in order to have right education? With Dick Ohmann, Stanley Aronowitz, Cary Nelson, and others, I think the "crisis of higher education" asks us to do more than think about education, educators, and the educated. It challenges us to make equality a reality. It asks us to identify the agencies of inequality in our lives (including the ideologies and institutions of professionalism), to find a basis for solidarity with inequality's antagonists, and to have hope for a better world on that basis.

For me, the basis of solidarity and hope will always be the collective experience of workplace exploitation and the widespread desire to be productive for society rather than for capital. So when we ask, "Why has higher education gotten more expensive?" we need to bypass the technocratic and "necessitarian" account of events, in which all answers at least implicitly bring the concept of necessity beyond human agency to bear ("costs 'had to' rise because . . ."). Instead, we need to identify the agencies of inequality and ask, "To whom is the arrangement of student debt and student labor most useful?" The "small narratives" of technocracy function to obscure the fundamental questions of distribution. Not just: Who pays for education? But: Who pays for low wages?

The employer doesn't pay. By putting students to work, UPS accumulates more than it would otherwise accumulate if it put nonstudents to work, because of the different material costs represented by persons who claim citizenship in the present, not citizenship in the future. These low wages aren't cheap to society; they're just cheap to employers. Students themselves subsidize this cheapness: by doubling the number of life hours worked, by giving up self-culture and taking on debt. The families of adult students subsidize the cheapness, both in direct labor time and in sacrificed leisure, in time lived together, and other emotional costs. Other service workers subsidize the cheapness, as the huge pool of cheap working students helps to keep down the price of nonstudent labor. And student workers, located, as I've said, in a kind of semiformal regulation environment, are themselves inevitably patrons of the larger informal economy of babysitters, handymen, and the cheap-work system of global manufacturing and agribusiness.

So, on the one hand, the labor time of the low-wage student worker creates an inevitable, embodied awareness that the whole system of our cheap wages is really a gift to the employer. Throwing cartons at 3:00 A.M. every night of one's college education, it becomes impossible not to see that UPS is the beneficiary of our financial aid, and not the other way around. As Dick Ohmann has commented of another group of campus flex-timers, the contingent faculty, there's some potential in this experience for militancy—for new kinds of self-organization for workplace security—and even a quest for new alliances with other hyperexploited and insecure workers. And in the United States, there are always more than 10 million people who are simultaneously workers and students at any given time, for many of whom the prospects of an "escape" from contingency are dim at best. Even under present conditions of extreme labor repression, the transformative agency of the millions of student employees is evident in the anti-sweatshop movement and in graduate-employee union movements, which have allied themselves with other insecure workers and not with the tenured faculty. "Professional" workers increasingly have interests and experiences in common with other workers.

On the other hand, especially for those for whom schooling does indeed provide an escape from contingency, these long terms of student work can also serve to reinforce commitments to inequality. The university creates professional workers who understand the work that everyone else does in a very particular way: they see manual work and service work through the lens of their own past, through their own sense of their past selves as students, likely comprising all of the feelings of the non-adult, of the temporary, of the mobile, of the single person. As one contributor to Bartlett's *Working Lives* site put it, it's "something I did once upon a time just to get through college." For the professional workers created by the university, these "other" workers, no matter their age or circumstances, are always doing the work of someone who isn't really a full citizen and who doesn't make the full claims of social welfare—just like themselves when they were not (yet) full adults and citizens. Their feeling is that these other workers, like the students who aped them for a few years, really ought to be moving on—out of the sphere of entitlement, out of "our" schools and hospitals, out of "our" public. The view of globalization from above is assisted by the voice of the beat cop to the guest worker loitering around the health-care system: move along, move along.

From here, we could go on to explore the meaning of contingency: not just part-time work but the insecurity and vulnerability of full-time workers. We could ask, for whom is this contingency a field of possibility? And for whom is contingency, in fact, a field of constraint?

It takes a village to pay for education and to pay for low wages and to pick up the cost for life injuries sustained by the absence of security and dignity. So perhaps the village should decide what education and wages should be, and the sort of dignity and security that everyone should enjoy, very much apart from the work they do.

5

Composition as
Management Science

Our basic claim is this: Though institutions are certainly powerful,
they are not monoliths; they are rhetorically constructed human
designs (whose power is reinforced by buildings, laws, traditions
and knowledge-making practices) and so are changeable. In other
words, we made 'em, we can fix 'em. Institutions R Us. Further, for
those of you who think such optimism is politically naïve and
hopelessly liberal and romantic, we believe that we (and you, too)
have to commit to this hypothesis anyway, the alternative—political despair—being worse.
                    —James Porter et al., "Institutional Critique," 2000

Time was, the only place a guy could expound the mumbo jumbo
of the free market was in the country club locker room or the
pages of *Reader's Digest*. Spout off about it anywhere else and
you'd be taken for a Bircher or some new strain of Jehovah's Witness. After all, in the America of 1968, when the great backlash
began, the average citizen, whether housewife or hardhat or salary-
man, still had an all-too-vivid recollection of the Depression. Not
to mention a fairly clear understanding of what social class was all
about. Pushing laissez-faire ideology back then had all the prestige
and credibility of hosting a Tupperware party.
                    —Thomas Frank, *The God That Sucked*, 2002

The first epigraph is drawn from the winner of the 2001
Braddock award for best essay published in a leading journal in the academic discipline of rhetoric and composition.

Rhet-comp is an emerging field with an especially vexed relationship
to the disciplinary history and practices of other fields in English studies, especially what David Downing characterizes as the "disciplinary

division of labor." As with any other academic field, its intellectual interests are wide ranging. These encompass classical rhetoric, cultural studies, rhetorical and communications theory, sociolinguistics, pedagogy, new media studies, organizational communications, and research into the composing process of countless genres of writing, from autobiography and narrative to "practical business writing," technical writing, and document design.

However, as Sharon Crowley points out, for the rest of the university, the field "rhet-comp" manifests itself in relation to one course, First-Year English. This course is widely staffed by persons working contingently, in what she and most observers agree are "unprofessional and unethical" conditions. Writing faculty generally work with diminished or nonexistent academic freedom protections, few resources, and often little acquaintance with the disciplinary knowledge of rhet-comp. While the course was commonly staffed by full-time lecturers and tenure-stream faculty until the 1940s, the expansion of higher education under the G.I. Bill initiated the practice of adjunct hiring and reliance on graduate employees to teach the course. By the mid 1960s, the casualization of writing instruction was institutionalized and massively expanded in order to fuel cross-subsidy of research and other university activities. During this expansion, a significant fraction of the collective labor of rhetoric and composition specialists was devoted to supervising and training the casualized first-year writing staff.

As a result, the disciplinary identity of tenurable faculty in rhetoric and composition has emerged in close relation to the permatemping of the labor force for first-year writing, creating what I've called the problem of "tenured bosses and disposable teachers." The negative consequences of this arrangement for students, faculty, the curriculum, and the discipline led Crowley to controversially suggest in 1990 that the first-year writing requirement be "abolished" as a step toward "unhooking" the discipline from the requirement. The permatemped workers who teach first-year writing didn't universally welcome this suggestion. Moreover, it has since become clear that permatemping extends far beyond first-year writing in English studies; it reaches throughout the university curriculum.

Crowley's "abolition" proposal inadvertently contributed to a significant trend within rhetoric and composition, what Eileen Schell and Patricia Lambert Stock call the attempt to reform academic labor practices "from above." In this chapter, I explore the way that a reform rhetoric "from above" increasingly dominates the discourse of the field, often doing much more to advance the interests of the supervisory class than the interests of the casualized. Crowley herself has ruefully reflected on the risks of "presuming to speak" for the casualized (239). Insofar as this book proceeds from my own experience as temporary faculty and a graduate employee, this chapter suggests—from that experience and perspective—the importance of setting aside managerial theories of agency and embracing, instead, the rhetoric and solidarities associated with the self-organization of casual labor.

Given the massive exploitation of part-time faculty and graduate employees in the field, most people working in rhet-comp instruction will agree with the general supposition of Porter et al. that the "institutions" of rhet-comp and higher education more generally are very much in need of "change," as well as with their basic and most urgent claim— that change is, in fact, possible.

Later on, I quarrel with the essayists' ramification of their argument, especially that change presupposes change agency from above, specifically a managerial insider prepared to make the sort of arguments by which universities are "likely to be swayed," to "ask for" resources using "effective rhetorical strategies," and to work to build "disciplinary status" that can be "parlayed into institutional capital" (Porter et al., 615–616).[1] This follows a general train of thinking in rhet-comp scholarship emphasizing how to "make arguments" that will be "convincing" to those "with the power" inside the institution (among many others, see Joseph Harris; Miller, "Arts of Complicity"; Murphy, "New Faculty"; Grimm).

Despite the evident sincerity of this line of inquiry, on the whole, I'm profoundly unconvinced that a management theory of agency and what I call the rhetoric of "pleasing the prince" is particularly useful—much less necessary—to the project of transforming institutions. I prefer instead a labor theory of agency and a rhetoric of solidarity, aimed at constituting, nurturing, and empowering collective action by persons in groups. I think most of the historical evidence shows that education management and its rhetoric of the past thirty years—"the mumbo jumbo of the free market"—has created the institutions we need to change. Similarly, I think the historical evidence shows that the primary agent of resistance and, ultimately, transformation are the organized efforts of those whose labor is composed by the university, including students.

In this chapter, I survey the degree to which managerial subjectivity predominates in composition, distorting the field's understanding of "materialism" and "critique" to the point that it consistently attempts to offer "solutions" to its "labor problem" without accounting for the historical reality of organized academic labor. There is, of course, a substantial countertrend in rhet-comp, including such voices as Eileen Schell, Chris Carter, Karen Thompson, Laura Bartlett, Patricia Lambert Stock, Tony Scott, David Downing, and Richard Ohmann. Nonetheless, the institutions of the field are overwhelmingly occupied by persons whose values are shaped in close relation to the practice, theory, and scholarship of the supervisory function. This has produced what I view as "managerial" theories of change: transformation by management for the good of labor, such as Porter et al.'s "Institutional Critique."

Observing the very different kinds and scope of accomplishments achieved by collective bargaining, I claim, instead, that "change" in composition depends primarily on the organized voice and collective action of composition labor. But insofar as "Institutional Critique" insists on the availability of alternatives to grotesque current realities, I'm prepared to make common cause with its authors. After all, Marx was among the first to insist that managers are workers too.

The "Heroic WPA"

> [Now capital] hands over the work of direct and constant supervision of the individual workers and groups of workers to a special kind of wage-laborer. An industrial army of workers under the command of a capitalist requires, like a real army, officers (managers) and N.C.O.s (foremen, overseers), who command during the labor process in the name of capital. The work of supervision becomes their established and exclusive function. (Marx, *Capital*, vol. 1, ch. 13)

The essay by Porter et al. makes several important points. Following a number of philosophers working in the Marxist tradition (David Harvey, Donna Haraway, and Iris Marion Young), their effort is at least partially an attempt to hold onto critical theory, to a commitment to justice, and to a materialist frame of analysis, and they make a point of reaching out to rhet-comp scholars engaging in cultural-studies practices, especially Jim Sosnoski and James Berlin. In particular, the piece emphasizes the necessity of critical theorizing to social change and, furthermore, that critical theorizing implies a materialist analytical frame and "an action plan" for transformation. Of special importance is the authors' suggestion, in allusion to leading criticism of exploitative labor practices, that transforming the practices of rhet-comp depends on transforming individual campuses and the material situation of those campuses. The authors are right to emphasize that the "disciplinary practices" of composition are not those that composition has imagined for itself in a vacuum; they are practices that have emerged in specific historical and material realities that themselves need to be changed in order to enable new disciplinary practices.

But for purposes of getting started in our own inquiry, the most interesting question raised by the Porter et al. essay is meta-discursive. Exactly what has gone on in the rhet-comp discourse that the essay's dramatic rhetoric frames the otherwise banal observation that "institutions can be changed" as a revelation to its readership? What hopeless structure of feeling so dramatically permeates the audience for this piece that such an uncontroversial claim needs to be advanced at all, much less receive the disciplinary equivalent of a standing ovation (the Braddock award)?

A big part of the answer has to do with current trends in the discourse: away from critical theory toward institutionally focused pragmatism, toward acceptance of market logic, and toward increasing collaboration with a vocational and technical model of education. This movement in rhet-comp follows the larger movement traced by Thomas Frank and others, the historical reemergence beginning about 1970 of substantial political support for the "market god," together with an accompanying revival of intellectual credibility for those "pushing laissez-faire ideology."

But perhaps the core understanding for our purposes is that the implied audience of the piece is lower-level management in the managed university. As Porter and Sullivan and their coauthors eventually make clear, the "we" who they are addressing in their research encompasses primarily "academics" with specific "professional class status," such as writing program administrators (WPAs) (634 n.3). While they mention the possibility of "groups" being involved in "effective strategies for institutional change," their real interest is in generating "rhetorical strategies" and "institutional capital" for individual writer rhetors: "This method insists that sometimes individuals . . . can rewrite institutions through rhetorical action" (613). Insisting that critique leads to action, the one example that the authors offer of a critique actually leading to change is their establishment of a business writing lab. This example falls well within the article's orientation toward the subjectivity of lower administration: "Those of us who are WPAs contend (if not outright *fight*) on a daily basis with our academic institutions for material resources, control over processes, and disciplinary validity" (614; emphasis in the original).

This is not to say that the authors don't mention other subjects, only that the administrative subjectivity is privileged. Ringing a variant on the "teacher hero" narratives of exploited pedagogical labor, we might call the familiar figure of Porter et al.'s narrative the "heroic WPA." They credit individual WPAs with two forms of "institutional action": the formation of graduate programs in rhetoric and composition, and the formation of undergraduate writing majors. Together with the establishment of the business writing lab at Purdue, these two forms of "action" are meant to serve as inspirational exemplars: "When we start to get discouraged about the possibility of rewriting institutions, we should remember our own history" (615). Throughout the article, meaningful change primarily refers to actions taken by individuals rather than groups, administrators rather than labor, and persons envisioning themselves belonging to a professional or managerial "class," but just barely, in connection with a "struggle for respectability" and "validity."

It is in the context of this specific positioning that the otherwise unremarkable claim that institutions can be changed requires the kind of urgency and repetition that it receives in the Porter et al. article. In the modern era, social transformation has transpired with many groups serving as the agent of change: students, political parties, trade unions, agrarian revolutionaries, and social movements animated by the experience of racial, ethnic, and gendered oppression, for example. Counterrevolutions have been led by military, industrial, and paramilitary interests; by the propertied classes; by superpower and colonial political surrogates; by fascist organizations; and by the intelligentsia. Professionals and managers, like most people, have been sometimes on one side and sometimes on the other of most transformative events. The professional-managerial group as a whole is conditioned by contradictory class status. On the one hand, they are persons who work to live (for most of their working lives, even the more highly paid physicians, lawyers, and managers cannot afford to stop working, tending to "cash in" toward the end of an arduous career). Nonetheless, the higher level of earnings associated with their position, as well as the status economy, tends to foster identification with the class that enjoys real wealth. This affective connection to real wealth leads professionals and managers to the purchase of consumer items intended to display their identification with bourgeois enjoyments: for most of her working life, the average member of the "professional-managerial class" is far more likely to own boat shoes than a boat.

It is not clear that "lower management" as a group has ever figured in any substantial transformation of society or its institutions, or that lower management represents a particularly strong standpoint for individuals "advocating" change to upper management. Indeed, despite the occasional exception, the opposite would seem to be the case. Lower management is particularly vulnerable, highly individuated, and easily replaced. Managers at the lowest level aren't usually even on the corporate ladder but are commonly "tracked" separately from upper-management echelons. In this way, persons managing a Taco Bell franchise are sometimes, but not often, the same persons who do management work at the parent TriCon Corporation.

Within academic capitalism, the heroic WPA might be seen as playing what Marx identified as the very working-class role of "a special kind of wage-laborer": the noncommissioned officer or foreman, the members of the working class whose particular labor is to directly administer the labor of other members of their class at the front line of the extraction of surplus value. (In Marx's view, which I share, the "commissioned officers" or upper managers are likewise workers whose special task is to creatively theorize and enact procedures to the disadvantage of other workers.)[2] As Richard Miller has observed, many professional compositionists will directly serve as lower management: he writes that "most" rhet-comp Ph.D.s will be "required" to manage a writing program, "oversee the labor of others," and perform "other such managerial tasks" (" 'Let's Do the Numbers,' " 98–99). Consistent with the general orientation of the article by Porter et al., Miller's observation suggests that professional compositionists more generally are interpellated as lower management: that is, even those holders of rhet-comp doctorates who evade the requirement to serve directly as lower managers will need to be viewed as theorizing or providing legitimation (through the production of scholarship, inventing classroom praxis, etc.) in connection with this front-line relationship between composition labor and "the work of supervision" performed by professional-managerial compositionists.

While the experience of promotion can be experienced subjectively as a change of class ("the working class can kiss me arse / I've got the foreman's job at last"), and is usually accomplished by material privileges, it is probably better to view the differences between lower-level management and labor as indicating a change of class loyalties, not an objective change of "class status."[3] Despite the quotidian-embodied intimacy that the WPA and composition scholars more generally share with the rank and file of composition labor (from which they sometimes have emerged; a significant number of rhet-comp doctorates appear to be awarded to persons who have served as adjunct comp labor), the lower-managerial lifeway of fighting for personal "control" over instructional "resources" and disciplinary status recognition is very different from the ethos of struggle that is usually associated with social and workplace transformation: the raising of consciousness, the formation of solidarities, coalition building, and so forth. If the analogy to the foreman or noncommissioned officer holds true, we would expect to find not only acquiescence to the "necessities" framed by the ruling class represented by upper management and commissioned officers, but even an enlarged loyalty to those imperatives. (As in the trope of the grizzled master sergeant who understands the "necessity" of sending troops under fire, while the new second lieutenant sentimentally condones desertion and "cowardice": the noncommissioned officer/WPA is still embodied enlisted labor, but as lower management is required to be even more "loyal" to the "necessities" maintaining the class structure than those who genuinely benefit from the class structure.) In this context, the "heroism" of the heroic WPA consists precisely in her capacity to represent the interests of the ruling class as the interests of the workers (teachers and students) in her charge. Jeanne Gunner is particularly trenchant in this connection, noting that the "tyrannical positions" held by many WPAs in relation to their writing staff are commonly justified by sincerely held convictions of "benevolence" (158–159).

Indeed, from the perspective of judicial opinion surrounding the National Labor Relations Act, which distinguishes the policy-setting "managerial" from the front-line "supervisory" functions, we might in legal terms find that historically the WPA performed a supervisory role. As Sharon Crowley notes, many WPAs don't hire, fire, or set policy regarding the people whose work they supervise—and gaining that power, especially the power to set policy regarding writing instruction, is one of the goals of the discourse. From this point of view, the WPA discourse is one of supervisors trying to join the managerial ranks, to more fully join the ranks of "decision makers," albeit at least partly with the intention of benefiting the superexploited working rank and file.

Certainly the "heroism" of the heroic WPA trades on the intimacy of the professional or managerial compositionist with the composition labor force. This intimacy is reflected by a certain ambiguity in the first-person plural in composition scholarship: Who is the "we" indexed by composition scholars? Who is meant by the term "compositionist"? Sometimes it means "those who teach composition"; sometimes it means "those of us who theorize and supervise the teaching of composition." The movement between these meanings always has a pronounced tendency to obscure the interests and voice of those who teach composition in subfaculty conditions, ultimately to the advantage of university management. At the same time, it imbues the ambition of the professional or managerial compositionist for respect and validity with the same urgency as the struggle of composition labor for wages, health care, and office space. Commonly, this confusion of the professional and lower-managerial interests with the labor struggle takes the form of suggesting that the set of demands overlap, or that the labor struggle depends on the prior satisfaction of the professional and managerial agenda. From a materialist standpoint, the intimacy enabling the multiple meanings of "we" becomes a vector for continuing exploitation. Understanding this intimacy as a structural relationship requires careful examination of the possibility that the heroic narrative of disciplinary "success" for professional and managerial compositionists has depended in part on the continuing *failure* of the labor struggle.

A materialist view of the disciplinarization of rhetoric and composition would situate this ascendance not simply in the heroic struggle of writing-program intellectuals for recognition and status but in the objective conditions of labor casualization created by upper management —the steady substitution of student and other nonfaculty, parafaculty, and subfaculty labor for teacher labor; the establishment of multiple tiers of work; the consolidation of control over the campus by upper administration, legislatures, and trustees; and so on. For instance, if we are to locate rhet-comp's ascendance in the years 1975–1995, then we must also acknowledge that this is a period of time in which undergraduate admissions substantially expanded—while the full-time faculty

were reduced by 10 percent, and the number of graduate student employees was increased by 40 percent (Lafer). How can composition's
"success" be separated from this story of failure for academic labor
more generally? Clearly, the emergence of rhetoric and composition into
some form of (marginal) respectability and (institutional-bureaucratic)
validity has a great deal to do with its usefulness to upper management,
by legitimating the practice of writing instruction with a revolving labor
force of graduate employees and other contingent teachers.

The discipline's enormous usefulness to academic capitalism—in delivering cheap teaching, training a supervisory class for the cheap teachers, and producing a group of intellectuals theorizing and legitimating
this scene of managed labor—has to be given at least as much credit in
this expansion as the heroic efforts that Porter et al. call the WPA's
"strong track record for enacting change" (614).

There is therefore a certain honesty in the tendency of some compositionists urging the rest of the discipline to "admit" and embrace their
"complicity" in a "corporate system" (Joseph Harris, 51–52; Miller,
"Arts of Complicity"). Indeed, in at least some cases, the advocacy of
certain "changes" in composition seems to follow well behind the curve
of academic capitalism's accomplished facts.

The Intricate Evasions of As: "How to Be One of the Gang When You're Not"

> The professional life of an adjunct comes with its own set of challenges.
> At Houghton Mifflin, we understand the valuable role that adjuncts
> play in higher education, and we hope the information on this web
> site helps you to negotiate those challenges. (Houghton Mifflin College
> Division)

Houghton Mifflin's college division registered the domain name www
.adjuncts.com and created the website Adjuncts.com primarily to introduce nontenurable faculty to its textbooks. The site additionally invites
visitors to use a variety of resources organized by field (under a menu
headed "Go to Your Discipline"), and tailored to what it describes as
the unique needs of the nontenurable faculty (their "own" challenges).
Houghton Mifflin's language of "understand[ing]" the "valuable role"
of adjunct labor is redolent of composition's professional-managerial

discourse on "the labor problem," which likewise features itself as offering help to composition labor in "negotiating" their "challenges." Most of the material on the site adopts the tone of a *Chronicle of Higher Education* advice column, such as Jill Carroll's "How to Be One of the Gang When You're Not," which urges adjunct labor to overcome the social "prejudice" of research faculty by "acting like" someone with a professorial job. This "acting like" includes showing up at guest lectures, eating at the faculty club, organizing conferences, volunteering for committee work, doing scholarship, writing items for the faculty newsletter, and attending department and campus meetings. Acknowledging that most of these actions constitute unwaged labor, Carroll represents that at least for "those" who have "made peace" with the "dominant facts of adjunct life" ("the low pay, the lack of respect, the lack of job stability"), all of this unpaid "acting like" a member of the professoriate might enable more "social interaction" with better-paid colleagues, ultimately paying off in the coin of emotion: "Relationships with other faculty members can be intellectually rich and one of the most satisfying aspects of the job."

A reading of Carroll's text could press in a number of directions—a reading that looked to the feminization of teaching work, in the vein of Eileen Schell's first book, for example, would comment on the concomitant feminization of reward in passages like this one, perhaps proceeding to critically explore the advocacy of a "service ethos" for composition labor in Richard Miller's work: How much of the uniqueness of adjunct life's special "challenges" and rewards, such as "service" and "relationships," are coded as opportunities for women? Another line of critique would drive at the fairness issues raised by a discourse urging professionalization of work ("Go to Your Discipline") in the absence of a concomitant professionalization of reward ("But Look for Your Paycheck Elsewhere"). These issues can be considered most vigorously by the growing literature on superexploitation or hyperexploitation, such as Andrew Ross's investigation of "The Mental Labor Problem," which names a radical erosion of the wage in many sectors of knowledge work, sometimes by substituting nonmaterial rewards such as the chance to work at an exciting, creative, and professional manner. "Being creative" or "being professional" in this respect substitutes for a substantial portion of the wage itself.

Perhaps the most interesting reading, to which I'll return in closing, would relate this problem of adjunct labor to the obsession among *yes*

professional compositionists with their disciplinary status, a structure of feeling that can easily be represented as "how to be one of the gang" of disciplines.[4] In my view, the problem of composition labor's felt exteriority to the gang of professors cannot be separated from the problem of composition management's felt exteriority to the gang of disciplines: the two structures of feeling are inseparably related along the "degree zero" of the material specificity of composition work—work conducted in the scene of managed parafaculty labor. I borrow the term "degree zero" from Paolo Virno, who uses it describe the "neutral kernel" of material determination that unites related but apparently contradictory structures of feeling. He asks, "What are the modes of being and feeling that characterize the emotional situations both of those who bow obsequiously to the status quo and those who dream of revolt?" *me* (28). That is: How is it that the same determining circumstances support those who go along and those who resist? *HW?*.

This problem is not composition's problem alone—foreign-language acquisition and health sciences are also particularly visible in this respect—but nowhere is the scene so prevalent and institutionalized as in composition, where the terminal degree does not presently signify certification of professional labor but, as Miller observes, testifies instead to the likely "requirement" of serving in lower management. Of course, this does not mean that the circumstance is composition's "fault"—far from it; only that it is a place of managed paraprofessional teaching where the conversion of the university to an "education management organization" (EMO) is visible, just as health sciences reveals the movement to managed care (the HMO).

Professional composition, in my view, will never feel like "one of the gang" of disciplines until its labor patterns are more like those in other fields. Of course, this equivalence could easily come about by the frightening but very real possibility—evidenced by clear statistical trends—that labor patterns in other disciplines will become more like those in composition, rather than the other way around. To put it in blunt terms, as long as composition's discourse remains a management science—or, alternatively, until history, engineering, and philosophy are management science to the same extent—it is likely to fail to enjoy the status it seeks: of a discipline among peers.

right

Nathaniel →

Insofar as we observe the continuing realization of the logic of the EMO, however, composition's "peerlessness"—its nonequivalence with the other disciplines—is likely to become increasingly visible as its "excellence," in Bill Readings's sense, with composition exemplifying the *scary!* ideal labor relation of the managed university to which all other disciplines must conform.

One interesting variant on this last reading would push the identity crisis of composition management yet further and critically examine the ways that composition management either tries to "be one" with the gang of composition labor or wants to demonstrate its understanding and appreciation ("I feel your pain" or "I hear your song"), coopting the voice of labor in the process. Yet another variant would reverse the observation that managers are workers too and investigate the degree to which the working subject is also a managerial subject, as well as rhet- comp's role in what Randy Martin, following a long line of cultural- studies critique of "the managed self" (Brantlinger; Watkins), describes as a campus-based "national pedagogy" promoting a "calculus of the self that eclipses labor's actual opportunities" ("Education," 26).

The urgency and interest of other readings notwithstanding, at this juncture my primary concern with Carroll's column is the overall strategy represented by the line of thought it exemplifies ("advice for adjuncts"). What characterizes this field of knowledge, much of it generated by adjuncts themselves (such as Carroll), is the dissemination of tactics for "getting ahead in the system as it is." The keynote of this genre is that there are facts of life in the corporate university, and most *exactly* possible versions of agency revolve around learning the ropes of the corporation rather than imagining alternatives to corporatism.

Most professional compositionists will recognize the emergence of this note in their own conversation in a twin sense. First, insofar as this kind of advice frequently comes from adjunct labor, this kind of discourse frequently is permitted to "pass" as the voice of composition labor—commonly to the exclusion or marginalization of the very different voice represented, for example, by the Coalition of Contingent Academic Labor (COCAL) or the fifty-campus movement of organized graduate employees. This other voice is committed not to the recognition of the inevitability of the corporate university but to struggling to- *yes* ward a different reality. Second, composition management deploys the value "getting ahead" together with a set of assertions about "the system as it is" in order to adopt a paternalist standpoint of care within a general strategy of lowered expectations: that is, given current "realities," the best "we can do" for the teachers and students in our care is to help them to get ahead. *right.*

In terms of theorizing "agency" and "change," therefore, a large sector of the composition discourse appears to be moving toward an extremely limited notion of both, characterized by a sense of belatedness, in exactly the sense of Francis Fukuyama's claim regarding the "end of history" or Daniel Bell's earlier claim of an "end to ideology." As noted above, the implications of an end of history for the discourse of managerial compositionists is that any changes that may be wrought in the future will be wrought within the frame of recognizing the inevitability of the corporate university or, as Miller puts it, "conceding the reality of academic working conditions" (*As if,* 22).

The recent calls in the rhet-comp mainstream for non-tenure-track instructorships as a "solution" to the superexploitation of composition labor is a good example of what is most disturbing about this line of thought (among many others, Murphy, "New Faculty"; Joseph Harris). While the subtitle of Murphy's piece suggests that he is writing, in September 2000, prospectively "toward a full-time teaching-intensive faculty track in composition" (as if such a thing required inventing), he confesses in his piece that he is really seeking only to "acknowledge what has *actually already taken place*" (23; emphasis in the original). Murphy means that part-time teachers are in most cases "really" full-time teachers, even if they have to teach at multiple institutions in order to do so. He cites his own case: teaching five courses per semester on two separate campuses, essentially, he writes, "splitting my appointment as a full-time teacher" (24). He goes on to propose that universities "formally recognize" this circumstance by "creating full-time [nontenurable] positions those teachers could grow into over the course of a career." The ultimate aim is that "teaching-intensive" faculty would participate in governance and administration and enjoy recognition as "legitimate full-time academic citizens," albeit with "salaries running parallel to, although always somewhat behind, those of traditional faculty" (25).

One may agree or disagree with this proposal; I, for one, feel constrained to point out that, historically, there have been plenty of "teaching-intensive" assistant professorships requiring little research and plenty of teaching, as in the community colleges and most liberal arts colleges—why not "advocate" for the creation or re-creation of teaching-intensive professorships rather than nontenurable instructorships? Insofar as many if not most "teaching-intensive" positions have traditionally been professorial, what exactly is the appeal of making them

TENURE

nontenurable, if not, as AAUP and the major academic unions have long observed, to consolidate managerial control?

Further, the invention of nontenurable instructorships, frequently paying less than $30,000 for teaching a 5–5 load, coincides with a radically gendered segmentation of the academic workforce: the persons being offered these jobs (involving more than full-time work but yielding less than full-time pay and rewards) are overwhelmingly women, whereas in higher education at large the tenured faculty and upper administration continue to be primarily men. Is the work nontenurable because it is done by women? Or is it "women's work" because it is nontenurable? (Minority faculty likewise are overrepresented in the ranks of the nontenurable full-time positions.)

And the leading studies of non-tenure-track faculty indicate that about half are dissatisfied with their job security, salaries, and ability to keep up with knowledge in their fields. Contrary to Murphy's projection of a stable non-tenure-track workforce, the full-time non-tenure-track population is characterized by high turnover. At any given moment, slightly more than half of non-tenure-track faculty expect to leave their current position "within three years," many of them for jobs outside of academe altogether (National Education Association, 1–4). Even *U.S. News and World Report*—never known for a bias in favor of labor —reports on the trend toward non-tenure-track instructorship under the headline of "The New Insecurity" and feels constrained to observe, in a featured box, that 57 percent of these jobs are held by women (as contrasted to 26 percent of tenured positions) (Shea). All of which is to say that, at the very least, rhet-comp's enthusiasm for this kind of appointment is up for debate. OK

Considering Murphy's article here is important because what he proposes "has actually already taken place" in a much more straightforward sense than he seems to be aware. Murphy acknowledges in a footnote that full-time non-tenure-track appointments "have already been experimented with" at a "surprising" number of schools" (37 n.2), but the reality was that all the major data sources at the time (most of them drawing from the NSOPF-93 dataset) already showed that as of fall 1992 more than 20 percent of the full-time faculty served in non-tenure-track positions—for a total of more than 100,000 persons employed in this "experimental" way. Furthermore, by April 1999, the *Chronicle of Higher Education* and other major education journals circulated the results of the Chronister-Baldwin study showing that the proportion of

now
491 in
eng

full-time faculty working off the tenure track had climbed to 28 percent by 1995 from 19 percent in 1975, while in the same period the proportion of those on the tenure track (but not yet tenured) dropped correspondingly, from 29 percent to 20 percent (Leatherman, "Use of Non-Tenure-Track Faculty"). To be fair to Murphy, we can say that perhaps he was attempting to affect the proportions within the mixed employment pattern that presently obtains in composition by increasing the percentage of the full-time lectureship relative to the number of part-time lectureships. Nonetheless, a kind of position held by between one-quarter and one-third of all full-time faculty and trending steadily upward really can't be framed as an "experiment" in "new" kinds of faculty work.[5] Even the somewhat less rigorous CAW voluntary survey—which probably undercounts nontraditional faculty work—showed that full-time non-tenure-track instructors accounted for close to one-fifth of the instruction in all English and freestanding composition departments (American Historical Association, tables 2, 2a, 2b).[6] Indeed, the NCES "New Entrants" white paper—commenting on the fact that persons beginning full-time academic employment in 1985 or later were more than twice as likely overall (33 percent) than persons hired before 1985 (17 percent) to serve off the tenure track—postulated that the eye-opening statistical change toward nontenurable work for the whole cohort of younger scholars had a lot to do with the "considerable number of non-tenure track appointments for foreign-language and writing specialists" (29).

In this instance, then, what passed for a "reasonable proposal" for rhet-comp—even, portentously, as a "new faculty for a new university"—was, in fact, a well-established practice in the management-dominated university by the mid 1980s. In this light, the proposal stands revealed not as the prospective and imaginary excursion into a better world but, to a certain disappointing extent, thoroughly reactive and even apologist, functioning to idealize after the fact, legitimating an already existing reality that pleases few people. The major source of data on the higher education workforce had already identified the creation of nontenurable full-time positions as a noteworthy trend particular to writing instruction fifteen years earlier. This disciplinary trend in new writing faculty was so pronounced that it affected the statistical profile of the pool of *all* entering faculty.

So the fact that Murphy's article has so far been eagerly taken up elsewhere in the rhet-comp literature as a genuinely innovative "proposal" for "new faculty" suggests a pervasive self-ignorance in the rhet-comp discourse. How does it come about that one of the discipline's two or three leading journals is prepared to publish a "practical pro-posal" regarding composition labor that is so out of touch with the sta-tistical reality of the composition workplace? This is ultimately not a question of Murphy's individual research but of the warm reception that this proposal-which-is-not-one received by professional composi-tionists (e.g., Joseph Harris, who congratulates Murphy for "doing the numbers," when, at least in this respect, Murphy hasn't done the num-bers at all).

So it is perhaps unsurprising that the readership of the Porter et al. article would need to be encouraged to believe in their own agency in regard to institutional transformation. After more than three decades of casualization, corporatization, and not incidentally disciplinary ad-vances for professional and managerial compositionists, most readers will have understood by now that their track record has everything to do with the *kinds* of change being enacted.[7] A lab for business writing? Sure. Salary, tenure, and research budget for writing program adminis-trators? No problem. A graduate program or certificate in rhet-comp? Go for it. But when it comes to employing the "institutional capital" that comes from overseeing a large, cheap labor force for purposes that run counter to institutional capitalism, such as addressing the scandal-ous working conditions of the labor force itself, the lower-management track record of enacting change is pretty poor. While there is substantial evidence that, even in this early stage of the movement, organized ad-junct faculty and graduate employees have the power to transform their working conditions—get health insurance, job security, the protections of due process, raises of 40 percent or more, and so on, often by acting collectively to change local and national law, struggling successfully with the frequently illegal actions of university management—there is little evidence that lower management has the same power for these kinds of change.[8]

There is an earnest materialism to the pessimistic structure of feeling addressed by the Porter et al. essay. Most professional and managerial compositionists want to do something about the exploitative system of academic labor. However, whether they do so logically, intuitively, or from the experience of essaying numerous "rhetorical strategies" with disappointing results, most also understand that there is little they can do about the labor system, either as individuals or as administrators.

depressing Indeed, perhaps the most important realization of the administrative subjectivity is that having administrative power is to be subject to administrative imperatives—that is, to be individually powerless before a version of "necessity" originating from some other source.

In part, this is the lesson of Annette Kolodny's compelling recent memoir of her deanship at the University of Arizona, a position she correctly dubs "academic middle management." She accepted the job in the belief that one committed administrator, "a feminist committed to both equity and educational excellence," could make the kind of difference that Porter et al. hope for the WPA, serving as "an instrument for progressive evolution." In doing so, she ultimately felt compelled, with many reservations, to employ the wiles of the canny bureaucrat: "If logic and hard data failed me and I thought it would help, I teased, I cajoled, I flirted, I pouted. I bought small gifts for one provost and always remembered the birthday of another" (21). And despite some modest successes, many of them the result of committed overexertion with consequences for her health, ideals, and friendships, she ultimately concludes she'd attempted something that couldn't be done by administrative agency. She devotes the last section of the book to rediscovering *own!* such agents of historical change as unionism and mass political movements—demanding, for example, a more just distribution of material wealth and opportunity.

As Kolodny's experience suggests, university administrators are doubly implicated in the set of transformations dubbed "academic capitalism," being required both to make the university responsive to "exterior market forces" and to actively cultivate "market behavior" in the faculty. In this context, it seems clear that administrators, especially lower administrators, are more—not less—subject to the dictates of academic capitalism than are the faculty. The faculty are at least free to resist marketization, albeit with varying degrees of success, whereas it seems that, at present, the work of academic managers fully overlaps with the project of marketization: there is literally no way to be a manager without feeling the need to adopt and promote market values. The installation of managerialism as the core subjectivity of the discipline of rhetoric and composition is therefore not so much an indicator of the field's success as it is evidence of its particular susceptability—the very terms of its intellectual evolution intertwined with the university's accelerated move toward corporate partnership, executive control, and acceptance of profitability and accumulation as values in decision-making.

The Hidden Idealism of Managerial "Materialism"

> Management theory has become so variegated in recent years that, for
> some, it now constitutes a perfectly viable replacement for old-fash-
> ioned intellectual life. There's so much to choose from! So many deep
> thinkers, so many flashy popularizers, so many schools of thought, so
> many bold predictions, so many controversies!
>
> For all this vast and sparkling intellectual production, though, we
> hear surprisingly little about what it's like to *be managed*. (Frank, *The*
> *God That Sucked*)

One consequence of the materialist self-understanding of the compositionist as a managerial intellectual has been a turn toward pragmatic
philosophies in the rhet-comp discourse. These urge the rhet-comp intellectual to acknowledge "complicity" and adopt the posture of a "canny
bureaucrat" (Miller, "Arts of Complicity"). Collapsing critical theory
and cultural studies into classroom manifestations, this standpoint tends
to characterize critical theory in crude terms (i.e., as the dosing of students with outmoded lefty truisms).

Its primary tactic is to attempt to turn the critique of enlightenment
theories of knowledge against its authors in critical theory, cultural
studies, and radical pedagogy. For instance, Freirean pedagogues elaborating a critique of the banking theory of knowledge are represented (or
misrepresented) by the pragmatist movement as themselves attempting
to deposit "out-of-date" anti-capitalisms in the helpless student brain.
For these pragmatists, the ideals of critical pedagogy are part of the
problem, insofar as these idealisms are inevitably out of touch with fundamental "realities" of the corporate university. Ultimately, this would-
be debunking of critical theory and cultural studies has acquired no
traction outside the field of rhetoric and composition. It probably offers
little of enduring interest within the field beyond the useful but unremarkable observations that classroom activities are an insufficient lever
for social change, and that it is possible for teachers to deploy radical
pedagogy in dominative ways. This last observation is indeed useful—
far too many teachers, just as Richard Miller suggests, adopt radical
pedagogy because it can be made to cover over our complicity with
domination, but in my view this usefulness hardly adds up to a convincing argument that the only remaining option is for teachers to adopt
a pedagogy that is overtly complicit with domination, or in Miller's

words, to "strategically deploy the thoughts and ideas of the corporate world" (" 'Let's Do the Numbers,' " 98).

Interestingly, this pragmatic movement has managed to conceal its own hidden idealism—its less than critical adherence to what Thomas Frank dubs the "market god" and its concomitant elevation of corporate management to a priestly class. By concealing its own market idealism underneath a rhetoric of exclusive purchase on "reality," pragmatist ideologues have had a fair amount of success at discouraging the effort to realize any *other* ideals than those of the market. (This is the imposition of what Fredric Jameson calls "the Reagan-Kemp and Thatcher utopias" and what David Harvey calls a "political correctness of the market.") Among the many useful observations of the critical tradition is that, despite the fantasies of those Marx loved to call the "vulgar political economists," markets don't exist transhistorically; they have "reality" to the extent that they are installed and maintained by human agents devoted to achieving particular market ideals. In contrast, pragmatist idealizations of the market conceal the human agency in the creation and maintenance of markets—what Sheila Slaughter and Larry Leslie describe as the conscious and deliberate "marketizing" of higher education in the United States and globally since the Nixon administration. Brought about not by necessity but by the planned and intentional defunding of public institutions, together with a corresponding diversion of public funds to private ventures ("corporate welfare"), market ideals were energetically wrestled into reality by embodied agents with political and economic force, in the process rolling back alternative ideals that themselves had been realized in law and policy by collective social action throughout the twentieth century (hence "neo"-liberalism, referring to the reinstallation of nineteenth-century laissez-faire or "liberal" economic policies).

Changing the managed university (and the "politics of work" therein) requires understanding that the "market fundamentalism" current among university managers has no more purchase on what is and what should be than any other system of foundational belief. Understood as a humanly engineered historical emergence of the past three decades, the "managed university" names a global phenomenon: the forced privatization of public higher education; the erosion of faculty, student, and citizen participation in higher education policy, except through academic-capitalist and consumer practices; the steady conversion of socially beneficial activities (cultivation of a knowledge commons, development of a democratic citizenry fit to govern itself) to the commodity form—the sale of information goods, such as patents and corporate-sponsored research, and the production of a job-ready workforce (Rhoades and Slaughter; Slaughter and Leslie; Martin, "Stat(e)ing the Obvious"). As Randy Martin makes clear, these circumstances are not brought about in the North American and European context because the state has "withdrawn" from higher education but because it "invests itself" ever more aggressively "in promoting an alignment of human initiative with business interest" ("Education as National Pedagogy," 7). Globally, the International Monetary Fund and the World Bank have actively promoted a similar reform agenda with respect to higher education. Using their power to impose involuntary privatization on national higher education systems, especially in Africa, they require tuition fees and effectively are "recolonizing" cultural and intellectual life throughout the global south, as their direct policy intervention, combined with neoliberal "constraints," caused universities to "substitute new staff, standardize pedagogical materials and marginalize local knowledges" (Levidow, para. 24–36).[9]

In all of these and most responsible materialist accounts, human agency drives history. But in the pragmatist-managerial version of materialism, collective human agencies are conspicuously absent. Even the agency of individuals is radically evacuated: for pragmatists, "markets" are real agents and people generally are not, except in their acquiescence to market dicta. Richard Miller, for example, writes, "the truth is that the question of who's qualified to teach first-year writing was settled long ago by the market" (" 'Let's Do the Numbers,' " 99). In a world of systems "governed" by the "arbitary," the "only possible" human agency becomes something like flexible self-specialization, the continuous retooling of self in response to market "demands," a subjectivity that Richard Sennett observes is just as unsatisfying a "corrosion of character" for those who win the market game as those who lose. In this view, persons can only be agents by adopting the arts of corporate domination and by fitting themselves to the demands of the market, "working within a system governed by shifting and arbitrary requirements" (Miller, "Arts of Complicity," 26). Representing corporate domination as a fact of life, this brand of pragmatism ultimately conceals a historically specific ideological orientation (neoliberalism) behind an aggressive redescription of "reality," in which "left-wing" bogeymen are sometimes raised as the threats to human agency—for example, Kurt

Spellmeyer's red-baiting review of *Left Margins*—when the real threat to human agency is the corporate-bureaucratic limits to human possibility established by the pragmatists themselves. The pragmatist turn has left its trace nearly everywhere in the composition discourse. Even while attempting to resuscitate the commitment to social transformation, following the lead of Marxist geographer David Harvey, Porter et al., for example, hold up the image of "academics railing at monopoly capitalism" as the straw man of "ineffectual" critique. Rather ironically for adherents of Harvey, they thereby reinscribe capitalist exploitation as the outer limit of change (and leave one wondering exactly how it is possible to read Harvey and not see a member of the academy railing at capitalist exploitation and attempting to map its exterior).

What most troubles me about the pragmatist movement is the way it seeks to curb the ambitions of our speech and rhetoric. In the pragmatist account, contemporary realities dictate that all nonmarket idealisms will be "dismissed as the plaintive bleating of sheep," but corporate-friendly speech "can be heard as reasoned arguments" (Miller, "Arts of Complicity," 27). I find this language intrinsically offensive, associating movement idealism and social-project identities and activist collectivity generally with the subhuman, rather than (as I see it) the fundamentally human capacity to think and act cooperatively. More important than the adjectives and analogies, however, is the substructure of assumptions about what rhetoric is for. The implicit scene of speech suggested here is of "pleasing the prince," featuring an all-powerful auditor with values beyond challenge and a speaker who is only able to share power by association with the dominating logic of the scene—a speaker whose very humanity depends on speaking a complicity with domination. As a cultural-studies scholar, I respect the lived realities of subjectivity under domination and thoroughly understand the need for frequent speech acts of "complicity." However, this does not suggest for me that this scene offers the central topos constitutive of human agency, or that the prince—however powerful—should be the object of our rhetoric.

Most astonishing about the recent success of claims that the logic and rhetoric of solidarity or justice "cannot be heard" is that these claims are so patently false, as a matter both of history and of contemporary reality. What do claims like these make of the achieved historical transformation associated with groups united by the idealism and critical imagination of rhetors such as Emma Goldman, W. E. B. DuBois, Eugene Debs, and Nelson Mandela? What of the gains of democratic revolutions after 1750? Or the nineteenth-century gains of abolition, decolonization, feminism, communism, and trades-unionism? Were any of these gains, together with the gains of the social movements after 1960, achieved by the sort of recognition of "institutional constraints" advocated by the pragmatists? And in the contemporary frame, despite the great success of corporate management at disorganizing labor, are the still-organized (and newly organized) voices of labor really "dismissed as the plaintive bleating of sheep" by management at Ford or in the California state universities? Hardly. The millions of dollars and dozens of managerial careers openly devoted to the perpetual struggle to contain and divide labor at both places suggests the magnitude of the power they are attempting to defuse. For example, the graduate employee union at the University of Michigan calculated that the annual salaries of the university's full-time bargaining team—$630,000—amounted to only slightly less than the cost of the contract improvements that the union was seeking: $700,000 per year. Likewise, are the nonprofit values of social entitlement, dignity, and equality advocated by the organized voices of the American Association of Retired Persons, the National Association for the Advancement of Colored People, and the National Organization of Women similarly "dismissed" by Washington bureaucrats? Not really.

So what should we make of a discourse that pretends that the organized voice of persons seeking social justice is impractical and sheeplike, and that agency is primarily possible in adopting a bureaucratic persona? In my view, we should call it a management discourse, of the sort that Thomas Frank barely exaggerates in suggesting threatens to take the place of intellectual life altogether. In holding our gaze on the managerialism of the composition discourse, we ultimately need to ask, *cui bono*? Who benefits? Despite its rhetoric of "student need" and "customer service," is the university of job-readiness really good for students? If it's designed to serve student needs, then why do so many students drop out in the first year and fail to graduate? If it's more efficient to reduce education to vocation, then why does it cost more and more money to go to college (certainly the salary costs for instruction aren't the reason)—exactly who receives the economic benefits (if any) of lowered salaries, reduced services, and lowered expectations? Why are so many young people underemployed if they are being increasingly well trained for corporate life? Or, as in David Brodsky's account, does the managed university primarily serve the interests of "the nomadic managerial hordes" that have "torn up the social contract" to govern in their own interest? It is not only adjunct faculty like Brodsky who suggest that the liberated self-interest of university management may not fully coincide with the interests of society. In an opinion piece excoriating the "dumbing down" of university leadership as a result of the ascent of managerialism and the market ethos, one university president observes that the "peripatetic" class of candidates for top administration "are more interested in landing better jobs than contributing to higher education" (Lovett).

In seeking to "transform institutions," then, the discourse of rhetoric and composition might share the skepticism of adjuncts like Brodsky at the claims of management discourse to deliver democratic outcomes through corporate processes and to promote change for the many by liberating the self-interest of a few. At its best, the managerial discourse in composition has an earnest commitment to bettering the circumstances of embodied composition labor and a real enthusiasm for a better world. Nonetheless, it has yet to acknowledge the limits presented by its failure to confront, in Thomas Frank's words, "what it's like to be managed."

Toward "A New Class Consciousness in Composition": *Writing without a WPA*

> The only worker who is productive is one who is productive *for capital*. [A] schoolmaster is productive when, in addition to belaboring the heads of his pupils, he works himself into the ground in order to enrich the owner of the school. That the latter has laid out his capital in a teaching factory, instead of a sausage factory, makes no difference to the relation. . . .
>
> To be a productive worker is therefore not a piece of luck, but a misfortune. (Marx, *Capital*, vol. 1, ch. 16)

At the beginning of this chapter, I suggested a willingness to make common cause with the administrative subject targeted by Porter et al. (because managers are workers, too). In closing, I'd like to expand on that willingness briefly, in connection with Joseph Harris's call for a "new class consciousness" in composition.

By a "new" class consciousness, Harris means "one that joins the in-

terests of bosses and workers around the issue of good teaching for fair
pay" (45). Living in a "right to work" state at the time, I have to say
that my first reading of this evidently sincere rubric literally gave me a
chill. At its most disturbing, this is Toyotist rhetoric clothed in academic
Marxism, grafting the total-quality "team" of management and labor
onto disciplinary identity, borrowing the term "class consciousness" to
add an aura of legitimacy to the plan. As in all Toyotist versions of an
"identity of interest" between management and labor, this plan simply
consolidates managerial control. Harris continues:

> What the director of a writing program wants is to be able to interview,
> hire, and train a teaching staff, to fire teachers who don't work out, to
> establish curriculum, to set policies and to represent the program as he
> or she sees best. What teachers want are reasonable salaries, benefits,
> working conditions, and job security; autonomy over their work; and to
> be treated with respect as colleagues. (57)

Leaving aside the question of whether this managerial portrait genuinely represents either "class consciousness" or "what teachers want," I
have to wonder by what mechanism would we adjudicate the conflicts
that inhere even in this rosy representation? That is: How does the
WPA's right to establish curriculum and set policies square with the
teachers' right to autonomy over their work? Who defines teaching that
doesn't "work out"? Why should it be the WPA and not other teachers,
as in other disciplines?

   To anyone familiar with labor history, this rhetoric isn't "new" at all
but sounds exactly like the old "partnership between labor and capital"
rhetoric of nineteenth-century anti-unionism, inked most famously by
the dean of American poltical cartoonists, Thomas Nast. In his most fa-
mous images on the theme, Nast opposed both organized (or "monopoly") capital and organized labor and insisted on a community of interest between the two. For instance, in a *Harper's Weekly* cartoon of November 23, 1878, he shows a smith using a hammer labeled "Labor" to
forge another hammerhead labeled "Capital" under the didactic headline: "One and Inseparable: Capital Makes Labor and Labor Makes
Capital." In the cartoon labeled "The American Twins" reproduced
here, Nash shows a worker and a top-hatted capitalist "boss" as Sia-
mese twins, joined at the hip. Under the rubric "The *Real* Union," the
reader is invited to see labor's interests as harmonizing with the "boss"

LABOR & CAPITAL

THE AMERICAN TWINS.
" United we stand, Divided we fall."

on exactly the sort of principle that Harris suggests ("good [work] for fair pay") rather than in collective bargaining.

Fortunately for the rest of us, the nineteenth-century labor movement rejected this rhetoric and worked in solidarity to establish the eight-hour day, reductions in the exploitation of youth and student labor, a more just wage, health benefits, released time for education and recreation, a safer workplace, and more. And the contemporary labor movement in the academy will reject Harris's rhetoric as well, in part because so many of these nineteenth-century demands are once again relevant and in part because it is in their power (and not lower management's) to accomplish these things.

What a large sector of composition labor (graduate employees and former graduate employees working off the tenure track) "really wants," is not to be "*treated . . . as* colleagues," but instead to *be* colleagues.

Nearly every participant in the composition conversation would like to see writing instructors become "more like" faculty—to have the chance to govern, enjoy an intellectual life and develop as an instructor, as well as enjoy better pay, benefits, protections, and security. But this hasn't translated into a consensus among professional and managerial compositionists that writing instructors should actually *be* faculty. Why not? Isn't composition work faculty work? Or is composition's "faculty work" the supervision of parafaculty? Harris's vision for "our joined interests as composition workers and bosses" appears really to mean accomplishing the disciplinary and managerial agenda of "more direct control over our curricula and staffing—within departments of English, or, if need be, outside them" (57–58).

It is hard to see how composition *labor* can have "more direct control" over "our" staffing without transcending the evasions of "as" and actually becoming colleagues who participate in a hiring and tenuring process, just "as" the faculty do. So, unsurprisingly, nowhere in the actually existing academic labor movement over the past century has anyone discovered that what academic labor really needs is for lower-level management to have more direct control of curricula and staffing (or to have the chance to set up new departments for disciplines that don't envision tenure for their workforce!). Somewhat predictably, this managerial plan for labor dignity is accompanied by digs at the Conference on College Composition and Communication statements on academic labor for the organization's "uncritical embrace of the tenure system as a guarantor of good teaching" (55).

OH! ok.

On what basis might a real class consciousness in composition unfold? One clear way to promote a genuine community of interest is in the mold of social-movement unionism, currently being practiced in a number of places in the academy, widespread in public-employee unionism more generally, and very significant in organizing efforts targeting the service economy. As explored by Chris Carter, academic movement unionism relates the public interest to the interest of the organized academic employee. As with public employees, many professionals, and the culture industry, the work of educators is the "production of society itself." (A position that can be found more theoretically elaborated in the tradition of Italian autonomist Marxism—for example, by Paolo Virno —but perhaps even more relevantly for the feminized labor of composition in the feminist political economy of Selma James and Maria Dalla Costa.) The "movement" union becomes a nexus for multiple struggles to converge and articulate an identity of interest in the project of transformation—a nexus of real-world agency through which organized humanity can once again see itself as the engine of history. The consciousness of class would invoke an identity of interests based not on workplace disciplines—"Oncologists unite!"—but on the common

258

not sure that this would work experience of selling one's labor in order to live, as well as on the wide-spread desire in the academy and in many sectors of service work to be productive for society rather than for capital.

But how could professional and managerial compositionists participate in this class consciousness or project identity? Certainly not as "managers" seeking "more direct control" of staff and curricula. Nevertheless, just as it is sometimes possible for deans and presidents to shed the administrative subjectivity and return to the labor of the professoriate, perhaps the professional and managerial compositionist can likewise shed the desire for control and embrace the reality of collective agency. Are we so sure after all that what the professional compositionist really wants is more control over people she must creatively treat "as" colleagues? Perhaps what the professional compositionist really wants is to lay down the requirement to serve as a WPA and to become a colleague among colleagues. Harris himself repeatedly identifies himself as a "worker" in a "collective educational project" and (unlike most contributors to the managerialist discourse) makes a point of endorsing collective bargaining and underlines the "structural and economic" nature of the problems we face. If we remove the taint of the pragmatist—the limits to the possible imposed by the intellectual-bureaucrat—we find in Harris's "boss" a worker struggling to make himself available to the rhetoric and social project of solidarity.

Ultimately, the efforts of Harris and Porter et al. are important not for their various complicities but for their genuine attempt to explore "a level of institutional critique . . . that we are not used to enacting in rhetoric and composition," including changing law and public policy. Nonetheless, since these are areas in which organized academic labor has been struggling, often effectively, for decades, Porter et al.'s statement that "we" are unused to acting in those arenas is false to an important extent. Indeed, any version of "us" that includes graduate-employee and contingent labor organizations would have to acknowledge that "we" are very much used to struggling at law with the university employer, and in the arena of policy with legislatures, labor policy boards, community groups, and the media. Which means that if "institutional critique" is the answer to the pessimistic structure of feeling that presently characterizes professional and managerial compositionists, it is a kind of critique that the professionals and managers will have to learn from the workers in their charge. In order to realize the scene of lower management learning to practice "institutional critique" and

They (WPAs) don't
have to "learn" this - Most of them
they already know it.

the "arts of solidarity" from labor, we will eventually have to reconsider the limits to thought imposed by pragmatism and learn once again to question the "inevitability" of the scene of managed labor to composition. In my view, composition's best chance to contribute to a better world and to achieve "disciplinary status" depends on learning to write as colleagues among colleagues—a condition predicated on working toward a university without a WPA.

The Rhetoric of "Job Market" and the Reality of the Academic Labor System

> The overall balance between supply and demand in academic labor markets will shift markedly, we believe, over the next few decades. The most dramatic changes will occur in the 1997–2002 period, when we project a *substantial* excess demand for faculty in the arts and sciences. If present trends persist, we would expect that there would be roughly four candidates for every five positions—a condition that could continue in subsequent years unless significant adjustments occur or policy changes occur. Although we project no comparable imbalance during the 1987–1992 period, we do expect some appreciable tightening of the academic labor markets to begin as early as 1992–1997.
> —William G. Bowen and Julie Ann Sosa, *Prospects for Faculty,* 1989 (emphasis in the original)

Given the dramatic and startling nature of its conclusions (that faculty jobs would soon appear like manna in the desert), and its origin in an unusual collaboration between a sitting university president (William Bowen) and an undergraduate student (Julie Ann Sosa, then the editor of the Princeton student newspaper), it's more than a little surprising that almost no one seems to have questioned the Bowen study before a 1994 blurb in the *Chronicle of Higher Education*—with the interesting exception of Lynne Cheney, who wrote an editorial for the *New York Times* assailing the assumptions that guided the Bowen study. Even after the report's projections proved wildly erroneous, few have troubled to analyze how those errors came about. Without anywhere confronting the organization's own history of enthusiasm for the

Bowen projections, the 1997 *Final Report of the MLA Committee on Professional Employment* (CPE) simply excludes the item from its bibliography. One goal of this chapter is to specify some of the failings of the study and to assess the causes and consequences of its startlingly uncritical reception in the academic community.[1]

It is also my hope to avoid scapegoating the Bowen project, which didn't create the conditions of its own reception. In understanding how the Bowen report succeeded with its audience of faculty and graduate students in the humanities, we may be able to move toward the more important understanding of the extent to which the flawed assumptions of the report are to an equal extent the flawed assumptions of its audience. That is, no one thought to treat Bowen's very surprising projections critically because, in creating them, Bowen simply applied the overwhelmingly dominant logic of the time.

For instance, if—as I argue here—the Bowen report erred by imposing market ideology on data about the structure and relations of academic labor, the uncritical reception of that error from 1989 through the present suggests a strong desire by faculty and many graduate students to believe that their work is indeed shaped by market logic. So a large part of this chapter is concerned with trying to explain how the idea of a "job market" came to acquire so much reality to so many members of the academy. If it's not a job market, why do we call it one anyway?

One way of describing the recent movement of thought about the academic labor system is as a series of waves. A "first wave" of labor consciousness emerged before 1970, propelling the self-organization of the academic workforce, especially in public institutions, where more than half the faculty are unionized. This labor awareness was contested by the administratively oriented second wave (of which Bowen's job-market study is emblematic), generally informed by a neoliberal ideology that idealizes market epistemology and naturalizes market relationships. Sweeping to dominance about 1980, this wave has the virtue of focusing on the connection of graduate education to the larger system of academic work (which the unions have been slow to do). In characterizing that connection primarily as a market relationship, administrative knowledge has been strongly contested by a third wave of knowledge produced by what is in North America a fifty-campus movement of graduate-employee unionists, or GEU (Coalition of Graduate Employee Unions). While far from dominant, the knowledge of the GEU movement is sharply ascendant in recent years, to the point where one *Chronicle of Higher Education* article on the graduate-employee coalition dubbed 2001 the year of the graduate student employee (Smallwood).

In this chapter, I explore the emergence of job-market theory in the discourse of academic professional associations. This was just one aspect of the market knowledge of the administrative second wave. For those of us in the humanities, market language gives the impression that we have collectively decided to put aside the playfulness of our cultural activities when talking about something as important as the situation that we also name the "job crisis."

The rhetorical richness of this market language has had a profound effect on how we think about graduate education. In particular, the rhetoric elaborating the market-crisis point of view sustains a general consensus that the system of graduate education is producing more degree holders than necessary and that this "overproduction" can be controlled "from the supply side" by reducing admissions to graduate programs.

This common sense is deeply flawed, to the point where I think we have to acknowledge that "market knowledge" is a rhetoric of the labor system and not a description of it. Because the incoming flow of graduate students is generally tightly controlled to produce "just enough" labor, graduate departments really can't reduce admissions without making other arrangements for the work that the graduate students would have done. Since the restoration of tenure-stream lines is rarely a department-level prerogative, a department with the power to reduce graduate-student admissions will generally be driven to substitute other casual appointments (postdocs, term lectureships, single-course piece workers). In terms of casualization, there is clearly no net improvement from this "supply-side" fix. Indeed, these other modes of casualized work are filled by persons who are themselves enmeshed in the system of graduate study. The system will continue to require "just enough" of these other term workers, all of whom will have had some experience of graduate education.[2]

This supply-side fantasy supports the most pernicious armchair activism of them all, persistently circulating the notion that graduate faculty can balance "the market" from the conference table at which they discuss the dossiers of applicants to their programs. On the one hand, of course, it is reasonable to imagine that reversing thirty years of casualization (i.e., by recovering jobs) will result in a reduced need for graduate students to do flexible labor. This could eventually reduce the graduate student population. On the other hand, however, it simply does not follow that reducing the graduate student population will alter the labor system. (This is like arguing that blowing smoke up a tailpipe makes a car run backward.) To a certain extent, the fantasy of supply-side control reflects the depoliticization and privatization of the professoriate: the desire to "be ethical" without having to enact a politics, to solve the problem with better management rather than struggle in solidarity with other persons who work.

Ultimately, the notion that the employment system can be controlled by the administration of graduate programs (i.e., by reducing Ph.D. "production") has to be seen as profoundly ideological. Even where there is a vigorous effort to diagnose the nature of the labor system, the ideology of the market returns to frame the solution, blocking the transformative potential of analysis that otherwise demonstrates the necessity of nonmarket responses. Encapsulating his own arguments on "Literary Study in the Transnational University," J. Hillis Miller enumerates "worldwide changes" that frame the material base of casualization, including the end of the cold war, the globalization of economies and media, and the conversion of the research university to a technological service mission, as well as the "concrete, material changes" of corporatization: defunding, growing class size, threats to tenure, the conversion to part-time faculty, underemployment of degree holders, and the commercialization of knowledge. And yet after providing a sweeping analysis uniting transformations in university work to structural realities on the global and continental scale, Miller has nothing more to offer in terms of a solution than the supply-side fantasy of clean hands: "It is not clear to me that it is ethically justifiable to go on producing new PhDs if there are not going to be jobs for them" ("Reply," 234).

Miller sees—he *knows*—that the problem is casualization, that graduate students and former grad students are flex labor, and that there are always "just enough" of them. And yet he retreats from the standpoint of globalization studies to speak in the folksy tones of the foreman at the plant when framing his solution: Well, I guess we better hold up the line and slow the production, boys; "demand" for our "product" is down. There is a steep-walled canyon between the analysis and the action plan that is not specific to Miller but, instead, is nearly uniform across the profession, which is reluctant to see the political nature of the struggle with casualization.[3] Insofar as the Fordist ideology of production and the neoliberal ideology of "markets in balance" provide false solutions to the post-Fordist academic economy, they help that post-Fordism along.

The Fordism of the discourse surrounding graduate education is a nearly unchanged survival of the dominant interpretive frame established between 1968 and 1970, when a freight train of scholarship decrying a cold-war "shortage" of degree holders suddenly reversed itself in attempting to account for a Vietnam-era "surplus." In what follows, I focus primarily on the development over time of the state-of-the-profession discourse of one organization, the Modern Language Association. MLA-centered communication does not fully encompass the discourse even of its "own" discipline, but there is remarkably little difference in the analytical frames employed by the various fields of study across disciplines: most appear to employ the market heuristic.[4] (If anything, the "hard sciences" appear more addicted to the ideological introjection of market values, perhaps because they are often less inclined to address casualization as a structural issue.) In addition, the MLA discourse appears to have influenced other humanities scholarship on employment issues and has been widely acknowledged by the mainstream press as authoritative on these questions. Featuring labor-intensive classes that often serve as university-wide requirements (writing, second-language acquisition, introductory cultural surveys), language departments have long been at the leading edge of casualization, together with mathematics and other humanities disciplines that provide general education. It is probably as a result of this early and extended experience of casualization that language and cultural-studies faculty are among the most visible authorities on the question. (Or, perhaps it is only because so many journalists have studied in English departments.) While there is unevenness in academic casualization, there are systematic consistencies across disciplines as well: in science and engineering, casual postdoctoral employment can last ten years before a full-time apppointment is secured (Regets). In any event, the MLA discourse does appear to fairly emblematize the general state of disciplinary discourse on higher ed workplace issues.

For language faculty, the Fordist rhetoric employed after World War II reached its peak in Don Cameron Allen's 1968 volume, financed by the MLA and the Danforth Foundation, *The Ph.D. in English and American Literature*. This was a book so overtaken by events that it was out of date at the moment it appeared in print. The 1968 and 1969 MLA conventions were turbulent for a number of reasons, including the sense by job seekers that for the first time in years there weren't enough jobs to go around, yet Allen's study was a mammoth survey of ways to increase the "production" of graduate schools. His proposals included abbreviated requirements and shorter dissertations, more funding and better advisement, the expansion of existing programs, and the development of new programs. Begun earlier in the 1960s, Allen's study responded to what he characterizes as nearly eight decades of "chronic shortage" of "trained English teachers" in higher education, from the 1890s to the "acute shortage" after 1950: "In fact, it was only in the unhappy period between 1931 and 1940 that there was any reasonable relationship between what was wanted and what was to be had" (16). For Allen and most others of his generation, a shortage of trained English teachers translated directly into a "scarcity of Ph.D.'s" in the field (84). While Allen also extensively discussed the viability of credentialing less arduous teaching-track degrees, the goal in increasing the "productivity" of graduate programs was to place degreed persons in jobs (rather than to substitute student labor for teacher labor).

For Allen, the application of Fordist rhetoric to graduate education still had the character of analogy. After surveying the number of degrees granted by the eighty-eight doctoral programs in English operating in 1965, Allen wrote, "It is as clear as a manufacturer's annual report that not all the plants are in full production" (22). How to fix this problem? Because "industrial production is increased by building more plants" and "streamlined production," the same might be true for graduate schools, so he recommended opening new graduate programs and shortening time to degree at existing programs to the four years recommended earlier by the Ford and Danforth Foundations (18, 30). The reform of graduate education takes the form of a modernization process, leading to a system that is "more rational, more attuned to our century and its demands" (89). While the language of industrial production in graduate education occurred as early as 1925 (Berelson, 29), it became widespread after the war in foundation-funded work like Bernard Berelson's 1960 Carnegie study, *Graduate Education in the United States*, which served up an institutional history of graduate education leading to an exposition of the crisis represented by the cold-war demand for "the doctoral product" (219), while strategizing means of supplying it. Most of Allen's 1968 recommendations to his disciplinary audience follow the general outlines laid out in Berelson's work, begun in 1957, the year Sputnik was launched.

Even at the time, this Fordist language was not adequate to the task of describing the structural transformation of the university, which was already beginning to disarticulate from the nation-state and retool itself into the transnational bureaucratic corporation described by Bill Readings. (Continuing the process observed by Clyde Barrow of the university's adopting a "corporate ideal" in the first decades of the twentieth century.) But Fordism provided an exceptionally powerful set of heuristics, values, and legitimations for the cold war expansion of what the era's ideologues were proud to call the "knowledge industry." Many more "plants" were built, a lot more doctoral product was moved, and "knowledge production" was enormously enlarged.

In other words, as long as demand for the doctoral product remained apparently limitless, Fordism was good knowledge, or at least it made sense. But between 1968 and 1970, the good knowledge of the cold war rapidly became the bad knowledge of retrenchment and casualization.

Initially, the term "job market" described an annual face-to-face event at the MLA convention, and not an ongoing systemic reality (as in "the market is really bad this year"). Inaugurated in 1955, the "Job Mart" (formally named the "Faculty Exchange") represented a modernization and rationalization of the hiring process that up to then had been conducted by the old-boy network. This was a two-room system. In one room, the association collected the dossiers of all job seekers for department chairs to peruse. In another room, job seekers waited for messages from chairpersons requesting interviews. This Job Mart operated a great deal like a face-to-face labor market in which persons certified to do higher education faculty work actually gathered in a room (somewhere between a marketplace and a shape-up hall) to "sell their labor." The system was not replaced until after 1969, when it "broke down" because the problem "was now one of locating jobs rather than candidates." At this point, the association dismantled the Job Mart and initiated the Job Information Service, which ceased to collect candidate dossiers and began to publish job listings (Association of Departments of English, i-ii).

To this moment, the 1971 inauguration of the Job Information Service, we can trace the first stroke of what I think we can accurately call the informationalization of the MLA. The job market was no longer the humble "mart," an event arranged by the association. Instead, it had become an external system or force that the association was obliged to provide information about: "The one thing needful—the one thing the profession has never had but which MLA is uniquely qualified to provide—is complete and detailed information on the job market at regular intervals throughout the year" (association officer William Schaefer, quoted in Association of Departments of English, ii). Not incidental to the emergence of this new "informational" mission is the pressure exerted by members of the association affiliated with the antiwar and other social movements for the association to figure as an instrument of social agency (which had resulted in, among other things, a successful effort by Paul Lauter and others to elect Louis Kampf to the presidency of the association in 1968).[5] Implicit in the informational mission was the disavowal of responsibility for making things happen; instead, the task is to describe, forecast, and advise—ideally, in exchange for a fee.

A key component of the informationalization process was the literalization of the market analogy, so that the market became something that needed to be reported on continuously (at "regular intervals throughout the year") and that such reporting could be construed as a useful contribution. At the 1969 meeting, the MLA voted to create a Job Market Study Commission, charged primarily with two responsibilities: "(1) examining the procedures of the Association as they have historically affected the market" and "(2) studying the operation of the market itself within the larger economic context" (Orr, 1185). The framing of these tasks clearly identifies "the market" as something external to the profession (and its association), something with an internal essence ("the market itself") unfolding in continuous and uniform time, embedded in an impersonal "larger economic context." No longer merely an analogy, the concept of job market now has empirical reality for humanities faculty and evidently borrows some of the aura and aspirations—the realpolitik and econometrics—of labor-market analysis, such as the 1969 Cartter study, "Academic Labor Market Projections and the Draft," designed to assure the wartime Congress that it could expect a comfortable "oversupply" of higher education faculty despite the prospect of expanded compulsory military service. The 1970 Orr report, "The Job Market in English and Foreign Languages," crystallized the terms of analysis that would be applied to what was then called retrenchment and which we now understand as casualization: the one-year drop in job availability was "but the first massive indication that supply and demand in these fields are seriously out of balance" (Orr,

1186). By 1971, a major "labor market" study in the sciences was in print, followed by Cartter's 1976 book. The notions of "Ph.D. oversupply," the fantasy of supply-side control, and the application of a "labor market" heuristic to professional work appeared to be instrinsically related. While the market analogy made the most sense from the perspective of the "buyer" in a "buyer's market"—that is, from the perspective of employers, such as industry, the state, and professional academic management—it made less sense from the point of view of the professional worker, who traditionally seeks collegial participation in determining the size, compensation, and composition of the workforce, including control of the terms under which apprentice professionals can be expected to serve. Rather than leave these considerations to a "market," professionals have tended to exert influence on at least a national scale by way of professional associations (which explains in part the degree to which many faculty seek the leadership of organizations like the MLA in these matters, perhaps even more than their union locals). In this context, the adoption by various disciplinary associations of the new "informational" mission needs to be seen as intrinsic to a neoliberal transformation, specifically underwriting knowledge of "the market" *against* the labor knowledge of structure and labor's consciousness of itself as a collective agent in the workplace and in the arenas of law, politics, and "the economy."

While both Berelson and Allen use the notion of "demand for faculty" and rely on graduate education as the supply of "product," both are much more invested in the Fordist production analogy than in the neoliberal language of "market." Berelson and Allen are concerned to describe things that the profession can do to "meet demand"—that is, produce more. When the question is of enlarging graduate education, the profession is willing to see itself as an agent. But when the situation is that of candidates unable to find employment, the profession is more concerned to describe the things it can't do. The literalization of "the market" has the effect of legitimating the passive, observational role of the informant; now the profession is a victim of forces beyond its control. The Orr report, for instance, cites "a number of economic and cultural trends [that] are finally reaching a dangerous convergence" (1185); "pressures upon us . . . national if not global in scope," the "limit to what the public will pay for [our] product," (1186), and so forth. The past thirty years of official "analysis" from disciplinary associations and foundations has for the most part simply replayed these chords—of trends, pressures, limits, and forces—all evidently transpiring in a field of titans, beyond the possibility of faculty contestation. The field of titans point of view leads to the dissemination of discursive constructions like the "lifeboat" analogy that is frequent in autobiographical and historiographic narratives of the profession. In lifeboat narratives, the era of "well-paid and secure" academic jobs figures as a historical accident (a peculiarity, brought about as a by-product of military-industrial expansion, or an unexpected historical gift dropped in the lap of a single cohort of the professoriate). From this perspective, succeeding generations are represented as, more naturally, drowning in the tide of history. Of course, the young "very much want, often desperately, to be let in, to climb aboard" (Tave, 7), but who can stem the tide?

The ideological content of the Orr report and its successors is exactly its tendency to represent limits and forces as beyond contestation. But in foreclosing the possibility of action at the level of structure, the market analogy also offers new fantasies of action, especially in relation to the concept of supply. One of the key contributions of the market heuristic to the Orr report and its successors is the problematization of the concept of supply, as in the now-familiar formulation that graduate programs are "turning out too many Ph.D.'s and M.A.'s for the market," that there is a state of "Ph.D. overproduction," leading to a Ph.D. "oversupply" (1190). While Hillis Miller's 1997 analysis almost exactly replicates Orr's 1970 formulation, Berelson and Allen in 1960 and 1968 rely on a different heuristic, largely innocent of the concepts of both market and supply. Berelson and Allen don't need the idea of "the market" because they don't need to fantasize an elastic relationship between demand and supply such that controlling the "supply" represents an action affecting the whole system. For Orr, the problematizing of the concept of supply is a real intellectual convenience, because it both (a) offers the fantasy of doing something to "the market" (i.e., balancing it) by "controlling" or "regulating" supply (1186, 1191), and (b) diverts attention from the real problems of "demand" (i.e., the willingness of administrations to use nondegreed flexible labor instead of degreed persons in jobs). Orr and his successors need "the market" to legitimate the fantasy of a supply-side fix, a fantasy that averts the consciousness of political struggle that would quickly transpire if the concept of "demand" were problematized.

Job-Market Theory as Second-Wave Knowledge

One might expect that from the perspective of forty years we would have a clearer view of casualization—that our understanding has gotten better and better, and that we are smarter than a naïve earlier generation. Unfortunately, this does not appear to be the case. Orr's 1970 report, while it does enthusiastically embrace the market heuristic and the new fantasy of supply-side influence, also provides a trenchant description of managerialism and casualization. Orr is perfectly aware that increased education work does not translate directly into increased professorial jobs, because "American society" is willing to accept colleges "staffed largely by persons trained differently from traditional professors" (1188). He is equally aware that the university has "welcomed new Ph.D. candidates with eagerness," not only to meet the "national emergency" of the cold war, "but also for another reason." This other reason? It doesn't seem to make any difference to them

> whether most freshmen and many sophomore courses in many areas, particularly English and foreign languages, are taught by experienced Ph.D.'s, by new M.A.'s, or by those even less qualified. Since B.A. graduate students or M.A.'s working toward the Ph.D. can be had at a lower cost per class than established professors, administrations have not overlooked the opportunity that presented itself. . . . Somewhat the same forces operated . . . in the many institutions which suddenly began to offer the M.A. (1190)

None of Orr's numerous suggestions for professional action actually address this process of substituting student labor for teacher labor, blaming impersonal "economic factors" and "certain forces" that "have caused" universities "to rely more heavily than before on Ph.D. candidates" to teach lower-division classes (1191), nor does he seem to care about lower-division teaching ("perhaps it really doesn't matter," he says). Nonetheless, he is very much aware of the extent and urgency of the casualization process, observing that an unnamed midwestern school, completely without doctoral instruction in 1955, by 1970 employed five graduate student teachers for each full-time teacher. He goes on to observe, complete with exclamation point, that at one "established school," the ratio of graduate employees to full-time faculty was 30 to 1. However appealing it found the market heuristic, Orr's report took it for granted that "the market" was merely one of many lenses for approaching graduate education.

Throughout the 1970s, there is a first wave of knowledge about the profession, supported in large part by active faculty unionism and movement politics, that struggled with the new ideological formation of the job market. In 1971, the young activist elected to the presidency of the MLA, Louis Kampf, elaborated the collective understanding that "unionization is a necessity" in his presidential address to the annual convention:

> We are workers under industrial capitalism. If we understand that, we can understand our alienation, our sense of powerlessness. For teaching, we collect wages: that is our basic connection to educational institutions, not the claims of humanist rhetoric. We are, in short, an intellectual proletariat. Consciousness of this condition can lead to self-hatred or cynical careerism. It can also lead to our uniting around the oppression we share with other alienated workers, the better to rid ourselves of the oppressors. (" 'It's Alright,' " 383)

It is hard to see that any subsequent awareness has improved upon Kampf's formulation, and insofar as the structures of feeling dominating the academy from the 1970s forward can be described as "self-hatred or cynical careerism," it has been a temptation for too many to see this unionist, intellectual workerism informed by commitments to a broad movement politics as the "lost cause" of the 1960s. In fact, graduate-employee unionism retained much of the movement commitments aired by Kampf. In contrast, although faculty unionism has rarely reached out to movements beyond the campus (or even to other workers on campus, including adjuncts and graduate employees), there was nonetheless a widespread labor consciousness. High points in this first-wave discourse include, especially, articles in 1974 and 1978 by Paul Lauter and others in *Radical Teacher* and *Universitas*, the journal of the SUNY union, later republished as "Retrenchment: What the Managers Are Doing" and "A Scandalous Misuse of Faculty: Adjuncts" (Lauter, *Canons and Contexts*, 175–197, 198–209). At this stage, buoyed by a militant labor movement on the national scene, even the discourse of department chairs was frequently pro-union: Marilyn Williamson's 1973 piece is fairly typical in arguing that "the union agreement holds many advantages," even for department administrators, and observing tartly that "to me as a chairman the word 'flexibility' has come to have one meaning: the ability to reduce my staff or my funds" (3–4). During the early 1970s, at least one anti-union article in the MLA newsletter for department chairs represented itself as an "alternative perspective" in the context of the general enthusiasm for collective bargaining (Alderman).

So, before 1975, it was common even for department chairs to recognize that the Fordist "production" analogy and neoliberal market analogies were "absurd" or "crude" and to insist that "concretely we are dealing with live human beings" (Adams, 7). In 1979, Paul Hunter understood that the replacement of full-time lines by graduate student labor constituted a virtual war on young people: "There is no youth in our profession any more," he wrote; "we face an immediate prospect of being in a profession that gets older every year, that fails to admit the young to its permanent numbers at all, that systematically excludes beginners from its ranks despite taunting them in graduate schools that foster both dreams and expectations" (7). He goes on:

> Once the MLA encompassed a variety of languages in its meeting halls. Now there are only two: the language spoken by the tenured and secure, a language of rationalized complacency; and the language of the unemployed, the underemployed, the temporarily employed, the part-time, the untenured, the uncertain, the paranoid, the disillusioned—a language of desperation, fury, and despair. It would be easy to be sentimental about their plight, but it would be trivial to treat the issue sentimentally and thus make it easy to comfort ourselves by the usual cynical reply, "But at least they are young, and their options are still open." (8)

Hunter has no quick solutions to offer, but his piece is in part an attempt to revive a generational frame of analysis, one that is inevitably significant for understanding how the transformation of higher education represents an increased exploitation of the young (which helps to explain why it is commonly students who are the most visible opponents of the corporate university).

By 1980, there was a fully developed second wave of response to casualization, one that no longer knew any exterior to market ideology. Second-wave knowledge takes "the market" as empirical reality and as the practical horizon of study: the question is no longer to understand or alter the structural forces shaping demand for degreed labor but simply to project and accommodate that demand. The practical consequence of second-wave thought was to generally contain and silence the interventionist labor knowledge of the 1970s and, more specifically, to enrobe the processes of casualization with an aura of market rationality and natural inevitability. Throughout the 1980s, the question of degree-holder "supply" remained highly problematized, with the primary discursive effect of rendering the structural transformation of "demand" relatively unproblematic. By naturalizing the notion of tidal or cyclic "fluctuations in demand," second-wave knowledge throughout the 1980s repeatedly concealed wholesale casualization beneath a circular and self-authenticating market rhetoric: because the system is a market, it naturally fluctuates; because the system fluctuates, it must be a market.

In this period, the annual publication by the MLA of charts showing hills and valleys in the number of jobs available from year to year bolstered this new common sense. The charts suggested that there was a kind of "business cycle" to academic job opportunities, from which tidal and cyclic rhythm would inevitably proceed both good times and bad. Accompanying staff essays explained how "outside economic forces" buoyed the occasional bull years and artificially extended the natural bearish periods. The profession was meant to understand that, although it was frequently a source of disappointment, "the market" operated according to perfectly understandable and rational principles. This new epistemology radically transformed disciplinary communication in the early part of the decade: whereas the 1981 official "working paper" on employment issues reiterated the 1970s call for "collective activism" in order to protect the workplace circumstances of young people, J. Hillis Miller in 1986 was able to brush aside the concerns of youth with the forecast of a better future, claiming that "demographic and actuarial changes [would] mean many new positions" in the mid 1990s (281). (Even at the time, it cannot have been clear that the appearance of jobs ten years in the future would address the circumstances of a typical forty-year-old degree holder visiting the convention as a jobseeker for the fifth year in a row.) What is important about this informatic futurology, however, is the exclusion during the early 1980s of structural knowledge from the professional discourse. Informationalization doesn't unfold only by installing the flexible work regime; it sustains the flex system continuously by interfering with the consciousness of flex workers. While the evidence and labor knowledge of casualization occasionally intruded on the flow of disciplinary information (e.g., Lauter, "Society and the Profession"), these emergent alarms were quickly muffled and explained away by the dominant heuristic of market.

The 1989 Bowen report is in many respects the fullest development of this mode of thinking, and one that appears to vigorously impose the ideology of "market" on data that virtually trumpets the structural reality of casualization. Subtitled "A Study of Factors Affecting Demand and Supply, 1987 to 2012," the Bowen project elaborates its view of the "roller-coaster pattern" of the business cycle in academic jobs in the first lines of its introduction: "periods of rapid expansion and retrenchment" after 1945, "swings that have been sharp and sometimes destabilizing" (3). (The cyclic long view over forty-five years is meant to lend credence to the report's projections of a quarter-century into the future.) Offering what it describes as a "highly quantitative analysis" aimed to enable university administrations to assure themselves of a smooth flow of "outstanding faculty," the project views its task as best accomplished by understanding the cycle of academic business: "We hope to provide a clearer sense of whether the 'boom' and 'bust' pattern of faculty staffing is likely to repeat itself and an improved understanding of how to avoid such disruptive and inefficient cycles" (4). While Bowen goes to a great deal of trouble to distinguish between "projections" and "predictions" (predictions describe what will happen; projections describe what will happen if specific assumptions are met), this distinction only highlights the counterfactual nature of the Bowen assumptions. It is only by actively excluding the evidence of structural transformation (the replacement of tenured faculty with managed labor, expanding reliance on graduate employees and other nondegreed teachers) that Bowen is able to impose this Platonic vision of the business cycle on the data, leading him to project that fantastic "massive upsurge" in "demand for faculty."

The most dramatic stroke in this regard was Bowen's decision, as he put it, "to define 'faculty' quite carefully." The universe of Bowen faculty included only the ladder ranks and full-time instructors, virtually excluding part-timers and faculty without the doctoral degree. The blundering represented by this decision is obvious in hindsight, though it's not been commented upon. Most observers have been content to accept Bowen's explanation that he couldn't have "predicted" what he called "massive cutbacks" in the 1990s (Magner, "Job Market Blues")

—as if retrenchment and casualization were a phenomenon of that decade and not well established twenty years earlier. As noted earlier, there was already a well-developed understanding of the exploitation of part-timers and graduate students, and plenty of hard quantitative data, too: the 1988 National Study of the Postsecondary Faculty counted hundreds of thousands of part-time faculty, a massive segment of the workforce that represents the near doubling of the ratio of part-time to full-time faculty in less than two decades, from about 20 percent in 1970 to nearly 40 percent in 1987. The fact that Lynne Cheney—of all people—was essentially alone in attempting to debunk the Bowen projections shows the staying power of the positivist market fantasy even in the most well meaning and politically committed quarters of the academy.

Bowen's error is in his attempt to understand the employment system *as* a system while excluding the largest categories of its working parts. Nonetheless, one might be able to excuse this decision as consequent upon the view from Princeton: from this standpoint, he naturally mistook the degree holder and the professoriate as the "real" faculty and was ill-positioned in the Ivy League to understand that nondegreed labor was the real labor of the new system. This could be true, except that Bowen's dogmatic imposition of market ideology took such acrobatic effort that it's nearly impossible for even the most generous observer to let him off the hook. For instance, faced with the evidence that increasing numbers of degree holders had been taking nonacademic work since the 1970s ("the movement away from academia that has been evident for some time now" [120]), Bowen rather perversely ignores the abundant testimony by graduate students that their dislocation was involuntary; expressing "considerable concern" about the larger numbers of degree holders who "chose [!] to pursue alternate careers" (13), he argues that this "trend" augurs a need to increase graduate school admissions (120). This is a breathtakingly flawed syllogism that imposes the market ideology of "free choice" on the statistical evidence of degree holders taking nonacademic jobs (ultimately generating the claim that even more people will "choose" similarly). This particular assumption is only one element of the overall error pattern of the Bowen projections, but this completely unwarranted imposition of free choice ideology is symptomatic of his general failure to process evidence of nonmarket structural relations.

Equally problematic are Bowen's suppositions regarding institutional decision-making. Despite enormous evidence to the contrary, Bowen

starts his calculation with the assumption that retiring and other depart-
ing faculty will be replaced by degree holders "on a one-for-one basis"
(25). Indeed, the reality for many departments since 1968 has been very
different from Bowen's assumption. Even in those circumstances where
the raw number of full-time faculty remains stable, there has commonly
been a substantial increase in the number of students; in other circumstances, the one-to-one replacement of full time faculty has meant the
substitution of non-tenure-track instructors for professorial labor. Overall, for most of the past thirty-five years, many departments have slowly
given up professorial lines or else counted themselves lucky when they
were able to hire one to one, despite a radically increased workload. But
rather than accounting for retrenchment and workload increases, and
lowering or contextualizing his projection of replacement demand,
Bowen actually adjusts his figures upward (by, correctly, assuming that
some of the new entrants will also need to be replaced). Convinced that
"replacement demand is much more stable over time than many have
assumed," Bowen selectively reports data in support of his understanding of the employment system as a rational "market," generating a pervasively rosy and ahistorical interpretation of otherwise alarming data.
Looking at the plummeting percentage of young people in the ladder
ranks (faculty under age forty were 42 percent of the total in 1977 and
just 22 percent of the total only ten years later, in 1987), Bowen fails to
consider the obvious reality that, in fact, there were more young people
than ever before working as higher education teachers (only they were
working "off the ladder" as graduate employees, part-timers, and nontenurable faculty). For more than ten years, young people had been
hired into the tenure stream in very small numbers; new tenurable hires
were older, having taken longer to complete a degree and to find a job
afterward, and so on. Although other observers noted the dramatic aging of the ladder faculty with concern, Bowen swept any consideration
of this peculiarity off the table, representing it as a systemic self-correc-
tion and declaring without evidence that the smaller number of young
faculty in 1987 was "more 'normal' " than the 1977 ratio, reflecting his
judgment of a system reaching balance and a "smooth" pattern of generational exit and replacement (16–27).

Bowen goes on to estimate various scenarios leading to a "net new-
position demand," based on the even more ahistorical assumption that
"institutions always *want* to have more faculty and will add faculty positions *when they can afford to do so*" (153). The emphasis is Bowen's

and probably reflects his moral certitude. Doubtless Bowen is right that
institutions should "want to have more faculty," but was there any basis in fact for this claim? The evidence clearly shows that the sort of
"faculty" that institutions have been "adding" has consistently been
term workers and graduate students. While there may well be occasional instances where administrations have chosen to increase the professorial faculty at the expense of other funding priorities (buildings and
sports facilities, information technology, etc.), these cases would run
against the general trend of administrative decision-making, and it
seems that the most successful pressure to increase tenure-track hiring
has come from academic unions. Bowen's ideas about what "institutions want" reflect the collegial common sense of Dink Stover at Yale
("Gosh, fellas, if the old u. could afford it, they'd keep you on for
sure!"), but it's not clear that they bear any documented relation to the
reality they purport to describe. Faced with the evidence of casualization advancing unevenly in the disciplines (i.e., a greater aging of tenurable faculty in the humanities), Bowen reads this datum exactly against
the trajectory of its meaning (i.e, that full-time positions for humanities
teachers have been more quickly converted to part-time slots, and therefore there will be fewer full-time positions to fill). Bowen instead manages to read this data as evidence that there will be *more* full-time hiring in the humanities—essentially saying that the slowed entry of young
people into the ladder ranks "means" that there will soon be more
young people in the ladder ranks (which is the same as saying that "because people have been eating less red meat lately, they'll soon need to
eat more red meat"). The closer one looks at Bowen's study, one has to
feel that Bowen sees more or less what he wants to see. Where nearly
every other observer saw steadily growing reliance on part-time faculty
—the ratio near doubling in twenty years—Bowen claims to see "no evidence of a significant trend in the part-time ratio" and, quite eccentri-
cally, assumes "no change" in that ratio while projecting the "demand"
for tenurable faculty over a quarter century (77 n.8).

One further example. With a similar commonsensicality, Bowen suggests that talent-rich doctoral "labor markets" lead to a more accomplished faculty, asserting that institutions are able "to raise hiring standards when there is a plentiful supply of talented young faculty." If
Bowen had looked more carefully, he might have seen what the 1992
NSOPF study was able to conclusively demonstrate: despite the "oversupply" of degree holders, "new entrants" to the ranks of full-time

faculty after 1985 were markedly less (not more!) likely to hold the Ph.D. than previous cohorts. Analysis of the "new entrants" data was completed some time after Bowen's study, but it's particularly helpful because it confounds cherished assumptions about the nature of the employment system. Startlingly, the group of junior faculty hired between 1985 and 1992 were almost 30 percent more likely to claim the B.A. or M.A. as their highest degree than were faculty hired any time earlier. This means that, under conditions of Ph.D. "oversupply," roughly 40 percent of the "new entrants" do not hold the doctorate. (By contrast, about 70 percent of the senior group of faculty, including many persons hired under the 1960s expansion cohort, hold the doctorate.) This pattern is consistent across institution type: research universities and other doctorate-granting institutions, as well as comprehensive and private liberal arts institutions, all show a substantial slide in the percentage of junior faculty holding the doctorate. The increase in nondoctoral faculty is stratified by discipline rather than by institution type: humanities and the fine arts show the most dramatic decline in doctorally degreed junior faculty, with a mere 55 percent of junior faculty in the humanities holding the Ph.D. (by contrast, 73 percent of senior faculty in the same fields hold the Ph.D.). But all program areas showed a substantial slide, with the exception of natural sciences, which showed a slight increase in doctorates among the new entrants (National Center for Education Statistics, "New Entrants," table 4.1).

Under the current system of academic work, the university clearly does not prefer the best or most experienced teachers; it prefers the cheapest teachers. Increasingly, that means the creation of nontenurable full-time instructorships and other casual appointments, a casualization that has unfolded unevenly by discipline and is especially pronounced in English and writing instruction. In this instance, Bowen has again simply applied the dominant logic and assumed that, even within the context of a general assault on the tenure system, "of course" the managers would hire the best "doctoral product" available. From the posture of common sense, it seems reasonable to assume—as many people have— that the replacement of tenured positions with "full-time" term contract positions means that persons holding doctorates will be awarded those jobs. The fashionable notion that we have an "oversupply" of degree holders sustains this assumption: many graduate faculty imagine that their students who don't get tenurable work will be leading contenders for contract positions, in which, it is further assumed, they will pursue the scholarship, teaching, and service that they would have done in a tenurable position, albeit on a more sped-up basis, less well paid, and without the protections of tenure. While it is true that numerous degree holders seek and would gladly accept these positions, the facts are quite clear: holders of doctorates have not enjoyed a preferential status for those jobs. Non-tenure-track positions have been awarded to persons without the doctorate in numbers large enough to substantially reduce the overall percentage of Ph.D. holders in the full-time workforce.

Taken as a whole, including trends in the use of graduate employees, part-time lecturers, and the number of non-Ph.D.s hired into full-time instructor positions, the academic labor system increasingly prefers teachers *without* the Ph.D.—even when, as in the languages, desperate and deeply indebted holders of the Ph.D. are willing to work without tenure and for salaries below $30,000. Bernard Berelson's 1960 study of graduate education was able to demonstrate, by survey of department chairs, an empirical preference for the doctoral degree holder as an undergraduate teacher (52–53). By contrast, thirty years later, Bowen can only offer an impressionistic assumption that the same holds true. (If he'd surveyed the literature, he would have found that academic management was busy developing a large discourse advertising the "quality of instruction" delivered with ever-fewer numbers of degreed faculty.) And in the circulation of this "bad information" through Bowen, despite what are certainly Bowen's individual good intentions and earnest scholarship, we begin to understand the real nature of an informationalized higher education: not the classic liberal and enlightenment fantasy of information that "wants to be free" for everyone, but the power of capital and the corporate university to make neoliberal ideology count as reality. When we think about it, of course, the information university doesn't "want" doctoral degree holders as faculty: as a general rule, the holders of doctoral degrees are disinclined to view students as information deficits or themselves as information-delivery devices. In believing that "education," "knowing," "research," and "study" are embodied human practices, dialectical or dialogic and not reducible to information transfer, the typical doctoral degree holder represents an obstacle to the fantasy of dollars for credits driving the managerial revolution toward a fully informationalized higher ed.

Through the 1980s and early 1990s, second-wave fantasies of the "job market," such as Bowen's, were all but unchallenged as they proceeded to do the corporate university the enormous service of covering up the processes of corporatization, managerialism, and casualization. It is important to understand that this supply-side second-wave knowledge does the same disservice even when it projects the opposite of Bowen's conclusions, as when the 1995 Massy-Goldman paper found "oversupply" and "overproduction" in the fields of science and engineering. (Though it is instructive to see the corporate university's swift response to small errors in that paper: the methodology of Massy and Goldman's study or "simulation" was carefully and promptly critiqued by staff employees at the Council of Graduate Schools [Syverson], in stark contrast to the uncritical celebration surrounding Bowen's projections.)

In acknowledging that Bowen's projections were flawed, the managers of university business have carefully conserved the neoliberal assumptions that created his projections in the first place, leaving their own agenda not only undisturbed but actually advanced, having given the clear impression that this "market" was volatile ("markets" always are) and difficult to predict, even by venerable experts, leading to an even larger interest in expert information. Through this period and to the present, the notion of a job market continues to provide the dominant narrative of academic work in the liberal and corporate media. Newspaper and Internet headlines scream the intelligible tale of second-wave knowledge: "Study Says U.S. Universities Produce Too Many Doctorates" (Magner); "A Surplus of Scholars Fight for Jobs in Academia" (Hodges); "Tenure Gridlock: When Professors Choose Not to Retire" (Wyatt); "Slaves to Science: For Post-docs, Finding a Supernova Is Easier Than Finding a Job" (Weed); "Oh, the Humanities! Pros Use Prose in Job-Hunting: Post-Tweed Breed of Professor Knows Marketing" (Argetsinger). At the present time, in the full ripening and apogee of second-wave knowledge, the system of graduate education is no longer understood as being "like" a market; it is generally understood, simply and self-evidently, that graduate education *is* a market.

By 1997, the dominance of market ideology had fully bloomed into a resplendently laissez-faire structure of feeling. In November of that year, Jules Lapidus, then president of the Council of Graduate Schools, took to the pages of the *Chronicle of Higher Education* to endorse a strong, free-market theory of graduate education, bolstered by a vigorously neoliberal ideology of the graduate student as consumer. Conceding that pursuing the Ph.D. is a "risky business" for many students, Lapidus agreed that it had "always" been so and vigorously opposed any regulation of the system: "The idea of developing some method to relate enrollments in graduate programs to projections of supply and demand in the job market runs counter to the American value of free choice." Concluding that "students have to decide for themselves if they believe that doctoral education is a good investment of their funds and their time," Lapidus seemed to feel that the ideology of choice ends the matter: "As far as I know, no one is being forced to study for the Ph.D."

The market epistemology is perhaps most distressing when it is adopted by those who are hurt most by it: graduate employees, term faculty, and junior members of the professoriate. As a historian in his early thirties and unable to find a permanent job despite having published three monographs, Robert E. Wright argued in his April 2002 *Chronicle* editorial, "A Market Solution to the Oversupply of Historians," that "the solution is clear. The salaries for new assistant professors [then about $40,000] should be lowered until the number of qualified job applicants . . . and the number of job openings become more equal." Being of a literary bent, and reading quickly, naturally I sought in Wright's proposal some satirical intent. I even heard an echo of "A Modest Proposal" in "A Market Solution." But on careful reading, Wright turns out to be in deadly earnest. An economic historian with a book published by Cambridge University Press, Wright sincerely means to propose that academic employers get together to fix the woes of the "market," not by intervening rationally (say, by restricting the use of graduate student labor and regulating the overuse of term faculty) but, rather, by further degrading the conditions of academic work. On the one hand, of course, the absurdities of what Wright calls his "market-oriented approach" are obvious: his plan would simply sort not for the best faculty but for the faculty that can afford to teach for smaller wages (by virtue of moonlighting, a pension, or other source of independent income); nor does it acknowledge the empirical, historical fact that the wage savings of the university's vast expansion of term labor have not so far been dedicated to creating new professorial jobs. What guarantee does he have that the university would dedicate these new wage savings to a larger pool of tenure-track faculty? And if we could find a mechanism to enforce such a guarantee, why not develop that enforcement mechanism without lowering wages in the first place?

Perhaps we should acknowledge the degree to which Wright's "proposal" simply realizes the absurd assumptions driving our own ideas about "the market" and academic work, especially our understandable but exaggerated sense of helplessness before its demands. What if, instead of constantly adjusting ourselves (and our compensation) to "meet the needs of the market," we started to adjust or regulate the "market" to meet *our* needs? This would mean, as a matter of course, that faculty would have to take more control of their workplaces and, rather than lowering faculty wages to the level of graduate employees and adjunct instructors (as Wright distressingly proposes), raise the wages of graduate employees and adjunct instructors to the level of the faculty (or even higher, in order to eliminate the motivation for replacing faculty workers with discounted labor). There is nothing utopian about this proposal: as true apprentice teacher-scholars and not cheap labor, most observers will agree that graduate employees should (a) teach no more than one course a year and (b) receive a living wage, currently in many major education centers ranging from $18,000 to $24,000.

One can easily argue that it should be more expensive to have a graduate program than not to have a graduate program (as it is in some of the less-exploitive circumstances at present and in many cases in the past). One might argue, likewise, that it should be more expensive to use flex labor than to use faculty labor (in the same way that it is more expensive to buy groceries at the convenience store). The base calculations for the salary of a part-time lecturer could begin at around $7,000 per class (one-eighth of a 4/4 load, with a starting salary near $50,000), and end up—after calculating fair health coverage, a retirement contribution, other benefits, a premium for "convenience," and a multiplier for years of experience—in the range of $9,000 to $11,000 per class, possibly quite a bit more for the term worker with many years of service.

Of course, at reasonable wages, the university has little motivation to admit "too many" graduate employees or rely unduly on term faculty. All of these calculations are perfectly rational—they can even be represented, if one wishes, as a "correction to the market" (à la Wright's pro-market plan to lower wages)—and have the advantage of being ethical. Furthermore, all of the problems of "the market" would vanish when fair wages were instituted across job descriptions. At the moment when everyone doing teacher work nonprofessorially is paid fairly, and far more expensively than heretofore, the assistant professor will become the cheapest labor available (relative to the fair wages of graduate employees and term faculty), and "demand" for assistant professors will cease to be a problem. Not coincidentally, in an environment of reasonable wages for everyone, Bowen's projections would in all likelihood have been more or less accurate.

At the forefront of this nonmarket or market-regulation approach to the "job crisis" are the union movements of graduate employees and adjunct academic labor. It is commonly remarked by members of the faculty that organized term faculty "are organizing themselves out of a job," as if by eliminating the university's motivation to hire them on exploitive terms, there will suddenly be no work for them. The same sentiments are commonly expressed in other workplaces, as in the railroads and in steel plants when white workers derided the efforts of African American workers to organize. It is, after all, the work of the proletariat to abolish itself. In actual fact, of course, the work of the academy will remain to be done: students will still need to taught, advised, and inspired. (Furthermore, in practical terms, since the turnover rate even of full-time term faculty is 30 percent a year, it is hard to imagine the need to "fire adjuncts" in order to create professorial jobs faster than the already existing attrition.) Even if it were true on some abstract or collective level that graduate employees and the former graduate employees working on a term basis were indeed organizing themselves out of a job, it is only to organize themselves collectively into better ones.

Certainly, not all graduate employees and term workers reject the "market-oriented" approach to their present and future work prospects. The *Chronicle of Higher Education* has been able to report on small groups of graduate employees who oppose unionization. Unionization votes by graduate employees have failed in a small minority of cases. And both graduate employees and term workers inevitably feel the pressure of having to "sell themselves" in a cruel, irrational, and exploitive workplace so that for many it feels, just as the *Washington Post* contends, that "job-hunting" in some sense equals "marketing." But an estimated 20 percent of graduate employees in the United States are now covered by union contracts (a figure that Gordon Lafer considers "comparable to the most highly organized states in the country and 50 percent above the national norm"). And there appear to be more contracts on the way. It is at least possible that soon enough the majority feeling among graduate employees (who eventually become all of the labor in the system, term faculty and tenure stream alike) will become the concerted will to make the "market" responsive to their needs, and not the other way around.

Appendix A

Yeshiva University 444 U.S. 672 (1980), *"Justice Brennan, Dissenting"*

MR. JUSTICE BRENNAN, with whom MR. JUSTICE WHITE, MR. JUSTICE MARSHALL, and MR. JUSTICE BLACKMUN join, dissenting.

In holding that the full-time faculty members of Yeshiva University are not covered employees under the National Labor Relations Act, but instead fall within the exclusion for [444 U.S. 672, 692] supervisors and managerial employees, the Court disagrees with the determination of the National Labor Relations Board. Because I believe that the Board's decision was neither irrational nor inconsistent with the Act, I respectfully dissent.

I

Ten years ago the Board first asserted jurisdiction over private nonprofit institutions of higher education. Cornell University, 183 N.L.R.B. 329 (1970). Since then, the Board has often struggled with the Procrustean task of attempting to implement in the altogether different environment of the academic community the broad directives of a statutory scheme designed for the bureaucratic industrial workplace. See, e.g., Adelphi University, 195 N.L.R.B. 639, 648 (1972). Resolution of the particular issue presented in this case—whether full-time faculty members are covered "employees" under the Act—is but one of several challenges confronting the Board in this "unchartered area." C. W. Post Center, 189 N.L.R.B. 904, 905 (1971).

Because at the time of the Act's passage Congress did not contemplate its application to private universities, it is not surprising that the terms of the Act itself provide no answer to the question before us. Indeed, the statute evidences significant tension as to congressional intent in this respect by its explicit inclusion, on the one hand, of "professional employees" under 2(12), 29 U.S.C. 152 (12), and its exclusion, on the other, of "supervisors" under 2(11), 29 U.S.C. 152 (11). Similarly, when transplanted to the academic arena, the Act's extension of coverage to professionals under 2(12) cannot easily be squared with the Board-created exclusion of "managerial employees" in the industrial context. See generally NLRB v. Bell Aerospace Co., 416 U.S. 267 (1974).

Primary authority to resolve these conflicts and to adapt the Act to the changing patterns of industrial relations [444 U.S. 672, 693] was entrusted to the Board, not to the judiciary. NLRB v. Weingarten, Inc., 420 U.S. 251, 266 (1975). The Court has often admonished that "[t]he ultimate problem is the balancing of the conflicting legitimate interests. The function of striking that balance to effectuate national labor policy is often a difficult and delicate responsibility, which the Congress committed primarily to the National Labor Relations Board, subject to limited judicial review." NLRB v. Truck Drivers, 353 U.S. 87, 96 (1957). Accord, Beth Israel Hospital v. NLRB, 437 U.S. 483, 501 (1978); NLRB v. Erie Resistor Corp., 373 U.S. 221, 235–236 (1963). Through its cumulative experience in dealing with labor-management relations in a variety of industrial and nonindustrial settings, it is the Board that has developed the expertise to determine whether coverage of a particular category of employees would further the objectives of the Act.[1] And through its continuous oversight of industrial conditions, it is the Board that is best able to formulate and adjust national labor policy to conform to the realities of industrial life. Accordingly, the judicial role is limited; a court may not substitute its own judgment for that of the Board. The Board's decision may be reviewed for its rationality and its consistency with the Act [444 U.S. 672, 694], but once these criteria are satisfied, the order must be enforced. See Beth Israel Hospital v. NLRB, supra, at 501.

II

In any event, I believe the Board reached the correct result in determining that Yeshiva's full-time faculty is covered under the NLRA. The

Court does not dispute that the faculty members are "professional employees" for the purposes of collective bargaining under 2(12), but nevertheless finds them excluded from coverage under the implied exclusion for "managerial employees."[2] The Court explains that "[t]he controlling consideration in this case is that the faculty of Yeshiva University exercise authority which in any other context unquestionably would be managerial." Ante, at 686. But the academic community is simply not "any other context." The Court purports to recognize that there are fundamental differences between the authority structures of the typical industrial and academic institutions which preclude the blind transplanting of principles developed in one arena onto the other; yet it nevertheless ignores those very differences in concluding that Yeshiva's faculty is excluded from the Act's coverage.

As reflected in the legislative history of the Taft-Hartley Amendments of 1947, the concern behind the exclusion of supervisors under 2(11) of the Act is twofold. On the one hand, Congress sought to protect the rank-and-file employees from being unduly influenced in their selection of leaders by the presence of management representatives in their union. "If supervisors were members of and active in the union which represented the employees they supervised it could be possible [444 U.S. 672, 695] for the supervisors to obtain and retain positions of power in the union by reason of their authority over their fellow union members while working on the job." NLRB v. Metropolitan Life Ins. Co., 405 F.2d 1169, 1178 (CA2 1968). In addition, Congress wanted to ensure that employers would not be deprived of the undivided loyalty of their supervisory foremen. Congress was concerned that if supervisors were allowed to affiliate with labor organizations that represented the rank and file, they might become accountable to the workers, thus interfering with the supervisors' ability to discipline and control the employees in the interest of the employer.[3]

Identical considerations underlie the exclusion of managerial employees. See ante, at 682. Although a variety of verbal formulations have received judicial approval over the years, see Retail Clerks International Assn. v. NLRB, 125 U.S. App. D.C. 63, 65–66, 366 F.2d 642, 644–645 (1966), this Court has recently sanctioned a definition of "managerial employee" that comprises those who " 'formulate and effectuate management policies by expressing and making operative the decisions of their employer.' " See NLRB v. Bell Aerospace Co., 416 U.S., at 288. The touchstone of managerial status is thus an alliance with management, and the pivotal inquiry is whether the employee in performing his duties [444 U.S. 672, 696] represents his own interests or those of his employer.[4] If his actions are undertaken for the purpose of implementing the employer's policies, then he is accountable to management and may be subject to conflicting loyalties. But if the employee is acting only on his own behalf and in his own interest, he is covered under the Act and is entitled to the benefits of collective bargaining.

After examining the voluminous record in this case,[5] the Board determined that the faculty at Yeshiva exercised its decisionmaking authority in its own interest rather than "in the interest of the employer." 221 N.L.R.B. 1053, 1054 (1975). The Court, in contrast, can perceive "no justification for this distinction" and concludes that the faculty's interests "cannot be separated from those of the institution." Ante, at 688.[6] But the Court's vision is clouded by its failure fully to discern and comprehend the nature of the faculty's role in university governance.

Unlike the purely hierarchical decisionmaking structure that prevails in the typical industrial organization, the bureaucratic foundation of most "mature" universities is characterized by dual authority systems. The primary decisional network [444 U.S. 672, 697] is hierarchical in nature: Authority is lodged in the administration, and a formal chain of command runs from a lay governing board down through university officers to individual faculty members and students. At the same time, there exists a parallel professional network, in which formal mechanisms have been created to bring the expertise of the faculty into the decisionmaking process. See J. Baldridge, Power and Conflict in the University 114 (1971); Finkin, The NLRB in Higher Education, 5 U. Toledo L. Rev. 608, 614–618 (1974).

What the Board realized—and what the Court fails to apprehend—is that whatever influence the faculty wields in university decisionmaking is attributable solely to its collective expertise as professional educators, and not to any managerial or supervisory prerogatives. Although the administration may look to the faculty for advice on matters of professional and academic concern, the faculty offers its recommendations in order to serve its own independent interest in creating the most effective environment for learning, teaching, and scholarship.[7] And while the administration may attempt to defer to the faculty's competence whenever possible, it must and does apply its own distinct perspective to those recommendations, a perspective that is based on fiscal [444 U.S. 672, 698] and other managerial policies which the faculty has no part in developing. The University always retains the ultimate decisionmaking authority, see ante, at 675–676, and the administration gives what weight and import to the faculty's collective judgment as it chooses and deems consistent with its own perception of the institution's needs and objectives.[8]

The premise of a finding of managerial status is a determination that the excluded employee is acting on behalf of management and is answerable to a higher authority in the exercise of his responsibilities. The Board has consistently implemented this requirement—both for professional and non-professional employees—by conferring managerial status only upon those employees "whose interests are closely aligned with management as true representatives of management." E.g., Sutter Community Hospitals of Sacramento, 227 N.L.R.B. 181, 193 (1976); Bell Aerospace, [444 U.S. 672, 699] 219 N.L.R.B. 384, 385 (1975); General Dynamics Corp., 213 N.L.R.B. 851, 857 (1974).[9] Only if the employee is expected to conform to management policies and is judged by his effectiveness in executing those policies does the danger of divided loyalties exist.

Yeshiva's faculty, however, is not accountable to the administration in its governance function, nor is any individual faculty member subject to personal sanction or control based on the administration's assessment of the worth of his recommendations. When the faculty, through the schools' advisory committees, participates in university decisionmaking on subjects of academic policy, it does not serve as the "representative of management."[10] Unlike industrial supervisors [444 U.S. 672, 700] and managers, university professors are not hired to "make operative" the policies and decisions of their employer. Nor are they retained on the condition that their interests will correspond to those of the university administration. Indeed, the notion that a faculty member's professional competence could depend on his undivided loyalty to management is antithetical to the whole concept of academic freedom. Faculty members are judged by their employer on the quality of their teaching and scholarship, not on the compatibility of their advice with administration policy. Board Member Kennedy aptly concluded in his concurring opinion in Northeastern University, 218 N.L.R.B. 247, 257 (1975) (footnote omitted):

> "[T]he influence which the faculty exercises in many areas of academic governance is insufficient to make them 'managerial' employees. Such

influence is not exercised 'for management' or 'in the interest of the employer,' but rather is exercised in their own professional interest. The best evidence of this fact is that faculty members are generally not held accountable by or to the administration for their faculty governance functions. Faculty criticism of administration policies, for example, is viewed not as a breach of loyalty, but as an exercise in academic freedom. So, too, intervention by the university administration in faculty deliberations would most likely be considered an infringement upon academic freedoms. Conversely, university administrations rarely consider themselves bound by faculty recommendations."

It is no answer to say, as does the Court, that Yeshiva's faculty and administration are one and the same because their interests tend to coincide. In the first place, the National Labor Relations Act does not condition its coverage on an antagonism of interests between the employer and the employee.[11] [444 U.S. 672, 701] The mere coincidence of interests on many issues has never been thought to abrogate the right to collective bargaining on those topics as to which that coincidence is absent. Ultimately, the performance of an employee's duties will always further the interests of the employer, for in no institution do the interests of labor and management totally diverge. Both desire to maintain stable and profitable operations, and both are committed to creating the best possible product within existing financial constraints. Differences of opinion and emphasis may develop, however, on exactly how to devote the institution's resources to achieve those goals. When these disagreements surface, the national labor laws contemplate their resolution through the peaceful process of collective bargaining. And in this regard, Yeshiva University stands on the same footing as any other employer.

Moreover, the congruence of interests in this case ought not to be exaggerated. The university administration has certain economic and fiduciary responsibilities that are not shared by the faculty, whose primary concerns are academic and relate solely to its own professional reputation. The record evinces numerous instances in which the faculty's recommendations have been rejected by the administration on account of fiscal constraints or other managerial policies. Disputes have arisen between Yeshiva's faculty and administration on such fundamental issues as the hiring, tenure, promotion, retirement, and dismissal of faculty members [444 U.S. 672, 702], academic standards and credits, departmental budgets, and even the faculty's choice of its own departmental representative.[12] The very fact that Yeshiva's faculty has voted for the Union to serve as its representative in future negotiations with the administration indicates that the faculty does not perceive its interests to be aligned with those of management. Indeed, on the precise topics which are specified as mandatory subjects of collective bargaining—wages, hours, and other terms and conditions of employment[13]—the interests of teacher and administrator are often diametrically opposed.

Finally, the Court's perception of the Yeshiva faculty's status is distorted by the rose-colored lens through which it views the governance structure of the modern-day university. The Court's conclusion that the faculty's professional interests are indistinguishable from those of the administration is bottomed on an idealized model of collegial decision-making that is a vestige of the great medieval university. But the university of today bears little resemblance to the "community of scholars" of yesteryear.[14] Education has become [444 U.S. 672, 703] "big business," and the task of operating the university enterprise has been transferred from the faculty to an autonomous administration, which faces the same pressures to cut costs and increase efficiencies that confront any large industrial organization.[15] The past decade of budgetary cutbacks, declining enrollments, reductions in faculty appointments, curtailment of academic programs, and increasing calls for accountability to alumni and other special interest groups has only added to the erosion of the faculty's role in the institution's decisionmaking process.[16] [444 U.S. 672, 704]

These economic exigencies have also exacerbated the tensions in university labor relations, as the faculty and administration more and more frequently find themselves advocating conflicting positions not only on issues of compensation, job security, and working conditions, but even on subjects formerly thought to be the faculty's prerogative. In response to this friction, and in an attempt to avoid the strikes and work stoppages that have disrupted several major universities in recent years, many faculties have entered into collective-bargaining relationships with their administrations and governing boards.[17] An even greater number of schools—Yeshiva among them—have endeavored to negotiate and compromise their differences informally, by establishing avenues for faculty input into university decisions on matters of professional concern. [444 U.S. 672, 705]

Today's decision, however, threatens to eliminate much of the administration's incentive to resolve its disputes with the faculty through open discussion and mutual agreement. By its overbroad and unwarranted interpretation of the managerial exclusion, the Court denies the faculty the protections of the NLRA and, in so doing, removes whatever deterrent value the Act's availability may offer against unreasonable administrative conduct.[18] Rather than promoting the Act's objective of funneling dissension between employers and employees into collective bargaining, the Court's decision undermines that goal and contributes to the possibility that "recurring disputes [will] fester outside the negotiation process until strikes or other forms of economic warfare occur." Ford Motor Co. v. NLRB, 441 U.S. 488, 499 (1979).

III

In sum, the Board analyzed both the essential purposes underlying the supervisory and managerial exclusions and the nature of the governance structure at Yeshiva University. Relying on three factors that attempt to encapsulate the fine distinction between those professional employees who are entitled to the NLRA's protections and those whose managerial responsibilities require their exclusion,[19] the Board concluded [444 U.S. 672, 706] that Yeshiva's full-time faculty qualify as the former rather than the latter. I believe the Board made the correct determination. But even were I to have reservations about the specific result reached by the Board on the facts of this case, I would certainly have to conclude that the Board applied a proper mode of analysis to arrive at a decision well within the zone of reasonableness. Accordingly, in light of the deference due the Board's determination in this complex area, I would reverse the judgment of the Court of Appeals.

NOTES

1. "It is not necessary in this case to make a completely definitive limitation around the term 'employee.' That task has been assigned primarily to the agency created by Congress to administer the Act. Determination of 'where all the conditions of the relation require protection' involves inquiries for the Board charged with this duty. Everyday experience in the administration of the statute gives it familiarity with the circumstances and backgrounds of employment relationships in various industries, with the abilities and needs of the workers for self-organization and collective action, and with the adaptability of collective

bargaining for the peaceful settlement of their disputes with their employers. The experience thus acquired must be brought frequently to bear on the question who is an employee under the Act. Resolving that question . . . 'belongs to the usual administrative routine' of the Board." NLRB v. Hearst Publications, Inc., 322 U.S. 111, 130 (1944). Accord, NLRB v. Seven-Up Bottling Co., 344 U.S. 344, 349 (1953).

2. Because the Court concludes that Yeshiva's full-time faculty are managerial employees, it finds it unnecessary to reach the University's contention that the faculty are also excluded as "supervisors" under 2(11). Ante, at 682. My discussion therefore focuses on the question of the faculty's managerial status, but I would resolve the issue of their supervisory status in a similar fashion.

3. See H.R. Rep. No. 245, 80th Cong., 1st Sess., 14 (1947):
"The evidence before the committee shows clearly that unionizing supervisors under the Labor Act is inconsistent with the purpose of the act. . . . It is inconsistent with the policy of Congress to assure to workers freedom from domination or control by their supervisors in their organizing and bargaining activities. It is inconsistent with our policy to protect the rights of employers; they, as well as workers, are entitled to loyal representatives in the plants, but when the foremen unionize, even in a union that claims to be 'independent' of the union of the rank and file, they are subject to influence and control by the rank and file union, and, instead of their bossing the rank and file, the rank and file bosses them."
See also S. Rep. No. 105, 80th Cong., 1st Sess., 3–5 (1947).

4. Section 2(11) of the Act requires, as a condition of supervisory status, that authority be exercised "in the interest of the employer." 29 U.S.C. 152 (11). See also NLRB v. Master Stevedores Assn., 418 F.2d 140 (CA5 1969); International Union of United Brewery Workers v. NLRB, 111 U.S. App. D.C. 383, 298 F.2d 297 (1961).

5. The Board held hearings over a 5-month period and compiled a record containing more than 4,600 pages of testimony and 200 exhibits.

6. The Court thus determines that all of Yeshiva's full-time faculty members are managerial employees, even though their role in university decisionmaking is limited to the professional recommendations of the faculty acting as a collective body, and even though they supervise and manage no personnel other than themselves. The anomaly of such a result demonstrates the error in extending the managerial exclusion to a class of essentially rank-and-file employees who do not represent the interests of management and who are not subject to the danger of conflicting loyalties which motivated the adoption of that exemption.

7. As the Board has recognized, due to the unique nature of their work, professional employees will often make recommendations on matters that are of great importance to management. But their desire to exert influence in these areas stems from the need to maintain their own professional standards, and

this factor—common to all professionals—should not, by itself, preclude their inclusion in a bargaining unit. See Westinghouse Electric Corp., 113 N.L.R.B. 337, 339–340 (1955). In fact, Congress clearly recognized both that professional employees consistently exercise independent judgment and discretion in the performance of their duties, see 29 U.S.C. 152 (12), and that they have a significant interest in maintaining certain professional standards, see S. Rep. No. 105, 80th Cong., 1st Sess., 11 (1947). Yet Congress specifically included professional within the Act's coverage. See NLRB v. Bell Aerospace Co., 416 U.S. 267, 298 (1974) (WHITE, J., dissenting in part).

8. One must be careful not to overvalue the significance of the faculty's influence on academic affairs. As one commentator has noted, "it is not extraordinary for employees to seek to exert influence over matters embedded in an employment relationship for which they share a concern, or that management would be responsive to their strongly held desires." Finkin, The NLRB in Higher Education, 5 U. Toledo L. Rev. 608, 616 (1974). Who, after all, is better suited than the faculty to decide what courses should be offered, how they should be taught, and by what standards their students should be graded? Employers will often attempt to defer to their employees' suggestions, particularly where—as here—those recommendations relate to matters within the unique competence of the employees.

Moreover, insofar as faculty members are given some say in more traditional managerial decisions such as the hiring and promotion of other personnel, such discretion does not constitute an adequate basis for the conferral of managerial or supervisory status. Indeed, in the typical industrial context, it is not uncommon for the employees' union to be given the exclusive right to recommend personnel to the employer, and these hiring-hall agreements have been upheld even where the union requires a worker to pass a union-administered skills test as a condition of referral. See, e.g., Local 42 (Catalytic Constr. Co.), 164 N.L.R.B. 916 (1967); see generally Teamsters v. NLRB, 365 U.S. 667 (1961).

9. The Board has also explained that the ability of the typical professional employee to influence company policy does not bestow managerial authority:

"Work which is based on professional competence necessarily involves a consistent exercise of discretion and judgment, else professionalism would not be involved. Nevertheless, professional employees plainly are not the same as management employees either by definition or in authority, and managerial authority is not vested in professional employees merely by virtue of their professional status, or because work performed in that status may have a bearing on company direction." General Dynamics Corp., 213 N.L.R.B., at 857–858.

10. Where faculty members actually do serve as management's representatives, the Board has not hesitated to exclude them from the Act's coverage as managerial or supervisory personnel. Compare University of Vermont, 223

N.L.R.B. 423 (1976) (excluding department chairmen as supervisors), and University of Miami, 213 N.L.R.B. 634 (1974) (excluding deans as supervisors), with Northeastern University, 218 N.L.R.B. 247 (1975) (department chairmen included within bargaining unit because they act primarily as instruments of the faculty), and Fordham University, 193 N.L.R.B. 134 (1971) (including department chairmen because they are considered to be representatives of the faculty rather than of the administration). In fact, the bargaining unit approved by the Board in the present case excluded deans, acting deans, directors, and principal investigators of research and training grants, all of whom were deemed to exercise supervisory or managerial authority. See ante, at 678, n.7.

11. Nor does the frequency with which an employer acquiesces in the recommendations of its employees convert them into managers or supervisors. See Stop & Shop Cos., Inc. v. NLRB, 548 F.2d 17, 19 (CA1 1977). Rather, the pertinent inquiries are who retains the ultimate decisionmaking authority and in whose interest the suggestions are offered. A different test could permit an employer to deny its employees the benefits of collective bargaining on important issues of wages, hours, and other conditions of employment merely by consulting with them on a host of less significant matters and accepting their advice when it is consistent with management's own objectives.

12. See, e.g., App. 740–742 (faculty hiring); id., at 232–233, 632, 667 (tenure); id., at 194, 620, 742–743 (promotion); id., at 713, 1463–1464 (retirement); id., at 241 (dismissal); id., at 362 (academic credits); id., at 723–724, 1469–1470 (cutback in departmental budget leading to loss of accreditation); id., at 410, 726–727 (election of department chairman and representative).

13. See 29 U.S.C. 158 (d).

14. See generally J. Brubacher & W. Rudy, Higher Education in Transition: A History of American Colleges and Universities, 1636–1976 (3d ed. 1976). In one of its earliest decisions in this area, the Board recognized that the governance structure of the typical modern university does not fit the mold of true collegiality in which authority rests with a peer group of scholars. Adelphi University, 195 N.L.R.B. 639, 648 (1972). Accord, New York University, 205 N.L.R.B. 4, 5 (1973). Even the concept of "shared authority," in which university decisionmaking is seen as the joint responsibility of both faculty and administration, with each exerting a dominant influence in its respective sphere of expertise, has been found [444 U.S. 672, 703] to be "an ideal rather than a widely adopted practice." K. Mortimer & T. McConnell, Sharing Authority Effectively 4 (1978). The authors conclude:

"Higher education is in the throes of a shift from informal and consensual judgments to authority based on formal criteria. . . . There have been changes in societal and legislative expectations about higher education, an increase in external regulation of colleges and universities, an increase in emphasis on managerial skills and the technocratic features of modern management, and a greater codification of internal decision-making procedures. These changes raise the question whether existing statements of shared authority provide adequate guidelines for internal governance." Id., at 269.

15. In 1976–1977, the total expenditures of institutions of higher education in the United States exceeded $42 billion. National Center for Education Statistics, Digest of Education Statistics 137 (Table 133) (1979). In the same year, Yeshiva University, a private institution, received over $34 million in revenues from the Federal Government. Id., at 132 (Table 127).

16. University faculty members have been particularly hard hit by the current financial squeeze. Because of inflation, the purchasing power of the faculty's salary has declined an average of 2.9 percent every year since 1972. Real salaries are thus 13.6 percent below the 1972 levels. Hansen, An Era of Continuing Decline: Annual Report on the Economic Status of the Profession, 1978–1979, 65 Academe: Bulletin of the American Association of University Professors 319, 323–324 (1979). Moreover, the faculty at Yeshiva has fared even worse than most. Whereas the average salary of a full professor at a comparable institution is $31,100, a full professor at Yeshiva averages only $27,100. Id., at 334, 348. In fact, a severe financial crisis at the University in 1971–1972 forced the president to order a freeze on all faculty promotions and pay increases. App. 1459.

17. As of January 1979, 80 private and 302 public institutions of higher education had engaged in collective bargaining with their faculties, and over 130,000 academic personnel had been unionized. National Center for the Study of Collective Bargaining in Higher Education, Directory of Faculty Contracts and Bargaining Agents in Institutions of Higher Education i–ii (1979). Although the NLRA is not applicable to any public employer, see 29 U.S.C. 152 (2), as of 1976, 22 States had enacted legislation granting faculties at public institutions the right to unionize and requiring public employers to bargain with duly constituted bargaining agents. Mortimer & McConnell, supra n. 14, at 53. See also Livingston & Christensen, State and Federal Regulation of Collective Negotiations in Higher Education, 1971 Wis. L. Rev. 91, 102.

The upsurge in the incidence of collective bargaining has generally been attributed to the faculty's desire to use the process as a countervailing force against increased administrative power and to ensure that the ideals of the academic community are actually practiced. As the Carnegie Commission found, "[u]nionization for [faculty] is more a protective than an aggressive act, more an effort to preserve the status quo than to achieve a new position of influence and affluence. . . ." Carnegie Commission on Higher Education, Governance of Higher Education 40 (1973). See also Mortimer & McConnell, supra n. 14, at 56; Lindeman, The Five Most Cited Reasons for Faculty Unionization, 102 Intellect 85 (1973); Nielsen & Polishook, Collective Bargaining and Beyond, The Chronicle of Higher Education 7 (May 21, 1979).

18. The Carnegie Commission, in concluding that "faculty members should have the right to organize and to bargain collectively, if they so desire," Carnegie Commission on Higher Education, supra, at 43, observed:

"We may be involved in a long-term period of greater social conflict in society and greater tension on campus. If so, it may be better to institutionalize this conflict through collective bargaining than to have it manifest itself with less restraint. Collective bargaining does provide agreed-upon rules of behavior, contractual understandings, and mechanisms for dispute settlement and grievance handling that help to manage conflict." Id., at 51.

19. Contrary to the Court's assertion, see ante, at 685, the Board has not abandoned the "collective authority" and "ultimate authority" branches of its analysis. See Reply Brief for Petitioner in No. 78–857, pp. 11–12, n.8. Although the "interest/alignment analysis" rationale [444 U.S. 672, 706] goes to the heart of the basis for the managerial and supervisory exclusions and therefore provides the strongest support for the Board's determination, the other two rationales are significant because they highlight two aspects of the university decisionmaking process relevant to the Board's decision: That the faculty's influence is exercised collectively—and only collectively—indicates that the faculty's recommendations embody the views of the rank and file rather than those of a select group of persons charged with formulating and implementing management policies. Similarly, that the administration retains ultimate authority merely indicates that a true system of collegiality is simply not the mode of governance at Yeshiva University. [444 U.S. 672, 707]

Appendix B

Brown University *1-RC-21368 (2004)*, *"Members Liebman and Walsh, Dissenting"*

Collective bargaining by graduate student employees is increasingly a fact of American university life.[1] Graduate student unions have been recognized at campuses from coast to coast, from the State University of New York to the University of California. Overruling a recent, unanimous precedent, the majority now declares that graduate student employees at private universities are not employees protected by the National Labor Relations Act and have no right to form unions. The majority's reasons, at bottom, amount to the claim that graduate-student collective bargaining is simply incompatible with the nature and mission of the university. This revelation will surely come as a surprise on many campuses—not least at New York University, a first-rate institution where graduate students now work under a collective-bargaining agreement reached in the wake of the decision that is overruled here.[2]

Today's decision is woefully out of touch with contemporary academic reality. Based on an image of the university that was already outdated when the decisions the majority looks back to, *Leland Stanford*[3] and *St. Clare's Hospital*,[4] were issued in the 1970's, it shows a troubling lack of interest in empirical evidence. Even worse, perhaps, is the majority's approach to applying the Act. It disregards the plain language of the statute—which defines "employees" so broadly that graduate students who perform services for, and under the control of, their universities are easily covered—to make a policy decision that rightly belongs to Congress. The reasons offered by the majority for its decision do not stand up to scrutiny. But even if they did, it would not be for the Board to act upon them. The result of the Board's ruling is harsh. Not only can universities avoid dealing with graduate student unions, they are also free to retaliate against graduate students who act together to address their working conditions.

I.

We would adhere to the Board's decision in *NYU* and thus affirm the Regional Director's decision in this case.

In *NYU*, applying principles that had recently been articulated in *Boston Medical Center*,[5] the Board held that the graduate assistants involved there were employees within the meaning of Section 2(3) of the Act, because they performed services under the control and direction of the university, for which they were compensated by the university. The Board found "no basis to deny collective-bargaining rights to statutory employees merely because they are employed by an educational institution in which they are enrolled as students." 332 NLRB at 1205. It was undisputed, the Board observed, that "graduate assistants are not within any category of workers that is excluded from the definition of 'employee' in Section 2(3)." Id. at 1206.

In turn, the Board rejected policy grounds as a basis for effectively creating a new exclusion. Rejecting claims that graduate assistants lacked a traditional economic relationship with the university, the Board pointed out that the relationship in fact paralleled that between faculty and university, which was amenable to collective bargaining. 332 NLRB at 1207–1208. The university's assertion that extending collective-bargaining rights to graduate students would infringe on academic freedom was also rejected. Such concerns, the Board explained, were speculative. Citing 30 years of experience with bargaining units of faculty members, and the flexibility of collective bargaining as an institution, the Board concluded that the "parties can 'confront any issues of academic freedom as they would any other issue in collective bargaining.'" Id., quoting *Boston Medical Center,* supra, 330 NLRB at 164.

Here, the Regional Director correctly applied the Board's decision in *NYU*. She concluded that the teaching assistants (TAs), research assistants (RAs), and proctors were statutory employees, because they performed services under the direction and control of Brown, and were compensated for those services by the university. With respect to the TAs, the Regional Director rejected, on both factual and legal grounds,

Brown's attempt to distinguish *NYU* on the basis that teaching was a degree requirement at Brown. Finally, she found that the TAs, RAs, and proctors were not, as Brown contended, merely temporary employees who could not be included in a bargaining unit. Accordingly, she directed a representation election, so that Brown's graduate students could choose for themselves whether or not to be represented by a union.

We agree with the Regional Director's decision in each of these respects.

II.

Insisting that it is simply restoring traditional precedent, the majority now overrules *NYU* and reverses the Regional Director's decision. It concludes that because graduate assistants "are primarily students and have a primarily educational, not economic, relationship with their university," they are not covered by the National Labor Relations Act and the Board cannot exercise jurisdiction over them. According to the majority, "[p]rinciples developed for use in the industrial setting cannot be 'imposed blindly on the academic world.'"[6]

There are two chief flaws in the majority's admonition. First, the majority fails to come to grips with the statutory principles that must govern this case. Second, it errs in seeing the academic world as somehow removed from the economic realm that labor law addresses—as if there was no room in the ivory tower for a sweatshop.[7] Before addressing those flaws, we question the majority's account of Board precedent in this area.

A.

Seeking to avoid the consequences of overruling such a recent precedent, the majority contends that *Leland Stanford*, not *NYU*, correctly resolves the issue presented here. The majority argues, moreover, that *Leland Stanford* itself was consistent with a decision that came before it, *Adelphi University*.[8] In fact, until today, the Board has never held that graduate teaching assistants (in contrast to certain research assistants and medical house staff) are not employees under the Act and therefore should not be allowed to form bargaining units of their own —or, indeed, enjoy any of the Act's protections.

In *Adelphi University*, decided in 1972, the Board excluded graduate assistants from a bargaining unit of faculty members because they did not share a community of interest with the faculty, not because they were not statutory employees. 195 NLRB at 640. The Board pointed out, among other things, that "graduate assistants are guided, instructed, and corrected in the performance of their assistantship duties by the regular faculty members to whom they are assigned." Id. Nothing in the Board's decision suggests that the graduate assistants could not have formed a bargaining unit of their own.

The *Leland Stanford* Board, as the majority acknowledges, "went further" in 1974. It concluded that because the research assistants (RAs) there were "primarily students" (citing *Adelphi University*), they were "not employees within the meaning of . . . the Act." 214 NLRB at 623. How the conclusion followed from the premise was not explained. The rationale of *Leland Stanford*, moreover, turned on the particular nature of the research assistants' work. The Board observed that:

> [T]he relationship of the RA's and Stanford is not grounded on the performance of a given task where both the task and the time of its performance is designated and controlled by the employer. Rather it is a situation of students within certain academic guidelines having chosen particular projects on which to spend the time necessary, as determined by the project's needs. Id. at 623.

This narrow rationale is not inconsistent with *NYU*, where the Board actually applied *Leland Stanford* to exclude certain graduate assistants from the bargaining unit. 332 NLRB at 1209 fn. 10.

Finally, the majority cites *Cedars-Sinai Medical Center*, 223 NLRB 251 (1976), and *St. Clare's Hospital*, supra, which involved medical interns, residents, and clinical fellows. The medical housestaff decisions, issued over the sharp dissents of then-Chairman Fanning, were correctly overruled in *Boston Medical Center*, supra, which the majority leaves in place.

Notably, in *St. Clare's Hospital*, the Board made clear that while "housestaff are not 'employees,' " the Board was *not* "renouncing entirely [its] jurisdiction over such individuals," but rather was simply holding that they did not have "bargaining privileges" under the Act. 229 NLRB at 1003 (footnote omitted). The majority here does not seem to make this distinction—which would give graduate assistants at least some protections under the Act—and thus itself seems to depart from the precedent it invokes.

In sum, while the *NYU* Board did not write on a clean slate, it hardly abandoned a long line of carefully reasoned, uncontroversial decisions. And, as we will explain, much has changed in the academic world since the 1970's.

B.

The principle applied in *NYU*—and the one that should be followed here—is that the Board must give effect to the plain meaning of Section 2(3) of the Act and its broad definition of "employee," which "reflects the common law agency doctrine of the conventional master-servant relationship." *NYU*, 332 NLRB at 1205, citing *NLRB v. Town & Country Electric*, 516 U.S. 85, 93–95 (1995). See also *Seattle Opera v. NLRB*, 292 F.3d 757, 761–762 (D.C. Cir. 2002), enfg. 331 NLRB 1072 (2000) (opera's auxiliary choristers are statutory employees, applying common-law test). Section 2(3) provides in relevant part that the "term 'employee' shall include *any* employee. . . ." 29 U.S.C. §152(3) (emphasis added). Congress specifically envisioned that professional employees —defined in Section 2(12) in terms that easily encompass graduate assistants—would be covered by the Act.

We do not understand the majority to hold that the graduate assistants in this case are *not* common-law employees, a position that only Member Schaumber reaches toward.[9] Here, the Board's "departure from the common law of agency" with respect to employee status is unreasonable. Compare *Town & Country Electric*, supra, 516 U.S. at 94 (upholding Board's interpretation of term "employee" as "consistent with the common law"). See also *Seattle Opera*, 292 F.3d at 765 fn. 11 (Board's hypothetical "neglect of the common law definition could have rendered its decision arbitrary and capricious").

Nothing in Section 2(3) excludes statutory employees from the Act's protections, on the basis that the employment relationship is not their "primary" relationship with their employer. In this respect, the majority's approach bears a striking resemblance to the Board's original "economic realities" test for employee status, which Congress expressly rejected when it passed the Taft-Hartley Amendments in 1947. That test was based on economic and policy considerations, rather than on common-law principles, but it did not survive.[10]

Absent compelling indications of Congressional intent, the Board simply is not free to create an exclusion from the Act's coverage for a category of workers who meet the literal statutory definition of employees. As the *NYU* Board observed, there is no such exclusion for "students." 332 NLRB at 1206. Cf. *Sure-Tan, Inc. v. NLRB,* 467 U.S. 883, 891–892 (1984) (observing that the "breadth of [the Act's] definition is striking" and noting lack of express exemption for undocumented aliens). Here, the majority cites nothing in the text or structure of the Act, nothing in the Act's legislative history, and no other Federal statute that bears directly on the issues presented. It goes without saying that the Board's own policymaking is bounded by the limits Congress has set.

The Supreme Court's decision in *Yeshiva,* supra, is instructive on this point. There, the Court considered whether university faculty members at one institution were managerial employees and so excluded from coverage. It observed that it could not decide this case by weighing the probable benefits and burdens of faculty collective bargaining. That, after all, is a matter for Congress, not this Court. 444 U.S. at 690 fn. 29 (citation omitted)

Other Federal courts have made similar observations in analogous cases, choosing to follow the plain language of the Act, rather than "attempting to 'second guess' Congress on a political and philosophical issue." *Cincinnati Assn. for the Blind v. NLRB,* 672 F.2d 567, 571 (6th Cir. 1982), cert. denied 459 U.S. 835 (1982) (refusing to find exception to Section 2(3) of the Act for disabled workers employed in sheltered workshops).[11] In a recent case where the Act's language was far less clear, our colleagues themselves have insisted that the statutory text alone dictated the outcome—indeed, they were content to "examine a particular statutory provision [Section 8(g) of the Act] in isolation" (to quote their words here).[12] The approach taken in this case stands in sharp contrast.

The majority never addresses the language of Section 2(3), which the Supreme Court has described as "broad." *Town & Country Electric,* 516 U.S. at 90 (citing dictionary definition of "employee" as including any "person who works for another in return for financial or other compensation"). Instead, it proceeds directly to consult "Congressional policies for guidance in determining the outer limits of statutory employee status." The majority cites the exclusion for managerial employees, which is not based on the Act's text. But in that example, as the Supreme Court explained, the "legislative history strongly suggests that there . . . were . . . employees . . . regarded as so clearly outside the Act that no specific exclusionary provision was thought necessary." *NLRB v. Bell Aerospace Co.*, 416 U.S. 267, 283 (1974). Graduate assistants simply do not fall into that category.

The Board's decision in *WBAI Pacifica Foundation*, 328 NLRB 1273 (1999), quoted by the majority, does not support its position here. That case involved the unpaid staff of a noncommercial radio station, who did not receive compensation or benefits of any kind, and whose work hours were "a matter within their discretion and desire." Id. at 1273. The Board found "*no* economic aspect to their relationship with the Employer, either actual or anticipated." Id. at 1275 (emphasis added). "Unpaid staff," the Board observed, "do not depend upon the Employer, even in part, for their livelihood or for the improvement of their economic standards." Id. at 1276. Rather, the Board explained, unpaid staff "work[ed] out of an interest in seeing the station continue to exist and thrive, out of concern for the content of the programs they produce, and for the personal enrichment of doing a service to the community and receiving recognition from the community." Id. at 1275.

The relationship between Brown and its graduate assistants is clearly different in nature. Teaching assistants, the Regional Director found, "perform services under the direction and control of Brown"—they teach undergraduates, just as faculty members do[13]—and "are compensated for these services by Brown," by way of a stipend, health fee, and tuition remission. As for research assistants in the social sciences and humanities (who were included in the bargaining unit), the Regional Director observed that they "have expectations placed upon them other than their academic achievement, in exchange for compensation."[14] The proctors, finally, are "performing services that are not integrated with an academic program," such as working in university offices and museums. Notably, the Regional Director found that Brown withholds income taxes from the stipends of teaching assistants, research assistants, and proctors and requires them to prove their eligibility for employment under Federal immigration laws.

The majority is mistaken, then, when it insists that the graduate assistants here do not receive "consideration for work," but merely financial aid. While it is true, as the majority observes, that "all the petitioned-for individuals are students and must first be enrolled at Brown to be awarded a TA, RA, or proctorship," that fact does not foreclose a meaningful economic relationship (as well as an educational relationship) between Brown and the graduate assistants. The Act requires merely the existence of such an economic relationship, not that it be the only or the primary relationship between a statutory employee and a statutory employer.[15]

C.

Even assuming that the Board were free to decide this case essentially on policy grounds, the majority's approach, minimizing the economic relationship between graduate assistants and their universities, is unsound. It rests on fundamental misunderstandings of contemporary higher education, which reflect our colleagues' unwillingness to take a close look at the academic world. Today, the academy is also a workplace for many graduate students, and disputes over work-related issues are common. As a result, the policies of the Act—increasing the bargaining power of employees, encouraging collective bargaining, and protecting freedom of association—apply in the university context, too. Not only is the majority mistaken in giving virtually no weight to the common-law employment status of graduate assistants, it also errs in failing to see that the larger aims of federal labor law are served by finding statutory coverage here. Indeed, the majority's policy concerns are not derived from the Act at all, but instead reflect an abstract view about what is best for American higher education—a subject far removed from the Board's expertise.

American higher education was being transformed even as the Board's "traditional" approach to graduate-student unionization developed. Nearly a decade before the Board decided *St. Clare's Hospital,* distinguished scholar and Columbia University administrator Jacques Barzun described changes that were tearing "apart the fabric of the former, single-minded" American university. He warned that "a big corporation has replaced the once self-centered company of scholars."[16] In deciding to exercise jurisdiction over private, non-profit universities more than 30 years ago (and reversing longstanding precedent in doing so), the Board recognized this development.[17]

After the 1980's, financial resources from governments became more difficult for universities to obtain.[18] "[A]s financial support for colleges and universities lag behind escalating costs, campus administrators increasingly turn to ill-paid, overworked part- or full-time adjunct lecturers and graduate students to meet instructional needs."[19] By December

2000, 23.3 percent of college instructors were graduate teaching assistants.[20]

The reason for the widespread shift from tenured faculty to graduate teaching assistants and adjunct instructors is simple: cost savings. Graduate student teachers earn a fraction of the earnings of faculty members.[21]

Two perceptive scholars have recently described the context in which union organizing among graduate students has developed. Their description is worth quoting at length:

> The post World War II expansion of universities is a well-documented phenomenon. Enrollments, resources, and activities increased and diversified. Universities were transformed into mega-complexes. But by the late 1980s and throughout the 1990s, the realization spread that expansion was not limitless. In response to heightened accountability demands, universities adopted management strategies that entailed belt-tightening and restructuring of the academic workplace. . . . [M]any universities replaced full-time tenure-track faculty lines with non-tenure-line and part-time appointments.
>
> . . .
>
> Expansion of doctoral degree production has continued nonetheless. . . . The discrepancy between ideals and realities prompt graduate students to consider unionization a viable solution to their concerns and an avenue to redress their sense of powerlessness.
>
> . . . .
>
> Among the primary reasons for graduate student unionization is the lengthened time required to complete a degree, coupled with an increased reluctance on the part of students to live in what they perceive as academic ghettos. Many older graduate students desire to start families, need health care coverage and job security, and perceive the faculty with whom they work to be living in comparative luxury. . . . *[D]ata show that the unionization of these individuals is driven fundamentally by economic realities.* Daniel J. Julius & Patricia J. Gumport, *Graduate Student Unionization: Catalysts and Consequences*, 26 REVIEW OF HIGHER EDUC. No. 2, 187 at 191, 196 (2002) (emphasis added; citations omitted).

Describing the same process, another scholar observes that the "increased dependence on graduate assistantships has created a group of workers who demand more economic benefits and workplace rights."[22] The question, then, is whether the collective efforts of these workers will be protected by federal labor law and channeled into the processes the law creates. Given the likelihood that graduate students will continue to pursue their economic interests through union organizing —even those who live the life of the mind must eat—there are powerful reasons to apply the Act and so encourage collective bargaining to avoid labor disputes, as Congress envisioned.[23] The prospect of continued labor unrest on campus, with or without federal regulation, is precisely what prompted the Board to assert jurisdiction over private nonprofit universities in the first place, three decades ago.[24]

The majority ignores the developments that led to the rise of graduate student organizing or their implications for the issue decided today. Instead, it treats the Board's 1974 decision in *Leland Stanford,* together with the 1977 decision in *St. Clare's Hospital,* as the last word. Like other regulatory agencies, however, the Board is "neither required nor supposed to regulate the present and the future within the inflexible limits of yesterday," but rather must "adapt [its] rules and practices to the Nation's needs in a volatile changing economy." *American Trucking Associations v. Atchison Topeka & Santa Fe Railway Co.,* 387 U.S. 397, 416 (1967).[25] The majority's failure to do so in this case is arbitrary.

III.

At the core of the majority's argument are the twin notions that (1) issues related to the terms and conditions of graduate student employment are "not readily adaptable to the collective-bargaining process," *St. Clare's Hospital,* 229 NLRB at 1002; and (2) imposing collective bargaining will harm "academic freedom" (as the majority defines it) and the quality of higher education. Neither notion is supported by empirical evidence of any kind. In fact, the evidence refutes them.

How can it be said that the terms and conditions of graduate-student employment are not adaptable to collective bargaining when collective bargaining over these precise issues is being conducted successfully in universities across the nation? New York University, ironically, is a case in point, but it is hardly alone. The recently-reached collective bargaining agreement there addresses such matters as stipends, pay periods, discipline and discharge, job posting, a grievance-and-arbitration procedure, and health insurance. It also contains a "management and academic rights" clause, which provides that:

> Decisions regarding who is taught, what is taught, how it is taught and who does the teaching involve academic judgment and shall be made at the sole discretion of the University. Collective Bargaining Agreement between New York University and International Union, UAW, AFL-CIO and Local 2110, Technical Office and Professional Workers, UAW (Sept. 1, 2001–Aug. 31, 2005), Art. XXII.[26]

The NYU agreement neatly illustrates the correctness of the *NYU* Board's view that the institution of collective bargaining is flexible enough to succeed in this context, as it has in so many others, from manufacturing to entertainment, health care to professional sports.

The NYU agreement cannot be dismissed as an anomaly. The amicus briefs to the Board submitted by the American Federation of Labor-Congress of Industrial Organizations (AFL-CIO) and the American Association of University Professors (AAUP) inform us of many other, established collective bargaining relationships between graduate student unions and universities.[27] To be sure, most involve public universities, but there is nothing fundamentally different between collective bargaining in public-sector and private-sector universities. www.nlrb.gov/nlrb/shared_files/decisions/342/342-42.htm_ftn59[28] The majority concedes that the subjects of graduate student collective bargaining "give the appearance of being terms and conditions of employment." Obviously, they *are* terms and conditions of employment, as found in a particular setting.

There remains the majority's claim that collective bargaining can only harm "academic freedom" and educational quality. Putting aside the issue of the Board's authority to serve as an expert guardian of these interests, the question is one of evidence. Here, too, the majority's claims are not simply unsupported, but are actually contradicted. The majority emphasizes that collective bargaining is "predicated on the collective or group treatment of represented individuals," while the "educational process" involves personal relationships between individual students and faculty members. The issue, if one is presented at all by this difference, is whether the two processes can coexist. Clearly, they can. The evidence is not just the ongoing collective-bargaining relationships between universities and graduate students already mentioned.

It also includes studies ignored by the majority, which show that collective bargaining has not harmed mentoring relationships between faculty members and graduate students.[29] These conclusions are not surprising. Collective bargaining is typically conducted by representatives of the university and graduate students' unions, not individual mentors and their students.

After a careful review, scholars Daniel Julius and Patricia Gumport, for example, concluded not only that "fears that [collective bargaining] will undermine mentoring relationships . . . appear to be foundationless," but also that data "suggest that the clarification of roles and employment policies can *enhance* mentoring relationships."[30] Scholar Gordon Hewitt reached a similar conclusion based on an analysis of the attitudes of almost 300 faculty members at five university campuses with at least four-year histories of graduate-student collective bargaining. Summarizing the results of his survey, Hewitt observes that:

> It is clear . . . that faculty do not have a negative attitude toward graduate student collective bargaining. It is important to reiterate that the results show faculty feel graduate assistants are employees of the university, support the right of graduate students to bargain collectively, and believe collective bargaining is appropriate for graduate students. *It is even more important to restate that, based on their experiences, collective bargaining does not inhibit their ability to advise, instruct, or mentor their graduate students.* Hewitt, supra, 29 JOURNAL OF COLLECTIVE NEGOTIATIONS IN THE PUBLIC SECTOR at 164 (emphasis added).

Amicus AAUP echoes these views in its brief to the Board. These findings should give the majority some pause, as should the obvious fact that whether or not the rights of graduate student employees are to be recognized under the Act, economic concerns have already intruded on academic relationships.

Finally, the majority invokes "academic freedom" as a basis for denying graduate student employees any rights under the Act. This rationale adds insult to injury. To begin, the majority defines "academic freedom" so broadly that it is necessarily incompatible with *any* constraint on the managerial prerogatives of university administrators. But academic freedom properly focuses on efforts to regulate the "content of the speech engaged in by the university or those affiliated with it." *University of Pennsylvania v. EEOC*, 493 U.S. 182, 197 (1990). On the majority's view, private universities should not be subject to the Act at all. But, of course, they are—just as are newsgathering organizations, whose analogous claims of First Amendment immunity from the Act were rejected by the Supreme Court long ago.[31]

The *NYU* Board correctly explained that the threat to academic freedom in this context—properly understood in terms of free speech in the university setting—was pure conjecture. 332 NLRB at 1208 fn. 9. We hasten to add that graduate students themselves have a stake in academic freedom, which they presumably will be reluctant to endanger in collective bargaining. As demonstrated in the amicus brief of the AAUP (a historical champion of academic freedom), collective bargaining and academic freedom are not incompatible; indeed, academic freedom for instructors can be strengthened through collective bargaining.[32]

IV.

"[W]e declare the federal law to be that graduate student assistants are not employees within the meaning of Section 2(3) of the Act," says the majority. But the majority has overstepped its authority, overlooked the economic realities of the academic world, and overruled *NYU* without ever coming to terms with the rationale for that decision. The result leaves graduate students outside the Act's protection and without recourse to its mechanisms for resolving labor disputes. The developments that brought graduate students to the Board will not go away, but they will have to be addressed elsewhere, if the majority's decision stands. That result does American universities no favors. We dissent.

Dated, Washington, D.C. July 13, 2004.

NOTES

1. See Neal H. Hutchens & Melissa B. Hutchens, *Catching the Union Bug: Graduate Student Employees and Unionization,* 39 GONZAGA L. REV. 105, 106–107 (2004) (surveying history and status of graduate student unions); Daniel J. Julius & Patricia J. Gumport, *Graduate Student Unionization: Catalysts and Consequences,* 26 REVIEW OF HIGHER EDUCATION 187, 191–196 (2002) (same); Grant M. Hayden, *"The University Works Because We Do": Collective Bargaining Rights for Graduate Assistants,* 69 FORDHAM L. REV. 1233, 1236–1243 (2001) (same); Douglas Sorrelle Streitz & Jennifer Allyson

Hunkler, *Teaching or Learning: Are Teaching Assistants Students or Employees,* 24 JOURNAL OF COLLEGE & UNIVERSITY LAW 349, 358–370 (1997) (same). By one recent count, 23 American universities have recognized graduate student unions or faculty unions including graduate students, beginning in 1969 with the University of Wisconsin–Madison. See Coalition of Graduate Employee Unions, *Frequently Asked Questions about Graduate Employee Unions* at www .cgeu.org/FAQ basics.html.

2. *New York University,* 332 NLRB 1205 (2000) (*NYU*).

3. *Leland Stanford Junior University,* 214 NLRB 621 (1974).

4. *St. Clare's Hospital & Health Center,* 229 NLRB 1000 (1977).

5. *Boston Medical Center,* 330 NLRB 152 (1999). That decision concerned hospital interns, residents, and fellows (house staff) involved in medical training as well as in patient care. In upholding their right to engage in collective bargaining, despite their status as students, the Board overruled *St. Clare's Hospital,* supra. The Board's decision today explicitly notes that it "express[es] no opinion regarding" *Boston Medical Center.* We believe that *Boston Medical Center* was correctly decided.

6. The majority quotes from the Supreme Court's decision in *NLRB v. Yeshiva University,* 444 U.S. 672, 680–681 (1980), in which the Court held that, given their role in university governance, the faculty members involved there were managerial employees, not covered by the Act. The Court made clear, however, that not all faculty members at every university would fall into the same category. 444 U.S. at 690 fn. 31. Following *Yeshiva,* the Board has continued to find faculty-member bargaining units appropriate. See, e.g., *Bradford College,* 261 NLRB 565 (1982).

7. Graduate assistantships are modest, even at top schools. The Regional Director found that at Brown the "basic stipend for a fellowship, teaching assistantship, research assistantship, or proctorship is $12,800 for the 2001–2002 academic year." According to a 2003 report, the "average amount received by full-time, full-year graduate and first-professional students with assistantships was $9,800." Susan P. Choi & Sonya Geis, "Student Financing of Graduate and First-Professional Education, 1999–2000," National Center for Education Statistics, Institute of Education Sciences, U.S. Dept. of Education 22 (2003). It stands to reason that graduate student wages are low because, to quote Sec. 1 of the Act, the "inequality of bargaining power" between schools and graduate employees has the effect of "depressing wage rates." 29 U.S.C. §151.

8. *Adelphi University,* 195 NLRB 639 (1972).

9. Member Schaumber asserts that "graduate student assistants fit poorly within the common law definition of 'employee.'" He maintains that graduate assistants are "not 'hired' to serve" in that capacity, that their work is "not performed 'for' the university, as such," and that their stipends "are not a quid pro quo for services rendered." We disagree in each respect, as a factual matter. As

the Regional Director found, graduate assistants carry out the work of the university, not their own projects, and they are compensated for it. There can be no doubt, of course, that Brown had the right to control the performance of the graduate assistants' work for the university, a key test for employee status at common law. See RESTATEMENT (SECOND) OF AGENCY §2(2) (1958) ("A servant is an agent employed by a master to perform service in his affairs whose physical conduct in the performance of the service is controlled or is subject to the right to control by the master"). Graduate students are clearly neither volunteers nor independent contractors.

10. See *NLRB v. United Insurance Co.*, 390 U.S. 254, 256 (1968) (discussing Congressional overruling of *NLRB v. Hearst Publications, Inc.*, 322 U.S. 111 (1944)). As we will explain, we believe that the economic realities here do support finding statutory coverage in any case.

11. See also *NLRB v. Lighthouse for the Blind of Houston*, 696 F.2d 399, 404 fn. 21 (5th Cir. 1983) (rejecting argument that [the] Board lacked jurisdiction over sheltered workshop and disabled workers employed there). We believe that the Board's approach in this area—the Board chooses to exercise jurisdiction only where the relationship between disabled workers and their employer is "typically industrial," as opposed to "primarily rehabilitative"—is ripe for reconsideration, particularly in light of the evolution of Federal policy toward disabled workers. See *NYU*, 332 NLRB at 1207 (discussing disabled-worker cases). The issue is now pending before the Board in *Brevard Achievement Center, Inc.*, No. 12-RC-8515 (review granted Aug. 23, 2000).

12. *Alexandria Clinic*, 339 NLRB No. 162, slip op. at 3 fn. 8 (2003).

13. The Regional Director found that the number of teaching assistantships, and the assignment of assistants to particular courses, is tied to undergraduate enrollment. She also found that Brown had "failed to demonstrate that most teaching assistantships at Brown are undertaken in order to fulfill a degree requirement."

14. The Regional Director found "insufficient evidence . . . upon which to conclude that as a general rule the RAs in the social sciences and humanities departments perform research as part of their studies in order to complete their dissertations," in contrast to RA's in the physical sciences, who were not included in the unit.

15. See, e.g., *Seattle Opera*, 292 F.3d at 762 ("[T]he person asserting employee status [under the Act] *does* have such status if (1) he works for a statutory employer in return for financial or other compensation . . . and (2) the statutory employer has the power or right to control and direct the person in the material details of how such work is to be performed").

16. Jacques Barzun, The American University: How It Runs, Where It Is Going 3 (1968).

17. See *Cornell University,* 183 NLRB 329, 331–333 (1970), overruling *Trustees of Columbia University,* 97 NLRB 424 (1951).

18. See, e.g., Clark Kerr, Troubled Times for American Higher Education: The 1990s and Beyond 3 (1994).

19. COMMITTEE ON PROFESSIONAL EMPLOYMENT, MODERN LANGUAGE AS-SOCIATION, FINAL REPORT 3 (1997) at www.mla.org/resources/documents/rep_ employment/prof-employment1 (examining higher education's pedagogical and professional crisis and proposing ways to increase the effectiveness of higher education).

20. *Reliance on Part-Time Faculty Members and How They Are Treated, Selected Disciplines,* CHRON. HIGHER EDUC., Dec. 1, 2000, available at chronicle .com/prm/weekley/v47/i14/14a01301.htm. See also Hutchens & Hutchens, supra, *Catching the Union Bug,* 39 GONZAGA L. REV. at 126 ("In an effort to contain costs, colleges and universities have increasingly relied on graduate students and non-tenure-track instructors"). Illustrating this trend, the New York Times recently reported that graduate students "teach more than half of the core courses that all Columbia [University] students must take." Karen W. Arenson, *Pushing for Union, Columbia Grad Students Are Set to Strike,* NEW YORK TIMES, p. A-11 (April 17, 2004).

21. Ana Marie Cox, *More Professors Said to Be off Tenure Track, for Graduate Assistants,* CHRON. HIGHER EDUC. (July 6, 2001) available at chronicle .com/prm/weekly/v47/i43/43a01201.htm. See also *Stipends for Graduate Assistants, 2001,* CHRON. HIGHER EDUC., Sept. 28, 2002, available at chronicle.com/ stats/stipends/.

22. Gordon J. Hewitt, *Graduate Student Employee Collective Bargaining and the Educational Relationship between Faculty and Graduate Students,* 29 J. COLLECTIVE NEGOTIATIONS IN THE PUBLIC SECTOR 153, 154 (2000). See also Hutchens & Hutchens, supra, *Catching the Union Bug,* 39 GONZAGA L. REV. at 126 ("[T]he reality at many institutions likely belies a picture of students carefully mentored by faculty in their employment capacities, especially in the context of teaching assistants.").

23. See Sec. 1, 29 U.S.C. §151.

24. See *Cornell University,* supra, 183 NLRB at 333.

25. The Board's recent failure to face contemporary economic realities threatens to become a recurring theme of its decisions. See *MV Transportation,* 337 NLRB 770, 776 (2002) (Member Liebman, dissenting) (criticizing [the] Board's reversal of successor-bar doctrine, despite [a] large increase in corporate mergers and acquisitions that destabilize workplaces).

26. The collective-bargaining agreement is posted on the University's Internet website at www.nyu.edu/hr/.

27. The AFL-CIO, for example, cites bargaining relationships at the Univer-

sity of California, the University of Florida, the University of South Florida, the University of Iowa, the University of Kansas, the University of Massachusetts, Michigan State University, the University of Michigan, Rutgers, the City University of New York, New York University, the State University of New York, the University of Oregon, Temple University, the University of Wisconsin, and Wayne State University. Brief of Amicus Curiae AFL-CIO in Support of Petitioner at 36 (May 20, 2002). See also Julius & Gumport, supra, *Graduate Student Unionization,* 26 REVIEW OF HIGHER EDUCATION at 192–193 (Table 1: "The Status of Graduate Student Unions in U.S. Institutions"). www.nlrb.gov/nlrb/shared_files/decisions/342/342-42.htm—_ftnref59

28. The majority points out that "states have the authority to limit bargaining subjects for public academic employees." But under the Act, not every subject of interest to graduate assistants would be a mandatory subject of bargaining. The Board presumably would be free to take into account the nature of the academic enterprise in deciding which subjects are mandatory and which merely permissive. See fn. 32, infra (discussing statutory bargaining obligations).

29. See Julius & Gumport, supra, *Graduate Student Unionization,* 26 REVIEW OF HIGHER EDUCATION at 201–209; Hewitt, supra, *Graduate Student Employee Collective Bargaining and the Educational Relationship between Faculty and Graduate Students,* 29 JOURNAL OF COLLECTIVE NEGOTIATIONS IN THE PUBLIC SECTOR at 159–164.

30. Julius & Gumport, supra, 26 REVIEW OF HIGHER EDUCATION at 201, 209.

31. *Associated Press v. NLRB,* 301 U.S. 103, 130–133 (1937).

32. The majority contends (1) that the "imposition of collective bargaining on the relationship between a university and its graduate students . . ." would limit the university's [academic] freedom to determine a wide range of matters"; and (2) that "because graduate student assistants are students, those limitations intrude on core academic freedoms in a manner simply not present in cases involving faculty employees." We disagree with both claims.

First, under Sec. 8(d) of the Act, collective bargaining would be limited to "wages, hours, and other terms and conditions of employment" for graduate student assistants. 29 U.S.C. §158(d). And with respect to those mandatory subjects of bargaining, the "Act does not compel agreements between employers and employees," just the "free opportunity for negotiation," as the NYU Board correctly observed. 332 NLRB at 1208, quoting *NLRB v. Jones & Laughlin Steel Corp.,* 301 U.S. 1, 45 (1937).

Second, the basis for the majority's distinction between faculty-member bargaining and graduate-assistant bargaining escapes us. In our view, there is no harm to genuine academic freedom in either case. But under the majority's view, faculty-member bargaining would interfere with the prerogatives of university management at least as much as graduate-student bargaining would. It is surely the subjects of bargaining that matter, not the identity of the bargaining party. In that respect, the similarities between graduate assistants and faculty members (in contrast to clerical or maintenance staff members, for example) is clear.

Notes

NOTES TO CHAPTER I

1. On the failure of professional associations to exert even modest influence on university employers, see Watt's entry, "The Modern Language Association" in *Academic Keywords* (169–178) and his "What Is the MLA?" As Lennard Davis observes in his "manifesto" against them, "the obvious thing about professional organizations in general is how well they dovetail with institutional agendas" (197).

2. One well-known survey of wages for casual academic teachers was conducted by the Coalition on the Academic Work Force (CAW). In English composition, fewer than one-third of the responding programs paid more than $2,500 a class. Nearly half (47.6 percent) paid less than $2,000 per class: teaching a full-time load of eight classes nets less than $16,000 annually, usually without benefits.

3. This can be described as a system of "all but unwaged" work, or a kind of volunteerism, like the Peace Corps, increasingly approachable through an ethos of service or creativity, as with the "avocational" and "supplemental" activities that generate a large fraction of web content. In 2000, Tiziana Terranova and Andrew Ross attempted to chart the strategic exploitation of "free labor" in both digital capitalism and the occupations of mental work more generally. As Ross observes: from the point of view of accumulation, the phenomenon of doctoral degree holders driving taxicabs does not represent a "waste" of education but testifies instead to its ruthless and systematic conversion of it to "un- or undercompensated labor" in ways we have yet to fully chart (27).

4. On academic unionism, professional work and social movements, see Rhoades; Martin, "Education as National Pedagogy" and "Stat(e)ing the Obvious"; Tirelli; Aronowitz, Nelson, *Manifesto* and *Academic Keywords*; Mark Kelley; and B. Bowen, "This Old House."

5. During this period, largely coterminous with Phyllis Franklin's unprecedented two decades as executive director of the MLA, numerous measures were employed by the association to contain dissent, including changing the organization's constitution. Some of these measures are discussed in Kelley and Christensen. For the association's official view of itself in relation to graduate-employee activism, see Showalter.

6. Interestingly, police officers and soldiers also frequently have the opportunity to seek new careers at age thirty-seven or thirty-eight. These retired servants of the state are typically homeowners and parents, enjoying annual pensions sometimes larger than faculty salaries and lifetime medical coverage: their years of service to the state have been amply rewarded. From the perspective of the legally enforced superexploitation of the graduate employee—the leading edge of the knowledge proletariat—the mere everyday exploitation of the working class has started to look pretty comfortable. Few members of the professoriate would complain if their contracts resembled the terms of service of these public employees: paid apprenticeship, twenty years of service, a decent wage, and a pension. (Nor is this mere speculation: two-thirds of higher education faculty in public institutions are unionized and enjoy rates of pay not very different from soldiers and police officers. From a labor point of view, faculty unions have been less successful than other public-employee unions in preventing a second tier of service—although outsourcing and casualization is a significant feature of the law-enforcement and military workplace as well.)

7. It has been suggested that the student movements of the 1960s, especially the Berkeley Free Speech Movement (FSM), gave rise to the graduate employee labor movement. It seems reasonable that the FSM and other movements for student power had a fair amount of influence on the mindset and commitments of grad employee unionists in early efforts, especially in the 1965 Berkeley effort. But by far the concerns of graduate employee unionists were in the early and mid 1970s the concerns of other unionists of that period, as well as of grad employee unionists today: workload, wages, health care, and grievance procedures. Rather than the "student power" movements, the most direct influence and often material support to grad employee unionists came from the individuals and institutions active in the movement to organize the tenure-stream faculty, as well as the legal and political environment fostered by the broader movement to organize public employees.

8. In 1970, with the first wave of academic labor organizing in high gear, the NLRB first began to assert jurisdiction over the teaching and nonteaching employees of private not-for-profit colleges and universities, where such institutions can be observed to "have a substantial effect on commerce." Most of the NLRB's higher education activity involved tenure-stream faculty and nonacademic staff, but in 1972, the Adelphi faculty union sought to include about 100 graduate teaching assistants in a bargaining unit with 600 tenure-stream faculty and librarians. The board excluded graduate employees from the faculty unit, on the grounds that faculty and graduate employees did not have sufficient community of interest to permit for effective bargaining. Left open was the question of whether the teaching assistants could form a unit of their own. Two years later, a small group of research assistants in the Stanford physics department

made such an attempt. The 1974 NLRB turned them down, observing that they were "primarily students." Involving fewer than 100 graduate employees in a single department, all engaged in research rather than teaching, this case also left the question of graduate employees serving as teachers unaddressed. In 1976 and 1977, the board denied bargaining rights to medical residents and interns using the "primarily students" criterion (even though they had received their medical degrees and were engaged in postgraduate employment). As Rohrbacher observes, the NLRB at this point codified the earlier decisions into the "primary purpose test," asserting that employees who sought work for "primarily educational" (as opposed to "primarily economic" reasons), did not enjoy the protections of the NLRA. Most damaging for graduate employees was the broad editorializing of the 1977 board on "the student-teacher relationship," using language that effectively denied students of private universities bargaining rights in nearly all circumstances for the next quarter-century.

9. The critique of the job market heuristic was first circulated on the discussion list of the Graduate Student Caucus (E-grad) during 1994 and 1995, by this author and others. It was read at an MLA welcome session in December 1996 and brought to the MLA Committee on Professional Employment conversation by Vicky Smallman and Pat Carter, the graduate student members of that committee. As with previous disciplinary incorporations of the work of Nelson, Bérubé, and countless intellectuals of the graduate employee union movement, the CPE obscures the origins of this critique and claims authorship for itself (MLA, *Final Report*, 12).

10. Indeed, the profit-driven U.S. health care system is hazardous to your health: according to one responsible estimate in *JAMA*, and killing 225,000 persons a year, errors and the "adverse consequences" of health care itself are the third-leading cause of death in the United States, closely following cancer and heart disease, but far in advance of stroke, which comes in a very distant fourth (Starfield).

NOTES TO CHAPTER 2

1. See, for example, the 1999 National Student Satisfaction Report, conducted by Noel-Levitz, a higher education consulting firm and subsidiary of the USA Group, the major education lender (which in 2000 merged with Sallie Mae). The report claims to reflect survey data from over half a million students at nearly 900 institutions. The survey is evidently based on the firm's trademarked Student Satisfaction Inventory, which is primarily used by client educators to "assess client [student] satisfaction" and is not offered here as an authentic record of the student voice. Nonetheless, it is clearly an instrument that serves as the authentic record of student voice or "demand" for at least some

university administrators, who have been investing heavily in the "parking, food and comfortable living quarters" that Noel-Levitz claims are the top issues for students, while continuing to divert funding from instructional labor, an area in which Noel-Levitz reports continuing high levels of "client satisfaction."

2. Throughout the body of the chapter, I am quoting from the widely available online versions of Noble's essays (I use the authoritative versions housed on the UCSD server), on the theory that these versions will continue to be more widely circulated than the hardbound volume from Monthly Review Press. Nonetheless, some readers will find citations to the monograph helpful. The claims regarding the "second phase" of education commodification are found on pages 26–27 and are elaborated in the introduction (x) and page 37: "For most of the last two decades this transformation has centered upon the research function of the universities. But it has now [!] shifted to the instructional function." In his extremely persuasive discussion of the relationship between correpondence schools at the turn of the last century and distance education, Noble associates the correspondence movement with the emergence of a "casualized workforce of 'readers' who worked part-time and were paid on a piecework basis per lesson or exam (roughly twenty cents per lesson in the 1920s). Many firms preferred 'sub-professional' personnel, particularly untrained older women, for routine grading. These people often worked under sweatshop conditions, having to deliver a high volume of lessons in order to make a living, and were unable therefore to manage more than a perfunctory pedagogical performance" (9). My quarrel is obviously not with Noble's historical observation here, or with his claim that more distance education will mean more deskilling of this kind, but with his exclusive association of commodification and deskilling with technology. The university has already an established preference for a gendered and "sub-professional" workforce apart from distance education or any potential future expansion of it. The massive casualized workforce already established in the managed university seems to me to call for additional analysis in the vein of Harry Braverman's work (in which office technology is seen as called forth to serve already-existing transformations in the management of office labor). That is: must we not see the technologization represented by online learning as at least partially the result of a rationalized ("scientifically managed"), casualized, and deskilled workforce, rather than its cause?

3. It's worth underscoring that my divergence from Noble is overall nonetheless primarily one of emphasis: he focuses on distance education, technologization, and the tenure stream, and I focus on casualization and the work of students and other contingent labor. Far more important than any differences, however, is our similar fundamental approach to academic work by applying a labor theory of value, in contrast to the predominant vision aptly described by Dan Schiller as an "information exceptionalism" that attempts to substitute a

"knowledge theory of value" (Schiller, "Information Commodity," 105–106). As indicated in detail above, I wish to associate myself firmly with Noble's analysis of education commodification more generally and with his indispensable ramification of that analysis for the traditional faculty.

4. This is not to suggest that there aren't circumstances where the notion of intellectual property rights, as in the struggle to resist the exploitation of indigenous knowledges, can't be mobilized with great tactical effectiveness (Coombe).

5. For an alternate view in the materialist tradition (of education as a "fictitious commodity"), see Noble, *Digital Diploma Mills, Part III,* 3.

6. Enrique Dussel continues to argue, from a standpoint including textual scholarship regarding what he views as the movement of Marx's intention in the project of *Capital,* that living labor represents a more valid "starting point" than analysis of the commodity form for the critique of capitalism. Certainly, commodification critique has in many instances been subject to incorporation, and nowhere more so than in the popular culture of the academy's liberal elite. Nonetheless, rather than attempting to describe one or the other as the "logical starting point," the position offered here is that critique should make more of an effort to sketch the relation between what Mosely, by analogy to Banaji, suggests is something more like a "double starting point" (7).

7. The data on this question varies by gender: in all four groupings of annual earnings (grades 9–11, high school, some college, B.A. or more), male incomes have dropped and female earnings have risen. The female earnings growth varies little by level of education and is modest in relation to the gendered earnings gap, with average female income at all education levels remaining well below average male earnings (evidently at least in partial relation to the exploitive feminization of occupation categories, such as nursing and teaching). Of course, there are many other factors, especially the changing composition of the workforce, the class-stratified patterns of dual-income households, and the dramatic change in the relative size of the groups represented by various "education levels." In addition, the years devoted to "some college" and "B.A. or higher" have increased, and the very nature of "higher education" has been transformed to involve very different activities between 1970 and the present. Above all, these data need to be read in connection with the political work of feminism. Nonetheless, all caveats considered, one of the more dramatic movements of the data is to suggest a growing economic penalty for remaining outside of the work regime represented by "higher education."

8. Some of the observations in this and a preceding paragraph regarding the work experience of North American "youth" were previously framed in a book chapter, Marc Bousquet, "Cultural Capitalism and the James Formation," in Susan Griffin, ed., *Henry James Goes to the Movies* (Lexington: University of Kentucky Press, 2001), 210–239.

NOTES TO CHAPTER 3

1. For a brief discussion of the failure of gender equity initiatives to have a long-term effect on equity in adjunct employment, see Hoeller ("Equal Pay"), who observes that the unions of full-timers, campus employers, and state governments all participate in the situation by negotiating regular raises for full-timers but not for the disproportionately female nontenurable faculty.

2. Susanne Palmer notes that that one "outcome of the Yeshiva decision is that universities have modeled their faculty self-governance committees after the Yeshiva model. The more self-governance and economic decision-making that is given to faculty the less likely that a collective bargaining unit can be certified by the NLRB" (5).

3. These data were computed by Ehrenberg et al. from the APPA data compiled by the Association of Higher Education Facilities Officers in 1999. Ehrenberg's econometric approach leads him to emphasize that these dramatic wage differentials "are raw differences that do not control for characteristics of the institutions or the areas in which the institutions are located, which might be expected to influence staff salaries independent of unionization" (216). By "controlling for the other characteristics . . . that influence salaries" besides unionization, including "the logarithm of the average math and verbal SAT seventy-fifth percentile SAT score for entering freshmen at the institution," Ehrenberg believes that the effects of unionization are smaller than the "raw differences" appear to suggest on their own. The problem with econometric modeling is that the assumptions are themselves rhetorical: by assuming that the SAT scores of entering students affect the wages of custodians, Ehrenberg reasons that because tenure-stream faculty at some selective institutions, such as Harvard, are paid more than at some less-selective institutions, custodians will be paid more at the same institutions. While plausible, this reasoning confounds the actual wages of custodians at places like Johns Hopkins and fails to account for the structural consequences of outsourcing, through which even prestige employers do not directly employ their staff but simply "pay a service." In this way, it is not Johns Hopkins who pays a subliving wage, but the contractor.

4. Newfield makes these observations about recent management theory and education administration in a book that stops at 1980 (*Ivy and Industry*). He promises a second volume regarding subsequent developments.

5. The currency of Toyotist liberation management theory with the professional-managerial class and representatives of the corporate media notwithstanding, few workers are persuaded. Even though the UAW leadership, themselves generally labor professionals and labor bureaucrats, initially bought into elements of Toyota's "team concept" during the late 1980s, a 1989 groundswell from the membership passed a resolution rejecting their leadership's position of cooperation with management, describing teams as "a managerial device which

encourages competition between workers in order to eliminate jobs, weaken solidarity, and help develop anti-union attitudes" (J. Slaughter 2).

6. Rather than emphasize the New Left social movements, Joseph Garbarino emphasizes the strong relationship between faculty unionism and the "revolution in public-employee relations that occurred in most of the major industrial states" (20) after John F. Kennedy issued presidential Executive Order 10988. He predicted, accurately, that the regulation environment would shape future growth: "As more states adopt supportive bargaining laws for public employees, the staff of institutions of higher education will be caught up in the movement" (254).

7. *AAUP Bulletin,* March 1972, quoted in Garbarino 86. The best account of the changes in AAUP policy toward collective bargaining in this period is Hutcheson, especially chapters 3 and 4, "Custodians of the Interests of Higher Education, or Employees?" and "The AAUP and Unionization, 1966 to 1971."

NOTES TO CHAPTER 4

1. Sources of the quotations in this chapter are from interviews and email exchanges.

2. The June 1, 2007, update of the partnership's website begins with the confession, "Despite its name, Metropolitan College is not a college" (Metropolitan College).

3. See chapter 2, note 7.

NOTES TO CHAPTER 5

1. "In effect, we are assuming that individuals and groups/communities can indeed change institutions. But we are also assuming an agent of fairly powerful status already working within an institution: probably a member of the managerial or professional class who has entered an institution (e.g. the corporation) in some employee status that allows him or her to begin to make changes at least at a local level" (Porter et al., 613, n.3).

2. For more on the labor of the professional-managerial class—which differs from real wealth despite its "elite" status in that each generation has to renew its "knowledge capital" through hard work (whereas the capital of real wealth seems to renew itself without effort)—see Ehrenreich. The fear of "falling" out of the professional-managerial fraction of the working class is a prospect that professionals and managers worry about, not just for their children but for themselves. The accelerated industrialization of knowledge work in the "knowledge economy" has meant that professionals and managers must continuously rehabilitate their knowledge just to maintain their own career prospects and status. The privations of severe discipline and continuous self-fashioning associated

with training and apprenticeship (in undergraduate, professional-school, and early-career pressures) have become lifetime requirements for professionals and managers.

3. My purpose in this section is not to critique the work of actually existing WPAs but to discuss the figure of the WPA as it interpellates rhet-comp scholarship more generally, as part of a historical turn toward practical and theoretical accommodation of the "realities" of the managed university. This would be a discussion of the WPA as canny bureaucrat/pragmatist boss, as constructed by Richard Miller and Joseph Harris among others, insofar as that constructed figure threatens to become the field's dominant subject position, and not the vexed and contradictory intentions and experiences of individuals. The real experiences of WPAs are simply too diverse to be addressed here. Not all WPAs, for example, are administrators: some serve as a kind of peer advisor in departments where most of the writing instruction is done by full-time faculty; some are adjuncts themselves; many are graduate students. Nor is it my goal for this essay to be part of an effort to "reform" the practices of actually existing WPAs (as if the "bad policy" of lower administration caused the labor system), nor would such suggestions be consistent with this project's larger commitments. In the big picture, my goal would be not to reform but to abolish the WPA as part of a more general abolition of the scene of managed labor in the academy. In disciplinary terms, this would form part of a process of founding rhet-comp teaching and scholarship on the basis of collegiality and self-governance that obtains elsewhere in the academy rather than in the managed relation so firmly crystallized in the bodies and figure of the actually existing WPA.

Nonetheless, it may be helpful for some readers to trace the real experience behind the rhetorical figure. For instance, tracing the risk of "schizophrenia" involved in moving from academic labor to academic lower management, Roxanne Mountford observes that "having once been one of the instructor-laborers," the WPA genuinely wants to consider herself a labor "insider" and even an advocate but discovers herself willy-nilly "a representative of institutional interests" who suffers a radical "change in values" in connection with upper management, becoming in effect, "one of them" (41–43). Diana George's collection of narratives by WPAs is particularly evocative for those interested in the complex movement of the class allegiances of the actual persons in the job. Nancy Grimm's "The Way the Rich People Does It" explores the strong equivalence between the diminished notion of what counts as "critical" for the members of her family who did maid service and the pragmatism of administration in a writing program: "For the Conroy women, a 'critical' approach to the habits of the rich people meant [correcting their relatives] whose habits fell short," a kind of pragmatic approach to the idea of the critical that Grimm calls "useful" in learning to "pay attention" to "things that matter" to the "rich people" of the academy (i.e., "the people in funding positions in the university"). In the same collection, Johanna Atwood Brown explores the problem of graduate students who serve as administrators of other graduate employees in a way ("the peer who isn't a peer") that can be extended analytically to the structure of feeling animating the whole field of composition. Doug Hesse explores the consequences in his own life of living the role of "WPA-as-father," in a set of paternalist iterations ranging from the mass-mediated images of paternal caretaking represented by Anthony Hopkins in *Remains of the Day*, David Bartholamae's image of the WPA as Michael Keaton's Batman "protecting and responsible, yet also brooding," and the images drawn from Hesse's own adolescence "climbing on and off a garbage truck" (47, 50). For a critique of the many ways that actually existing WPAs become subject to the various ideologies of paternalism and benevolence, and the way in which even a shared sense of speaking from the "outside" can be mobilized by the administrative subject "in defense of tyranny," see Jeanne Gunner. For a discussion of the WPA as a worker with little control over the disposition of her own labor, see Laura Micciche.

4. David Downing's "Beyond Disciplinary English" systematically relates the operation of disciplinarity in English to the exploitative division of labor in the field, a formation he calls "managed disciplinarity" (28).

5. An opinion piece by Michael Murphy appeared in the *Chronicle of Higher Education* while I was revising an earlier version of this chapter. Overall, the later piece retains the rhetoric of the first ("We should formalize the . . . heterogeneity that actually exists in higher education") but substantially modifies his proposal in two respects. First, he now proposes creating tenure-track positions for full-timers who concentrate on teaching; second, he limits the proposal to "institutions where other faculty members now get significant load reductions for research and where large numbers of part-timers are now used" (B15). Insofar as these kinds of institutions already have a full-time faculty comprised of between 17and 28 percent non-tenure-track faculty, many of whom concentrate on teaching (some are non-tenure-track researchers), one has to ask, *even if* the "new" full-time positions were created by combining the part-time faculty positions into new tenure-track teaching positions, how would these new tenure-track teaching positions relate to the huge number of already existing non-tenure-track teaching positions? Or is Murphy now just arguing for the tenure eligibility of persons who concentrate on teaching, consistent with past academic practice at many institutions and the policies of all academic unions (as well as with my own views)? One still has to ask why does he now exclude non-research-oriented schools from his new recommendations, where the tenuring of faculty on the basis of teaching is common practice?

6. The survey breaks down teaching by department into "introductory," "all other," and "all" undergraduate courses. In English and free-standing composition courses, this schematic doesn't quite capture the role of writing instruction, which comprises a significant percentage of "introductory" courses but is far

from the total. Similarly, a great deal of writing instruction takes place in upper-division classes, such as business and professional writing, writing about literature and culture, and so on. The survey represents that 17–18 percent of "introductory" courses in the English and free-standing composition departments surveyed are taught by full-time non-tenure-track faculty.

7. For a skeptical account of what happens to proposals for change that threaten the "structural base" of disciplinary power, as well as the measure of improvements in "professional conditions" ("basically, the tenure rate for WPAs"), see Gunner 154, 160.

8. For instance, the UAW-affiliated NYU graduate-employee union won raises of $5,000 per year in its first contract (2002) for more than a third of its membership, with stipends increasing as much as 38 percent over the life of the contract, plus 100 percent health coverage. By 2004, the minimum graduate-employee stipend at NYU was $18,000 for a twenty-hour week. Similar gains were expected by the bargaining unit for non-tenure-track faculty on the same campus, the largest unit of its kind in the country. At the University of Michigan, the Graduate Employees Organization negotiated almost half a million dollars in additional child care subsidy from its employer, to $1,700 per semester for the first child plus $850 per semester per child thereafter. Similarly, at the largest public university system in the country, California State, the union's 2002 contract compelled the university to hire 20 percent more tenure-track faculty in each year of the contract, as well as provide expanded benefits and security for existing non-tenure-track faculty, including three-year contracts for those with six years of service (Phillips). For more details, see Gordon Lafer on graduate employee unionism, Susan Griffin on contingent-faculty unionism in composition, the Coalition of Graduate Employee Unions' website (www.cgeu.org), and *Workplace: A Journal for Academic Labor* (www.workplace-gsc.com).

9. In an article titled "The Worldwide Rise of Private Colleges," David Cohen in the *Chronicle of Higher Education* portrays privatization as a kind of corporate "white knight" that emerges in aftermath of the "failure" of the public sector: "As the world's hunger for higher education has outstripped the ability of many governments to pay for it, a type of institution has come to the rescue that is well established in the United States . . . private colleges." Associating the "public" with failure, scarcity, and famine ("world hunger"), the piece assigns heroic agency to market institutions and the United States. On this wildly rhetorical foundation, the piece proceeds to a stunningly propagandistic reversal of cause and effect in describing the privatization process: "In Mexico, a nine-month strike last year over the introduction of tuition at the country's largest public institution, the National Autonomous University, drove some middle-class students who were impatient with the strike's socialist ideals onto the campuses of private colleges" (A47–48). It is, of course, the forced introduction of tuition in a public institution that led to the nine-month strike, so if

there is a cause for middle-class flight from public institutions, it is not the "strike" or "socialist ideals" but the prior act of de-funding. One must ask, why does the article install "impatient middle class students" as the normative subjectivity, rather than the subject that is actually the norm on the scene—that is, a striking student subject engaged in a heroically protracted resistance to privatization?

NOTES TO CHAPTER 6

1. Of course, there have been complaints about the Bowen study, some of them quite heated. Dubbing Bowen the "Robert McNamara of the academic world" (a reference to Eugene McCarthy's quip that the trouble with McNamara was that he made no *small* mistakes), one reviewer compares the study to medical malpractice and complains that "a similar performance on the part of a mutual fund manager or CEO would mean the end of a career" (Rice). It's remarkable how rare such complaints have been. Moreover, the danger with this category of response is that by complaining of Bowen's "bad management," we grant the necessity for econometric, neoliberal, and managerialist leadership in the first place. The problems of academic labor won't be solved by more and better management but by repudiating academic managerialism more generally.

2. A more theoretical discussion of these issues and a critique of the related idea that degree holders are the "product" of graduate education is presented in the introduction.

3. Reminding us that "markets" are social formations, Evan Watkins calls academic-disciplinary responses of which Miller's is typical, "an interesting notion of 'ethical'" that "folds neatly" into marketization processes more generally: "Thus 'economic realities' don't intrude from the outside to set a limit on how many Ph.D.'s we should 'ethically' produce; economic practices are part of the training from the beginning" (164).

4. For example, see the mathematician Geoff Davis, whose model and recommendations are widely quoted by university administrations (University of Washington, for example). Claiming that the "history of mathematics Ph.D. production" is one of "perpetual instability" and "continual alternation" between shortage and surplus, Davis models a "10-year boom-bust cycle" in the job market. The positive "knowledge" represented by this model leads Davis to claim that "there are straightforward ways to remedy the situation," primarily better modeling and the "rationalizing" of "Ph.D. production."

5. Richard Ohmann discusses these events in chapter 2 of *English in America,* "MLA: Professors of Literature in a Group" (27–50). See also Kampf, "It's Alright, Ma" and interviews with Lauter and Kampf by student activists (Pannapacker and Parascondola, 1998), together with Kampf's letter of resignation from the Job Market Study Commission, appended to the Orr report (1198).

Works Cited

Adams, Richard P. "Nobody Wins the Numbers Game." *ADE (Association of Departments of English) Bulletin* 43 (1974): 6–8.

Alderman, Taylor. "Collective Bargaining: Another Viewpoint." *ADE (Association of Departments of English) Bulletin* 42 (September 1974): 34–36.

Allen, Don Cameron. *The Ph.D. in English and American Literature.* New York: Modern Language Association, 1968.

American Federation of Teachers. "Film Captures Adjunct Plight." No date. Available at: www.aft.org (accessed February 1, 2006).

American Historical Association. "Summary of Data from Surveys by the Coalition on the Academic Workforce." November 2000. Available at: www.theaha.org/caw/cawreport.htm (accessed May 15, 2007).

American Philosophical Association. "APA Statement to Prospective Graduate Students." No date. Available at: w3.arizona.edu/~phil/grad.htm (accessed February 10, 2001).

Argetsinger, Amy. "Oh, the Humanities! Pros Use Prose in Job-Hunting: Post-Tweed Breed of Professor Knows Marketing." *Washington Post,* December 30, 2000, C1.

Arnold, Gordon B. *The Politics of Faculty Unionization: The Experience of Three New England Universities.* Westport, Conn.: Bergin and Garvey, 2000.

Aronowitz, Stanley. *The Knowledge Factory: Dismantling the Corporate University and Creating True Higher Learning.* Boston: Beacon Press, 2000.

Aronowitz, Stanley, and William DiFazio. "Unions and the Future of Professional Work." Chapter 7 of *The Jobless Future: Sci-Tech and the Dogma of Work.* Minneapolis: University of Minnesota Press, 1994, 202–225.

Association of Departments of English. "From the Editor." *ADE (Association of Departments of English) Bulletin* 72 (Summer 1982): i–iii.

Ausubel, Jesse. "Virtual U: Origins and New Release; Remarks to the First Adopters Workshop." University of Pennsylvania, February 1, 2002. Available at: www.virtual-u.org/documentation/ausubelremarks.asp (accessed August 8, 2006).

Barrow, Clyde W. *Universities and the Capitalist State: Corporate Liberalism and the Reconstruction of American Higher Education, 1894–1928.* Madison: University of Wisconsin Press, 1990.

Bartlett, Laura, ed. *The Working Lives of College Students.* Includes contributions titled "Work, Meet Education, Your New Roommate," "The School-Work Connection," "Wonderful World of Work," "A Rude Awakening," and others. Available at: www.composition.dc-marion.ohio-state.edu/workinglives (accessed November 27, 2005).

Battista, Robert, Peter C. Schaumber, and Ronald Meisberg. "Decision on Review and Order." *Brown University and UAW* (Case no. 1-RC-21368). National Labor Relations Board, July 13, 2004.

Bell, Daniel. "By Whose Right?" In Harold Hodgkinson, ed., *Power and Authority: Transformation of Campus Governance.* San Francisco: Jossey-Bass, 1971, 151–173.

Berelson, Bernard. *Graduate Education in the United States.* New York: McGraw-Hill, 1960.

Berry, Joseph. "Contingent Faculty in Higher Education: An Organizing Strategy and Chicago Area Proposal." Ph.D. dissertation, Union Institute, Chicago, 2002. Available at: www.cewaction.org (accessed February 1, 2006).

Bérubé, Michael. *The Employment of English: Theory, Jobs, and the Future of Literary Studies.* New York: New York University Press, 1998.

Birnbaum, Robert. *How Colleges Work: The Cybernetics of Academic Organization and Leadership.* San Francisco: Jossey-Bass, 1988.

———. "The Latent Organization Functions of the Academic Senate." In Christopher M. Brown, ed., *Organization and Governance in Higher Education,* 5th ed. Boston: Pearson, 2000, 232–243.

Blumenstyk, Goldie. "For-Profit Colleges Face New Scrutiny." *Chronicle of Higher Education.* May 14, 2004. Available at: www.chronicle.com (accessed March 1, 2006).

———. "For-Profit Education: Online Courses Fuel Growth." *Chronicle of Higher Education.* November 25, 2005. Available at: www.chronicle.com (accessed March 1, 2006).

Bok, Derek. *Universities in the Marketplace: The Commercialization of Higher Education.* Princeton, N.J.: Princeton University Press, 2004.

Bok, Derek, and John T. Dunlop. *Labor and the American Community.* New York: Simon and Schuster, 1970.

Bousquet, Marc. "The Waste Product of Graduate Education: Toward a Dictatorship of the Flexible." *Social Text* 20 (Spring 2002): 81–104.

Bousquet, Marc, Tony Scott, and Leo Parascondola, eds. *Tenured Bosses and Disposable Teachers: Writing Instruction in the Managed University.* Carbondale: Southern Illinois University Press, 2004.

Bowen, Barbara. "Interview by Ann Wallace." *Workplace: A Journal for Academic Labor* 3.1 (January 2000). Available at: www.louisville.edu/journal/workplace/issue5/bowen.html.

———. "This Old House: Renovating the House of Labor at the City University of New York." *Workplace: A Journal for Academic Labor* 1.1 (January 1998). Available at: www.workplace-gsc.com/features1/bowen.html.

Bowen, William G., and Julie Ann Sosa. *Prospects for the Faculty in the Arts and Sciences: A Study of Factors Affecting Demand and Supply, 1987 to 2012.* Princeton, N.J.: Princeton University Press, 1989.

Bowles, Samuel, and Herbert Gintis. *Schooling in Capitalist America: Education Reform and the Contradictions of Economic Life.* New York: Basic Books, 1976.

Brantlinger, Patrick. *Crusoe's Footprints: Cultural Studies in Britain and America.* New York: Routledge, 1990.

Braverman, Harry. *Labor and Monopoly Capital: The Degradation of Work in the Twentieth Century.* New York: Monthly Review Press, 1974.

Brenner, Johanna. "On Gender and Class in U.S. Labor History." In Ellen Meiksins Wood, Peter Meiksins, and Michael B. Yates, eds., *Rising from the Ashes? Labor in the Age of "Global" Capitalism.* New York: Monthly Review Press, 1998, 110–126.

Brodsky, David. "Democratic vs. Corporate Governance." *Workplace: A Journal for Academic Labor* 4.2 (February 2002). Available at: www.workplace-gsc.com.

Bronfenbrenner, Kate, and Robert Hickey. "Winning Is Possible: Successful Union Organizing in the United States—Clear Lessons, Too Few Examples." *Multinational Monitor.* June 2003. Available at: www.multinationalmonitor.org (accessed July 10, 2005).

Brown, Christopher M., ed. *Organization and Governance in Higher Education,* 5th ed. ASHE Reader Series. Boston: Pearson, 2000.

Brown, Johanna Atwood. "The Peer Who Isn't a Peer: Authority and the Graduate Student Administrator." In Diana George, ed., *Kitchen Cooks, Plate Twirlers and Troubadors: Writing Program Administrators Tell Their Stories.* Portsmouth N.H.: Boynton/Cook Heinemann, 1999, 120–126.

"Brown Blood" (pseud.). Weblog Profile. Available at: community.livejournal.com/brown_blood (accessed December 10, 2006).

Bureau of Labor Statistics. *Union Members in 2006.* Available at: www.bls.gov/news.release/union2nrO.htm (accessed June 4, 2007).

Caffentzis, George. "Why Machines Cannot Create Value; or, Marx's Theory of Machines." In Jim Davis, Thomas Hirschl, and Michael Stack, eds., *Cutting Edge: Technology, Information Capitalism and Social Revolution.* London: Verso, 1997, 29–56.

Camhi, Joe. *Screw U., A Play in One Act.* Available at: www.cewaction.org (accessed February 1, 2006).

Campbell, Roald, Thomas Fleming, L. Jackson Newell, and John W. Bennion. *A

History of Thought and Practice in Educational Administration. New York: Teachers College Press, 1987.

Carnegie Commission on Higher Education. *The Governance of Higher Education: Six Priority Problems.* New York: McGraw-Hill, 1973.

Carroll, Jill. "How to Be One of the Gang When You're Not." *Chronicle of Higher Education,* January 18, 2002. Available at: www.chronicle.com (accessed March 1, 2006).

→ **✕✕** Carter, Christopher. *Rhetoric and Resistance in the Corporate Academy.* Cresskill, N.Y.: Hampton, 2008.

Cartter, Allan M. *Ph.D.'s and the Academic Labor Market.* New York: McGraw-Hill, 1976.

Cartter, Allan M., and R. L. Farrell. "Academic Labor Market Projections and the Draft." In *The Economics and Financing of Higher Education in the United States.* Washington, D.C.: Joint Economic Committee of the Congress, 1969, 357–374.

Castells, Manuel. *The Information Age: Economy, Society and Culture.* Vol. 1 in *The Rise of the Network Society,* 2nd ed. Malden, Mass.: Blackwell, 2000.

Chaffee, Ellen, and William Tierney. *Collegiate Culture and Leadership Strategies.* New York: American Council on Education, 1988

Cheney, Lynne V. "The Phantom Ph.D. Gap." *New York Times,* September 28, 1989, A27.

Cho, Hanah. "For-Profit Schools at 'Tipping Point.'" *Baltimore Sun,* February 28, 2006, 1D.

Christensen, Kirsten M. "On Fostering (In)Civility and Feeling (Un)Welcome. *minnesota review* 50/51 (Spring/Fall 1998): 263–269.

Clawson, Dan. *The Next Upsurge: Labor and the New Social Movements.* Ithaca, N.Y.: Cornell University Press, 2003.

Coalition on the Academic Workforce. *1999 Staffing Survey.* Available at: www.historians.org/caw/caw report.htm (accessed December 15, 2006).

Coalition of Graduate Employee Unions. *Casual Nation.* December 2000. Available at: www.cgeu.org.

Cohen, David. "The Worldwide Rise of Private Colleges." *Chronicle of Higher Education,* March 9, 2001, A47–A49.

Cohen, Michael, and James G. March. "Leadership in an Organized Anarchy." In Christopher M. Brown, ed., *Organization and Governance in Higher Education,* 5th ed. Boston: Pearson, 2000, 16–35.

Collins, Doug. "Second-Class Treatment for Adjuncts in Faculty Unions." *Chronicle of Higher Education,* December 16, 2005. Available at: www.chronicle.com (accessed February 1, 2006).

Conference on College Composition and Communication. "Statement of Principles and Standards for the Postsecondary Teaching of Writing." 1989. Available at: www.ncte.org/12/sub/state3.html.

Conway, Charnley. "Metropolitan College Develops Skilled Workers." *Business First of Louisville,* April 15, 2005. Available at: louisville.bizjournals.com.

Coombe, Rosemary. "Intellectual Property, Human Rights and Sovereignty." *Indiana Journal 4, Global Legal Studies* 59 (Fall 2998): 1–41.

Cox, Ana. "None of Your Business: The Rise of the University of Phoenix—and Why It Will Fail Us All." In B. Johnson, P. Kavanagh, and K. Mattson, eds., *Steal This University: The Rise of the Corporate University and the Academic Labor Movement.* New York: Routledge, 2003, 15–32.

Crowley, Sharon. *Composition in the University.* Pittsburgh: University of Pittsburgh Press, 1998.

Damrosch, David. *We Scholars: Changing the Culture of the University.* Cambridge: Harvard University Press, 1995.

"The Dance That Is My Life." Weblog. Available at: www.walkingingrace.spaces.live.com (accessed December 2006).

Davis, Geoff. "Employment Picture for New Ph.D.s: Rationalizing Ph.D. Production." *Science's Next Wave* (American Association for the Advancement of Science). March 7, 1997. Available at: www.nextwave.sciencemag.org/cgi/content/full/1998/03/29/73.

Davis, Jim, Thomas Hirschl, and Michael Stack, eds. *Cutting Edge: Technology, Information Capitalism and Social Revolution.* London: Verso, 1997.

Davis, Lennard J. "Dancing in the Dark: A Manifesto against Professional Organizations." *minnesota review* 45/46 (Fall 1995/Spring 1996): 197–214.

DeCew, Judith Wagner. *Unionization in the Academy: Visions and Realities.* Lanham, Md.: Rowman and Littlefield, 2003.

Dew, John Robert, and Molly McGowan Nearing. *Continuous Quality Improvement in Higher Education.* Westport, Conn.: ACE/Praeger, 2004.

Dill, David. "The Management of Academic Culture." In Christopher M. Brown, ed., *Organization and Governance in Higher Education,* 5th ed. Boston: Pearson, 2000, 261–272.

Downing, David. "Beyond Disciplinary English: Integrating Reading and Writing by Reforming Academic Labor." In David B. Downing, Claude Mark Hurlburt, and Paula Mathieu, eds., *Beyond English Inc.: Curricular Reform in a Global Economy.* Portsmouth, N.H.: Boynton/Cook Heinemann, 2002, 23–38.

———. *The Knowledge Contract: Politics and Paradigms in the Academic Workplace.* Lincoln: University of Nebraska Press, 2005.

Draut, Tamara. *Strapped: Why America's 20- and 30-Somethings Can't Get Ahead.* New York: Doubleday, 2006.

Dubson, Michael. "Address for COCAL IV." Presented at San Jose, California, January 12, 2001.

———. *Ghosts in the Classroom: Stories of College Adjunct Faculty—and the Price We All Pay.* Boston: Camel's Back Books, 2001.

Duryea, E. D. "Evolution of University Organization." In Christopher M. Brown, ed., *Organization and Governance in Higher Education,* 5th ed. Boston: Pearson, 2000, 3–15.

Dussel, Enrique. "The Four Drafts of *Capital:* Toward a New Interpretation of the Dialectical Thought of Marx." *Rethinking Marxism* 13.1 (Spring 2001): 10–26.

Dyer-Witheford, Nick. *Cyber-Marx: Cycles and Circuits of Struggle in High-Technology Capitalism.* Urbana-Champaign: University of Illinois Press, 1999.

Eble, Kenneth Eugene. *The Art of Administration.* San Francisco: Jossey-Bass, 1978.

Ehrenberg, Ronald, Daniel B. Klaff, Adam Kezsbom, and Matthew P. Nagowski. "Collective Bargaining in Higher Education." In Ronald Ehrenberg, ed., *Governing Academia.* Ithaca, N.Y.: Cornell University Press, 2004, 209–234.

Ehrenreich, Barbara. "Class Struggle 101." *Progressive,* November 2003. Available at: www.progressive.org/nov03/ehr1103.html (accessed April 15, 2005).

Ehrle, Elwood. *Managing the Academic Enterprise. Case Studies for Deans and Provosts.* New York: American Council on Education/Macmillan, 1988.

Eliot, Charles. *University Administration.* Boston: Houghton Mifflin, 1908.

Euben, Donna. "Academic Labor Unions: The Legal Landscape." *Academe.* January/February 2001. Available at: www.aaup.org/publications/Academe.

Fife, Jonathan D. "Review of *Management Fads in Higher Education* by Robert Birnbaum." *Journal of Higher Education* (July/August 2003): 469–472.

Finkelstein, Martin J., Robert Seal, and Jack Schuster. *New Entrants to the Full-Time Faculty of Higher Education Institutions.* NCES 98-252. Washington, D.C: U.S. Department of Education, National Center for Education Statistics, 1998. Available at www.nces.org (accessed March 10, 2001).

Fitts, Karen, and Alan France, eds. *Left Margins: Cultural Studies and Composition Pedagogy.* Albany: SUNY Press, 1995.

Flynn, Elizabeth Gurley. "Sabotage: Its Necessity in the Class War." Part 1 of *Sabotage: The Conscious Withdrawal of the Workers' Industrial Efficiency.* Cleveland: IWW, 1916. Available at: www.iww.org/culture/library/sabotage (accessed April 20, 2001).

Fogg, Piper. "NYU Settles Case with Professor over Denial of Tenure." *Chronicle of Higher Education,* May 7, 2002. Available at: www.chronicle.com (accessed February 20, 2006).

Frank, Thomas. "The God That Sucked." *Baffler* 14 (2002). Available at: www.thebaffler.com/gts.html (accessed July 1, 2003).

———. *One Market under God: Extreme Capitalism, Market Populism, and the End of Economic Democracy.* New York: Anchor, 2001.

Gappa, Judith, and David Leslie. *The Invisible Faculty.* San Francisco: Jossey-Bass, 1993.

Garbarino, Joseph. *Faculty Bargaining: Change and Conflict.* New York: Carnegie Foundation/McGraw-Hill, 1975.

George, Diana, ed. *Kitchen Cooks, Plate Twirlers and Troubadors: Writing Program Administrators Tell Their Stories.* Portsmouth, N.H.: Boynton/Cook Heinemann, 1999.

Giammarese, Kate. "Surviving the Fast-Food Chain Gang (review of Tannock, *Youth at Work*)." *Madison* (Wisconsin) *Capital Times.* June 1, 2001. Available at: www.captimes.com/books/reviews/1614.php (accessed July 1, 2002).

Gilbert, Sandra. "Bob's Jobs: Campus Crises and 'Adjunct' Education." In *Profession 1998.* New York: Modern Language Association, 1998.

Goral, Tim. "Making Peace with the Marketplace: Interview with David Kirp." *University Business.* No date. Available at www.universitybusiness.com.

Gottfried, Barbara, and Gary Zabel, "Social Movement Unionism and Adjunct Faculty Organizing in Boston." In B. Johnson, P. Kavanagh, and K. Mattson, eds, *Steal This University: The Rise of the Corporate University and the Academic Labor Movement.* New York: Routledge, 2003, 207–220.

Greenhouse, Steven. "Overtime Rules Dispute Is a Numbers Game." *New York Times,* August 31, 2004. Available at www.nytimes.com (accessed November 27, 2005).

Greenhouse, Steven, and David Leonhardt. "Real Wages Fail to Match a Rise in Productivity." *New York Times,* August 28, 2006. Available at: www.nytimes.com (accessed September 15, 2006).

Griffin, Susan. "Speaking from the Middle." *CCC (College Composition and Communication)* 50 (September 1998): A4–A5.

Grimm, Nancy. " 'The Way the Rich People Does It': Reflections on Writing Center Administration and the Search for Status." In Diana George, ed., *Kitchen Cooks, Plate Twirlers and Troubadors: Writing Program Administrators Tell Their Stories.* Portsmouth N.H.: Boynton/Cook Heinemann, 1999, 14–25.

Grossman, Lev. "They Just Won't Grow Up." *Time,* January 24, 2005, 42–54.

Gunner, Jeanne. "Among the Composition People: The WPA as English Department Agent." *JAC (Journal of Advanced Composition)* 18.1 (1998): 153–165.

Hammers, Maryann. "Wanted: Part-timers with Class: UPS Launches Earn and Learn." *Workforce* (Crain Communications, New York), June 2003. Available at: www.workforce.com (accessed October 1, 2005).

Hankin, Joseph. "TD4020: College and University Organization and Administration: Spring 2002." Syllabus, Columbia University. Available at: www.virtualupdate.org/Features/Previous%20Issues/V1N2featuresA.html.

Haraway, Donna J. *Simians, Cyborgs, and Women: The Reinvention of Nature.* New York: Routledge, 1991

Hardy, Cynthia. *The Politics of Collegiality.* Montreal: Queens University Press, 1996.

Harris, John W. "Key Concepts of Quality Improvement in Higher Education." In John W. Harris and Mark Baggett, eds., *Quality Quest in the Academic Process.* Birmingham, Ala.: Samford University, 1992, 7–19.

Harris, Joseph. "Meet the New Boss, Same as the Old Boss: Class Consciousness in Composition." *CCC (College Composition and Communication)* 52.1 (September 2000): 43–68.

Harvey, David. *Spaces of Hope.* Berkeley: University of California Press, 2000.

Heller, Scott. "The Expected Turnaround in the Faculty Job Market May Come Too Late for 'Lost Generation' of Scholars." *Chronicle of Higher Education,* May 13, 1990. Available at: www.chronicle.com (accessed February 1, 2006).

Herman, Deborah, and Julie M. Schmid. *Cogs in the Classroom Factory: The Changing Identity of Academic Labor.* Portsmouth, N.H.: Praeger, 2003.

Hesse, Doug. "The WPA as Father, Husband, Ex." In Diana George, ed., *Kitchen Cooks, Plate Twirlers and Troubadors: Writing Program Administrators Tell Their Stories.* Portsmouth N.H.: Boynton/Cook Heinemann, 1999, 44–55.

"hitchhiker42" (pseud.) "I Hate How UPS Is Always Fucking You Over." Weblog post to "Brown Blood," May 26, 2006. Available at: www.community.livejournal.com/brown_blood/ (accessed December 2006).

Hodges, Jane. "A Surplus of Scholars Fight for Jobs in Academia." *New York Times,* January 16, 2000, sec. 3, p. 15.

Hoeller, Keith. "Equal Pay Means Equal Raises, Too." *Chronicle of Higher Education,* August 16, 2005. Available at: www.chronicle.com (accessed September 5, 2005).

———. "Treat College Part-Time Faculty Fairly." *Tacoma News-Tribune,* October 7, 2006. Available at: coastcca.com (accessed January 15, 2007).

Houghton Mifflin College Division. *So Much to Teach, So Little Time.* No date. Available at: www.adjuncts.com (accessed January 15, 2003).

Howington, Patrick. "Students May Fill Many New Jobs." *Louisville Courier-Journal,* May 18, 2006. Available at: www.courier-journal.com (accessed July 10, 2006).

Hunter, J. Paul. "Facing the Eighties." *ADE (Association of Departments of English) Bulletin* 62 (September/November 1979): 1–9.

Hutcheson, Philo. *A Professional Professoriate: Unionization, Bureaucratization, and the AAUP.* Nashville: Vanderbilt University Press, 2000.

"Invisible Adjunct." Weblog. No date. Available at: www.invisibleadjunct.com/ (accessed February 1, 2006).

Irvine, Martha. "More Americans Find Themselves in 'Delayed Adulthood.'" *Louisville Courier Journal,* 27 October 2003, A4.

Ivey, Julie. "We Are Teachers!" No date. Available at: www.cewaction.org (accessed February 1, 2006).

Jameson, Fredric. "Culture and Finance Capital." Chapter 7 in *The Cultural Turn.* London: Verso, 1998, 136–161.

Janakos, Linda. *The President Makes a Commercial.* No date. Available at: www.cewaction.org (accessed February 1, 2006).

———. *Teachers on Wheels.* No date. Film distributed by the author.

Jencks, Christopher, and David Reisman. *The Academic Revolution.* Garden City, N.Y.: Doubleday, 1969.

JobVent. Weblog. No date. Available at: www.jobvent.com (accessed December 15, 2006).

Johnson, Benjamin, Patrick Kavanagh, and Kevin Mattson, eds., *Steal This University: The Rise of the Corporate University and the Academic Labor Movement.* New York: Routledge, 2003.

Kamenetz, Anya. *Generation Debt: Why Now Is a Terrible Time to Be Young.* New York: Riverhead, 2006.

Kampf, Louis. "'It's Alright, Ma (I'm Only Bleeding)': Literature and Language in the Academy." MLA Presidential Address: Chicago, December 27, 1971. *PMLA* 87.3 (May 1972): 377–383.

———. "I Want to Resign." Letter dated July 6, 1970. Reprinted in David Orr, "The Job Market in English and Foreign Languages." *PMLA* 85.5 (October 1970): 1198.

Karman, John. "Delivering an Education: UPS Boosts Its Recruiting Effort Outside Jefferson County for Metropolitan College." *Business First of Louisville.* March 24, 2000. Available at: www.louisville.bizjournals.com/louisville/stories/2000/03/27/story3.html.

Karman, John, and Brent Adams. "Close Ties among UPS, Government and Development Officials Helped Package Come Together Quickly." *Business First of Louisville.* May 19, 2006. Available at: www.louisville.bizjournals.com/louisville/stories/2006/05/22/story1.html.

Kelley, Mark. "On Incivility in Academe." *minnesota review* 50/51 (Spring/Fall 1998): 243–248.

Kelley, Robin D. G. "The Proletariat Goes to College." In Cary Nelson, ed., *Will Teach for Food: Academic Labor in Crisis.* Minneapolis: University of Minnesota Press, 1997, 145–152.

Kemerer, Frank, and J. Victor Baldridge. *Unions on Campus.* San Francisco: Jossey-Bass, 1975.

Kerr, Clark. "Society: Industrial Relations and University Relations" (1968). In Kerr Clark, *The Great Transformation in Higher Education, 1960–1980.* Albany: SUNY Press, 1991, 181–188.

Kerr, Clark. "Unions' Effects on Labor's Share" from *Labor's Income Share and the Labor Movement* (1957) and "International Comparisons" from *The Future of Industrial Societies: Convergence or Continuing Diversity* (1983), in Clark Kerr and Paul D. Staudohar, eds, *Economics of Labor in Industrial Society.* San Francisco: Jossey-Bass, 1986, 236–242, 266–269.

———. *The Uses of the University.* 5th ed. Cambridge: Harvard University Press, 2001.

Kirp, David. *Shakespeare, Einstein, and the Bottom Line : The Marketing of Higher Education.* Cambridge: Harvard University Press, 2004.

Kloss, John. "An Amazing Circus," "Full-Time Activist," "It's Alive," and "Misadventures of a Freeway Flier" (cartoons). No date. Available at: www.cewaction.org (accessed February 1, 2006).

"Kody" (pseud). Weblog. April 28, 2005. Available at: basildangerdoo.blogspot.com (accessed December 2006).

Kolodny, Annette. *Failing the Future: A Dean Looks at Higher Education in the Twenty-First Century.* Durham, N.C.: Duke University Press, 1998.

Ladd, Everett Carll, Jr., and Seymour Martin Lipset. *Professors, Unions, and Higher Education.* New York: McGraw-Hill, 1973.

Lafer, Gordon. "Graduate Student Unions Fight the Corporate University." *Dissent.* Fall 2001. Available at: www.dissentmagazine.org/archive/fa01/lafer.shtml.

Lapidus, Jules. "Why Pursuing a Ph.D. Is a Risky Business." *Chronicle of Higher Education,* November 14, 1997, A60.

LatinoLA. "Earn and Learn: UPS Offers Part-Time Work, Tuition Assistance, and Forgivable Loans." September 28, 2002. Available at: www.latinola.com/story.php?story=493 (accessed March 2007).

Lauter, Paul. *Canons and Contexts.* New York: Oxford University Press, 1991.

———. "Content, Culture, Character." *Works and Days* 21.1–2 (2003): 51–56.

———. "Society and the Profession, 1958–1983." *PMLA* 99.3 (May 1984): 414–426.

Lawrence, David. "From the Editor." *ADE (Association of Departments of English) Bulletin* 94 (Winter 1989): 1–3.

Lazerson, Marvin, Ursula Wagener, and Larry Moneta. "Like the Cities They Increasingly Resemble, Colleges Must Train and Retain Competent Managers." *Chronicle of Higher Education,* July 28, 2000, A72.

Lazzarato, Maurizio. "Immaterial Labor." In Paolo Virno and Michael Hardt, eds., *Radical Thought in Italy: A Potential Politics.* Minneapolis: University of Minnesota Press, 1996, 133–147..

Leatherman, Courtney. "Part-Time Faculty Members Try to Organize Nationally." *Chronicle of Higher Education,* January 26, 2001, A12–13.

———. "Use of Non-Tenure-Track Faculty Members Is a Long-Term Trend, Study Finds." *Chronicle of Higher Education,* April 9, 1999, A14–A16.

Lederman, Doug. "N.Y. Reigns in For-Profit Colleges." *Inside Higher Education.* January 23, 2006. Available at: www.insidehighered.com (accessed March 1, 2006).

Levidow, Les. "Marketizing Higher Education: Neoliberal Strategies and Counter-Strategies." *Cultural Logic* 4.1 (Winter 2001). Available at: www .eserver.org/clogic/4-1.

Levin, John S. "Faculty Work: Tensions between Educational and Economic Values." *Journal of Higher Education* 77.1 (January/February 2006): 62–88.

Lovett, Clara. "The Dumbing Down of College Presidents." *Chronicle of Higher Education,* April 5, 2002, B20.

Lyman, Rick. "Movie Stars Fear Inroads by Upstart Digital Actors." *New York Times,* July 8, 2001. Available at: www.nytimes.com/2001/07/08.

Magner, Denise. "Job Market Blues: Instead of the Anticipated Demand, New Ph.D.'s Are Finding Few Openings." *Chronicle of Higher Education,* April 27, 1994, A17.

———. "Study Says U.S. Universities Produce Too Many Doctorates." *Chronicle of Higher Education,* June 30, 1995, A16.

Martin, Randy, ed. *Chalk Lines: The Politics of Work in the Managed University.* Durham, N.C.: Duke University Press, 2000.

———. "Education as National Pedagogy." In Randy Martin, ed., *Chalk Lines: The Politics of Work in the Managed University.* Durham, N.C.: Duke University Press, 2000, 1–32.

———. *Financialization of Daily Life.* Temple University Press, 2002.

———. "Stat(e)ing the Obvious." *Workplace: A Journal for Academic Labor* 2.2 (May 2000). Available at: www.workplace-gsc.com/issue4/martinintro .html.

Marx, Karl. *Capital: A Critique of Political Economy,* vol, 1. Trans. Ben Fowkes. Intr. Ernest Mandel. New York: Penguin/New Left Review, 1996.

Masland, Andrew. "Organizational Culture in the study of Higher Education." In Christopher M. Brown, ed., *Organization and Governance in Higher Education,* 5th ed. Boston: Pearson, 2000, 145–152.

Massy, William, "Reengineering Resource Allocation Systems" and "Lessons from Health Care." In William Massy, ed., *Resource Allocation in Higher Education.* Ann Arbor: University of Michigan Press, 1996, 15–48, 193–222.

Massy, William, and Charles Goldman. *The Production and Utilization of Science and Engineering Doctorates in the U.S.* Palo Alto, Calif.: Stanford, 1995.

Massy, William, et al. *Virtual U Strategy Guide.* Available at: www.virtual-u .org/downloads/vu-strategy-guide.pdf (accessed August 10, 2005).

McIntosh, Don. "Skit Protests Oppression of Banana Workers in Guatemala." *Northwest Labor Press,* February 4, 2000. Available at: www.nwlaborpress .org/2000/2-04-00guate.html (accessed August 10, 2006).

McPhee, John. "Out in the Sort: Lobsters, Bats, and Bentleys in the UPS Hub." *New Yorker,* April 18, 2005, 161–173.

Metropolitan College. *Who We Are.* Available at: www.metro-college.com (accessed June 2,2007).

Micciche, Laura. "More Than a Feeling: Disappointment and WPA Work." *College English* 64.4 (March 2002): 432–458.

Miller, J. Hillis. "Reply." In *Profession 1997.* New York: Modern Language Association, 1997, 233–235.

———. "The Triumph of Theory, the Resistance to Reading, and the Question of the Material Base." MLA Presidential Address 1986. *PMLA* 102.3 (May 1987): 281–291.

Miller, Richard. "The Arts of Complicity: Pragmatism and the Culture of Schooling." *College English* 61.1 (September 1998): 10–28.

———. *As if Learning Mattered: Reforming Higher Education.* Ithaca, N.Y.: Cornell University Press, 1998.

———. " 'Let's Do the Numbers': Comp Droids and the Prophets of Doom." In *Profession 1999.* New York: Modern Language Association, 1999, 96–105.

Modern Language Association. *Final Report of the MLA Committee on Professional Employment.* December 1997.

———. "Working Paper of the Commission on the Future of the Profession, May 1981." *PMLA* 96.4 (September 1981): 525–540.

Morgenson, Gretchen. "Some Things You Just Can't Teach." *New York Times,* May 15, 2005, business sec., p 1.

Morris-Suzuki, Tessa. "Capitalism in the Computer Age" (rev., with a new Afterword). In Jim Davis, Thomas Hirschl, and Michael Stack, eds., *Cutting Edge: Technology, Information Capitalism and Social Revolution.* London: Verso, 1997, 57–72.

———. "Robots and Capitalism." In Jim Davis, Thomas Hirschl, and Michael Stack, eds., *Cutting Edge: Technology, Information Capitalism and Social Revolution.* London: Verso, 1997, 13–28.

Mortenson, Tom. "I Worked My Way through College. You Should, Too. 1964–65 to 2002–03." Spreadsheet. Available at: www.postsecondary.org/archives/Reports/Spreadsheets/1251102WorkedShould.pdf (accessed November 27, 2005).

Mosely, Fred. Introduction to "The Four Drafts of *Capital:* Toward a New Interpretation of the Dialectical Thought of Marx." *Rethinking Marxism* 13.1 (Spring 2001): 1–10.

Moten, Fred, and Stefano Harney. "The Academic Speed-Up." *Workplace: A Journal for Academic Labor* 2.2 (May 2000). Available at: www.workplace-gsc.com/issue4/harneymoten.html.

———. "Doing Academic Work." In Randy Martin, ed., *Chalk Lines: The Pol-*

itics of Work in the Managed University. Durham, N.C.: Duke University Press, 2000, , 154–180.

Mountford, Roxanne. "From Labor to Middle Management: Graduate Students in Writing Program Administration." *Rhetoric Review* 21.1 (2002): 41–53.

Murphy, Michael. "Adjuncts Should Not Just Be Visitors in the Academic Promised Land." *Chronicle of Higher Education,* March 29, 2002, B14–15.

———. "New Faculty for a New University: Toward a Full-Time Teaching-Intensive Faculty Track in Composition." *CCC (College Composition and Communication)* 52.1 (September 2000): 14–42.

Nast, Thomas. "The American Twins" (cartoon). *Harper's Weekly,* February 7, 1874, 136.

National Center for Education Statistics, U.S. Department of Education. "The Condition of Education 2000." Summary document of various NCES publications, html version. 2000. Available at: www.NCES.ed.gov.

———. "Instructional Faculty and Staff in Higher Education Institutions: Fall 1987 and Fall 1992." Analysis of NSOPF-93 and NSOPF-88. NCES Publication 97-470. 1997. Available at: www.NCES.ed.gov.

———. *National Study of the Post-Secondary Faculty, 1993.* NSOPF-93. 1993. Available at: www.nces.org.

———. "New Entrants to the Full-Time Faculty of Higher Education Institutions." Analysis of NSOPF-93 and NSOPF-88. NCES Publication 98-252. 1998. Available at: www.NCES.ed.gov.

———. *Profile of Undergraduates in U.S. Postsecondary Institutions: 1999–2000.* NCES Publication 2002-168. Washington, D.C.: National Center for Education Statistics, 2002.

———. *Work First, Study Second: Adult Undergraduates Who Combine Employment and Postsecondary Enrollment.* NCES Publication 2003-167. Washington, D.C.: National Center for Education Statistics, 2003.

National Education Association. "Full-Time Non-Tenure-Track Faculty." Redaction of NSOPF-93. *Update* 2.5 (September 1996). Available at: www2 .nea.org/he/heupdate/images/v2no5.pdf (accessed July 10, 2005).

NEA Higher Education Research Center. "The Other Staff: Non-Teaching Employees Make Up the Majority of Higher Education Staff." *NEA Update* 9.2 (February 2003): 1–4.

Nelson, Cary. "Contingent Faculty Seek Equity." *Academe,* March/April 2001. Available at: www.aaup.org (accessed February 1, 2006).

———. *Manifesto of a Tenured Radical.* New York: New York University Press, 1997.

———, ed. *Will Teach for Food: Academic Labor in Crisis.* Minneapolis: University of Minnesota Press, 1997.

Nelson, Cary, and Stephen Watt. *Academic Keywords: A Devil's Dictionary for Higher Education.* New York: Routledge, 1999.

――――. *Office Hours: Activism and Change in the Academy.* New York: Routledge, 2004.

Neumann, Anna. "The Social Construction of Resource Stress." In Christopher M. Brown, ed., *Organization and Governance in Higher Education,* 5th ed. Boston: Pearson, 2000, 389–405.

Newfield, Christopher. *Ivy and Industry: Business and the Making of the American University: 1880–1890.* Durham: Duke University Press, 2003.

――――. "Jurassic U: The State of University-Industry Relations." *Social Text* 22.2 (Summer 2004): 37–66.

Newton, Jethro. "Views from Below: Academic Coping with Quality." *Quality in Higher Education* P.1 (April 2002): 39–61.

Noble, David. *Digital Diploma Mills: The Automation of Higher Education.* New York: Monthly Review Press, 2002.

――――. *Digital Diploma Mills, Part I: The Automation of Higher Education.* October 1997. Available at: communication.ucsd.edu/dl/ddm1.html.

――――. *Digital Diploma Mills, Part II: The Coming Battle over Online Instruction* (Confidential Agreements between Universities and Private Companies Pose Serious Challenge to Faculty Intellectual Property Rights). March 1998. Available at: communication.ucsd.edu/dl/ddm2.html.

――――. *Digital Diploma Mills, Part III: The Bloom Is off the Rose.* November 1998. Available at: communication.ucsd.edu/dl/ddm3.html.

――――. *Digital Diploma Mills, Part IV: Rehearsal for the Revolution.* November 1999. Available at: communication.ucsd.edu/dl/ddm4.html.

――――. *Digital Diploma Mills, Part V: Fool's Gold.* March 2001. Available at: communication.ucsd.edu/dl/ddm5.html.

Ohmann, Richard. *English in America: A Radical View of the Profession.* New York: Oxford University Press, 1976.

Orr, David. "The Job Market in English and Foreign Languages." *PMLA* 85.5 (October 1970): 1185–1198.

Osterman, Rachel. "Trump's Pitch: I'll Teach You to Be Rich." *Sacramento Bee,* January 28, 2006, business sec., p. D1.

Palmer, Susanne. *A Brief History of Collective Bargaining in Higher Education.* Available at: home.comcast.net/~erozycki/HECollectBar.html.

Pannapacker, William. "Arrested at the M.L.A. Convention: A Conversation with Louis Kampf." *Workplace* 1.2 (December 1998). Available at: www.cust .educ.ubc.ca/worplace/workplace2/kampf2.htm (accessed January 15, 2001).

Parascondola, Leo. "Interview with Paul Lauter." *Workplace* 1.2, December 1998. Available at: www.cust.ubc.ca/workplace/workplace2/lauter.html (accessed January 15, 2001).

Peterson, Marvin, and Melinda G. Spencer. "Understanding Academic Culture and Climate." In Christopher M. Brown, ed., *Organization and Governance in Higher Education,* 5th ed. Boston: Pearson, 2000, 170–181.

Phillips, Peter. "A Win for Higher Education in California." Press release, Sonoma State University, California Faculty Association, March 28, 2002. Available at: www.projectcensored/org.

Porter, James, Patricia Sullivan, Stuart Blythe, Jeffry T. Grabill, and Libby Miles. "Institutional Critique: A Rhetorical Methodology for Change." *CCC (College Composition and Communication)* 51.4 (June 2000): 610–641.

Poster, Mark. *The Mode of Information: Poststructuralism and Social Context.* Chicago: Polity Press, 1990.

Readings, Bill. *The University in Ruins.* Cambridge: Harvard University Press, 1996.

Regets, Mark. "Employment Picture for Ph.D.s: 1995 NSF Data on Labor-Market Conditions for New Ph.D. Recipients." *Science's Next Wave* (American Association for the Advancement of Science). March 7, 1997. Available at: nextwave.sciencemag.org/cgi/content/full/1998/03/29/76.

Reisman, David. *On Higher Education.* San Francisco: Jossey-Bass, 1981.

Rhoades, Gary. *Managed Professionals: Unionized Faculty and Restructuring Academic Labor.* Albany: SUNY Press, 1998.

Rhoades, Gary, and Christine Maitland. "The Hidden Campus Workforce: (De)Investing in Staff." *NEA Almanac of Higher Education* (1998): 109–118.

Rhoades, Gary, and Sheila Slaughter. *Academic Capitalism and the New Economy.* Baltimore: Johns Hopkins University Press, 2004.

Rice, William Craig. "The Robert McNamara of the American Academy." *Idler* 1.19 (August 2, 1999). Available at: www.the-idler.com/vIn19.html.

Rohrbacher, Bernhard Wolfgang. "After *Boston Medical Center:* Why Teaching Assistants Should Have the Right to Bargain Collectively." *Loyola of Los Angeles Law Review* 33 (June 2000): 1849–1918.

Ross, Andrew. "The Mental Labor Problem." *Social Text* 18.2 (Summer 2000): 1–31.

Runkel, Ross. *NLRB Reversals during the Bush Administration.* Available at: www.lawmemo.com/articles/nlrbreversals.html (accessed September 15, 2006).

"saintteamo." "End UPS Part Time Poverty." Weblog post to "BrownCafe," January 21, 2003. Available at: www.browncafe.com/forum/66078-post11 .html (accessed August 1, 2006).

Saltman, Ken. "Rehabilitation for Milken's Junk Habit." In: M. Bousquet and K.Wills, eds., *The Politics of Information: The Electronic Mediation of Social Change.* An e-book from Alt-X Press (2004). Available at: www.altx .com/ebooks/download.cfminfopol.pdf (accessed March 1, 2006).

Saltzman, Gregory M. "Higher Education, Collective Bargaining, and the Law." *NEA Almanac of Higher Education* (2001): 45–58.

———. "Legal Regulation of Collective Bargaining in Colleges and Universities." *NEA Almanac of Higher Education* (1998): 45–63.

Saltzman, Gregory M. "Union Organizing and the Law: Part Time Faculty and Graduate Teaching Assistants." *NEA Almanac of Higher Education* (2000): 43–55

Sassen, Saskia. *Informalization in Advanced Market Economies.* Geneva: International Labour Organization, 1997. With a preface by Samir Radwan. Available at: www.ilo.org/public/english/employment/strat/publ/iddp20.htm.

———. *The Mobility of Labor and Capital.* Cambridge: Cambridge University Press, 1988.

Sawyer, Ben. *Serious Games: Improving Public Policy through Game-Based Learning and Simulation.* Washington, D.C.: Woodrow Wilson Center, 2001.

Schell, Eileen. *Gypsy Academics and Mother-Teachers: Gender, Contingent Labor, and Writing Instruction.* Portsmouth, N.H.: Boynton/Cook-Heinemann, 1997.

Schell, Eileen, and Patricia Lambert Stock. *Moving a Mountain: Transforming the Role of Contingent Faculty in Composiion Studies and Higher Education.* Urbana, Ill.: National Council of Teachers of English, 2001.

Schiller, Dan. *Digital Capitalism: Networking the Global Market System.* Cambridge: MIT Press, 2000.

———. "The Information Commodity: A Preliminary View." In Jim Davis, Thomas Hirschl, and Michael Stack, eds., *Cutting Edge: Technology, Information, Capitalism, and Social Revolution.* London: Verso, 1997, 103–120

Schlosser, Eric. *Fast Food Nation.* New York: Harper, 2005.

Sennett, Richard. *The Corrosion of Character: The Personal Consequences of Work in the New Capitalism.* New York: Norton, 1998.

Serrou, Melanie. Testimony before the Portland Community College Board. October 20, 2005. Mpeg sound file. Available at: pccff.org/cewboard.htm (accessed February 1, 2006).

Seymour, Daniel T. *On Q: Causing Quality in Higher Education.* Phoenix: Oryx Press, 1993.

Shea, Rachel Hartigan. "The New Insecurity." *U.S. News and World Report,* March 25, 2002. Available at: www.usnews.com/issue/020325/ideas/25tenure.htm (accessed April 15, 2003).

Showalter, Elaine. "Taming the Rampant Incivility in Academe." *Chronicle of Higher Education,* January 15, 1999, B4.

Silverman, Daniel. "Decision and Direction of Election." *New York University and United Auto Workers* (Case No. 2-RC-22082). New York: National Labor Relations Board Region 2, 2000.

Slaughter, Jane. "Management by Stress." *Multinational Monitor,* January/February 1990. Available at: www.multinationalmonitor.org (accessed June 30, 2006).

Slaughter, Sheila, and Larry L. Leslie. *Academic Capitalism: Politics, Policies and the Entrepreneurial University.* Baltimore: Johns Hopkins University Press, 1997.

Smallwood, Scott. "Success and New Hurdles for T.A. Unions." *Chronicle of Higher Education,* July 6, 2001, A10.

Smith, Paul. *Millenial Dreams: Contemporary Culture and Capital in the North.* New York: Verso, 1997.

Smith, Tom W. *Coming of Age in 21st-Century America.* General Social Survey Report. Chicago: University of Chicago, 2003.

"Snowe, Lucy" (pseud.). "Why Do I Do This?" *Chronicle of Higher Education,* October 15, 2004, C1–4.

Soley, Lawrence. *Leasing the Ivory Tower: The Corporate Takeover of Academia.* Boston: South End, 1995.

Spellmeyer, Kurt. "Out of the Fashion Industry: From Cultural Studies to the Anthropology of Knowledge." *CCC (College Composition and Communication)* 47.3 (October 1996): 424–436.

Sperber, Murray. *Beer and Circus: How Big-Time College Sports Is Crippling Undergraduate Education.* New York: Owl, 2000.

Starfield, Barbara. "Medical Errors: A Leading Cause of Death." *Journal of the American Medical Association (JAMA)* 284 (July 2000): 483–485.

Stephenson, Neal. *Cryptonomicon.* New York: Avon, 2002.

Strickland, Donna. "The Managerial Unconscious of Composition Studies." In Marc Bousquet, Tony Scott, and Leo Parascondola, eds., *Tenured Bosses and Disposable Teachers: Writing Instruction in the Managed University.* Carbondale: Southern Illinois University Press, 2004.

SUNY Oswego Fact Book. No date. Available at: www.oswego.edu/administration/institutional_research/fact.html (accessed August 19, 2005).

"SUNY Oswego Fast Facts." No date. Available at: www.oswego.edu/about/facts/ (accessed November 27, 2005).

"SUNY Oswego Student Employment." No date. Available at: www.oswego.edu/admissions/costs/financial/employment.html (accessed August 19, 2005).

"supergirl" (pseud.) Weblog. March 1, 2005. Available at jealousthendead.livejournal.com (accessed December 7, 2006).

Sykes, Charles J. *Prof Scam: Professors and the Demise of Higher Education.* Washington, D.C.: Regnery Gateway, 1988.

Syverson, Peter D. *When Simulation Becomes Reality: Press Reaction to Massy/Goldman Study Creates Erroneous Message.* Council of Graduate Schools Research Center, 1997. Available at: www.cgsnet.org/vcr/cctr508.htm.

Tannock, Stuart. *Youth at Work: The Unionized Fast-Food and Grocery Workplace.* Philadelphia: Temple University Press, 2001.

Tave, Stuart. "The Guilt of the Professor." *ADE (Association of Departments of English) Bulletin* 59 (1978): 6–12.

Terranova, Tiziana. "Free Labor: Producing Culture for the Digital Economy." *Social Text* 18.2 (Summer 2000): 33–58.

Thelin, John. *A History of American Higher Education.* Baltimore: Johns Hopkins University Press, 2004.

Tierney, William G. *Building the Responsive Campus: Creating High Performance Colleges and Universities.* Thousand Oaks, Calif.: Sage, 1999.

Tirelli, Vincent. "Adjuncts and More Adjuncts: Labor Segmentation and the Transformation of Higher Education." In Randy Martin, ed. *Chalk Lines: The Politics of Work in the Managed University.* Durham, N.C.: Duke University Press, 2000, 181–201.

University of Washington Graduate School. "Ph.D. Career Paths." May 1998. Available at: www.grad.washington.edu/stats/phd_survey/phd_survey.htm.

UPS. *Earn and Learn Fact Sheet.* Available at: pressroom.ups.com/mediakits/factsheet/0,2305,777,00.html (accessed May 15, 2007). Updated April 25, 2005.

USA Group. *Noel-Levitz National Student Satisfaction Report, 1999.* Denver: Noel-Levitz, 1999. Available at: www.usagroup.com/borrowing/news/090899pr.htm (accessed January 25, 2001).

Vaughn, William. "I Was an Adjunct Administrator." In Marc Bousquet, Tony Scott, and Leo Parascondola, eds., *Tenured Bosses and Disposable Teachers: Writing Instruction in the Managed University.* Carbondale: Southern Illinois University Press, 2004, 165–170.

Virno, Paolo. "The Ambivalence of Disenchantment." In Michael Hardt and Paolo Virno, eds., *Radical Thought in Italy: A Potential Politics.* Minneapolis: University of Minnesota Press, 1996, 13–36.

Walzer, Michael. "The Underworked American." *New Republic,* September 22, 1997. Available at: www.tnr.com.

Washburn, Jennifer. "Studied Interest: How Industry Is Undermining Academia." *American Prospect.* February 2005. Available at: www.prospect.org (accessed March 1, 2006).

——. "University, Inc.: 10 Things You Should Know about Corporate Corruption on Campus." *Campus Progress* (2005). Available at: www.campusprogress.org (accessed March 1, 2006).

——. Washburn, Jennifer. *University, Inc.: The Corporate Corruption of American Higher Education.* New York: Basic Books, 2005.

Watkins, Evan. "The Educational Politics of Human Resources: Humanities Teachers as Resource Managers." *minnesota review* 45/46 (Fall 1995/Spring 1996): 147–166.

Watt, Stephen. "What Is an Organization Like the MLA?" *Workplace* 1.1 (February 1998). Available at: www.cust.educ.ubc.ca/workplace/features1/watt.html (accessed December 5, 2005).

Weed, William Speed. "Slaves to Science: For Post-docs, Finding a Supernova Is

Easier Than Finding a Job." *Salon.com.* February 28, 2000. Available at: www.salon.com/books/it/2000/02/28/postdoc/index.html (accessed March 10, 2001).

Weissman, Robert. "Global Management by Stress." *Multinational Monitor,* July/August 2001. Available at: multinationalmonitor.org (accessed July 21, 2006).

Westheimer, Joel. "Tenure Denied: Union Busting in the Corporate University." *Workplace: A Journal for Academic Labor* 4.2 (February 2002). Available at: www.workplace-gsc.com.

White, Geoffry, ed. *Campus, Inc.: Corporate Power in the Ivory Tower.* Buffalo, N.Y.: Prometheus Books, 2000.

Williams, Jeffrey. "Debt Education." *Dissent* (Summer 2006): 55–61.

———. "The Post-Welfare State University." *American Literary History* 18 (2006): 190–216.

Williamson, Marilyn L. "An English Chairman Looks at Unionization." *ADE (Association of Departments of English) Bulletin* 39 (December 1973): 3–6.

Wolf, Barbara. *A Simple Matter of Justice: Contingent Faculty Organize.* Film. 2002.

———. *Degrees of Shame: Part-time Faculty. Migrant Workers of the Information Economy.* Film. 1999.

Wright, Robert E. "A Market Solution to the Oversupply of Historians," Editorial. *Chronicle of Higher Education,* April 12 2002, B20.

Wyatt, Edward. "Tenure Gridlock: When Professors Choose Not to Retire." *New York Times,* February 16, 2000, sec. 3, p. 15.

Yates, Michael. "Lambs to the Slaughter." *Workplace: A Journal for Academic Labor* 1.2 (December 1998). Available at: www.workplace-gsc.com.

Index

Academic labor system, academic labor markets. *See* System of academic labor

Accreditation system, limited ability to restrain for-profits, 9

Accumulation of capital by nonprofits, 7, 28–29, 83–84

Adelphi University, 243n8

Adjunct faculty. *See* Faculty

Adjuncts.com, 167–168

Administrators: administrative solidarity, 11, 91–93, 98–102; compared to health-care management, 1–2; cybernetic systems model of university leadership, 72–79; degradation of faculty working conditions, 4; culture of struggle with faculty, 12–14, 92–94, 102–103; defiance of law, 33–35; leadership discourse, 99–101, 105; "management of meaning," 102–103; management by stress, 104–108; perpetators of the real "prof scam," 3; retaliation against union supporters, 31; perceive tenure as an obstacle to institutional mission, 73, 76–79; salary, xviii, 6; spending on facilities, sports, and pet projects, 7, 56; spending on union-busting corporate law firms, 34

Allen, Don Cameron, 190–191, 194, 195

Alternate careers for Ph.D. holders, 26, 45

American Association for Higher Education (AAHE), 105

American Association of Retired Persons (AARP), 179

American Association of University Professors (AAUP), 13, 18, 53–54, 96, 110, 114–116, 123

American Federation of State, County, and Municipal Employees (AFSCME), 53, 96, 115

American Federation of Teachers (AFT), 8, 18, 33, 34, 53, 96, 115, 123

American Philosophical Association (APA), 16

Apprenticeship model, failure of, xiv

Aronowitz, Stanley, 58, 81, 90, 154

Association for the Study of Higher Education (ASHE), 75

Baldridge, J. Victor, 114

Baldridge, Malcolm, 103, 106

Barrow, Clyde, 9, 18, 64, 123, 192

Bartlett, Laura, 147, 160

Bell, Daniel, 99–100, 170

Berelson, Bernard, 191, 194, 195, 200

Berlin, James, 160

Berry, Joe, 14, 97

Berube, Michael, 29, 31, 45

Birnbaum, Robert, 72, 74–76, 97, 105–106

Bok, Derek, 9, 114, 117–118

Bowen, Barbara, 243n4

Bowen, William G., 14–18, 186–187, 200–206, 253n1

Braverman, Harry, 62

Brennan, Justice William, 95, 109–110

Brenner, Johanna, 97–98

Brodsky, David, 179–180

Bronfenbrenner, Kate, 97

Brown University, 36, 224–241 (Appendix B)

Caffentzis, George, 83

California Faculty Association, 57

California Federation of Teachers, 49

California State University system, 252n8

"Job market." *See* System of academic labor

Job-market theory, 14, 45, 187, 192–209; Bowen report, 15–18, 200–206; consequences for self-understanding of graduate employees and faculty serving contingently, 20–21; as instance of managerial knowledge, 19; Job Market Study Commission (MLA, 1969), 193 253n5; Job Mart (MLA, 1955), 192

Kamenetz, Anya, 137
Kampf, Louis, 193, 197, 253n5
Kemerer, Frank, 114
Kerr, Clark, 10, 19, 74, 99–102, 103, 118–122
Kirp, David, 9, 77
Kloss, John, 49–53
Kolodny, Annette, 174

Labor-market analysis: contrasted to job-market theory, 19–20, 190–198, 200–206; elimination of "surplus" degree holders by re-creating tenure-track positions, 41; professionals and labor monopoly, 22–23; segmentation by gender, 22
Ladd, Everett, 114, 118
Lafer, Gordon, 96, 209, 252n8
Lauter, Paul, 78, 193, 197, 253n5
Lawrence, David, 16
Lazzarato, Maurizio, 61
Leadership discourse. *See* Administrators
Leslie, Larry, 10, 107, 176
Lipset, Seymour, 114, 118

Managed higher education: compared to managed health care, 1–2, 55–56, 76, 168; corporate university, corporatization, xvi; corporate-style administration, 9–15, 19; early twentieth-century imposition of scientific management, 18; university casualization in context of global permatemping, 44; ways nonprofits are managed to benefit corporate shareholders, 5. *See also* Administrators; For-profit institutions; Management theory
Management theory, 101–103, 175–185
Marketization, 1–2, 176–177, 207–209
Martin, Randy, 30, 31, 169, 177

Massy, William, 22, 71–79, 106–107
Media coverage of academic labor issues, 30
Mental labor, crippling exceptionalism, 28; bohemian ideology, 63; immaterial labor, 61
Metropolitan College. *See* UPS and Metropolitan College
Milken, Michael, 9
Miller, J. Hillis, 189, 195, 199
Miller, Richard, 159, 163, 167, 175–178
Modern Language Association: enthusiasm for Bowen report, 16–17; excludes Nelson, Berube, and Graduate Student Caucus from bibliography of report on professional employment, 45, 245n9; opposition to organizational reform initiated by graduate employees, xiii–xiv, xvii, 31; produces "job-market" discourse, 190–199. *See also* Faculty; Graduate employees; Graduate Student Caucus
Monster.com, MonsterTRAK, 150
Murphy, Michael, 159, 170–172, 251n5

Nast, Thomas, 181–182
National Association for the Advancement of Colored People (NAACP), 179
National Autonomous University of Mexico, 252n9
National Education Association (NEA), 53, 96, 105, 115–116, 123
National Labor Relations Act (NLRA), 27, 29, 32
National Labor Relations Board (NLRB), 29, 32, 36–40, 95, 117, 244n6
National Organization of Women (NOW), 179
Nelson, Cary, 29, 45, 154; direct action by grad employees, 35; foreword, xiii–xviii; "lumpen professoriate," 2
Neoliberalism, 19
Newfield, Christopher, 9, 18, 103, 123, 248n4
New York University, 30, 31, 36–40, 77, 224–241 (Appendix B), 252n8
Noble, David, 9, 57–60, 80, 246n2, 246n3

Ohmann, Richard, 154, 155, 160, 253n5
Organizational-culture approach to struc-

About the Authors

Marc Bousquet is a tenured associate professor of English at Santa Clara University. Active in the Graduate Student Caucus throughout the 1990s, he currently serves on the National Council of the American Association of University Professors (AAUP). He is the founding editor of *Workplace: A Journal for Academic Labor* (www.workplace-gsc.com). His essays on academic labor have appeared in such journals as *Social Text, Journal of Advanced Composition, College English, minnesota review,* and *Cinema Journal*. His contributions to academic labor studies have been the subject of a special double issue of the journal *Works and Days* (41/42, 2003). His previous books include *Tenured Bosses and Disposable Teachers* (2003) and *The Politics of Information* (2004).

Cary Nelson is Jubilee Professor of Liberal Arts and Sciences and Professor of English at the University of Illinois at Urbana-Champaign. His twenty-five authored or edited books include *Higher Education under Fire: Politics, Economics, and the Crisis of the Humanities* (1994), *Will Teach for Food: Academic Labor in Crisis* (1997), *Academic Keywords: A Devil's Dictionary for Higher Education* (1999), and *Office Hours: Activism and Change in the Academy* (2004). He is the author of over 100 essays, including a number published in *Academe, The Chronicle of Higher Education,* and *Inside Higher Education*. He is the forty-ninth president of the American Association of University Professors.